Naked & Unashamed

WHAT PEOPLE ARE SAYING

"*Naked and Unashamed* is the most urgently needed Bible study of our time! Judy Rossi and Sandy Troutman have done an extraordinary job of developing a resource that combines illustrations of real-life issues that are tearing our society apart with solid, well-researched truth, relevant applications, and action steps that produce healing and hope. This is a study that should be offered in every church on an annual basis. It provides a safe place for women to find answers to hard questions. I give it my highest recommendation!"
Carol Kent, Speaker and Author
Unquenchable: Grow a Wildfire Faith that Will Endure Anything (Zondervan)

"Finally a book that's a real *Bible Study* on sex! You'll be enriched by time in God's word, encouraged by personal application, and given hope for yourself and for others."
Susan Alexander Yates, author and speaker
31 Days of Prayer for My Teen (Baker Books)

"In this world of brokenness and sexual sin, there is good news. In *Naked and Unashamed*, Judy Rossi and Sandy Troutman teach and mentor; they beautifully describe God's design for sex and sexuality with truth and compassion. This Bible study does not merely inform, it transforms. If you're ready to be free from the ravages of pornography, adultery, abuse, and the gamut of sexual counterfeits, THIS is the study for you."
Lisa E. Nelson, Speaker and Author
A Woman's Guide to Fasting (Bethany House)

"Rich in biblical truth and godly wisdom, *Naked and Unashamed: Choosing God's Divine Design for Sex* addresses issues too long considered taboo. Judy and Sandy have written a powerful Bible study 'for such a time as this!' They point us to God's Word as the authority for life, and the source of hope and healing.
Brenda Pace, Speaker and Author
The One Year Yellow Ribbon Devotional (Tyndale House), *Medals above My Heart* (B&H Books) and *The Journey of a Military Wife: God's Truth for Every Step* (American Bible Society)

FOLLOWING GOD
CHRISTIAN LIVING
BIBLE STUDY SERIES

A 12 WEEK BIBLE STUDY

Naked & Unashamed

CHOOSING GOD'S DIVINE DESIGN FOR SEX

JUDY ROSSI and SANDY TROUTMAN

AMG
PUBLISHERS
ADVANCING THE MINISTRIES
OF THE GOSPEL

Following God

Naked and Unashamed: Choosing God's Design for Sex

ISBN: 978-0-89957-287-1
First Printing, 2015

Cover design by Michael Largent
at InView Graphics, Chattanooga, TN (www.imagewright.net)

Editing by Agnes Lawless and Rick Steele

Typesetting and page layout by Jennifer Ross

Printed in Canada
20 19 18 17 16 15 –MAR– 6 5 4 3 2 1

CONTENTS

Naked and Unashamed: Choosing God's Divine Design for Sex offers straight talk about a difficult topic. This study is for women of all ages and backgrounds. Many of us have husbands, children, other family members, friends, those we mentor, or who ourselves wrestle with the multifaceted issues of a sexually broken world. Many have experienced its impact on our lives, in our marriages, in our homes, on our college campuses, and in our workplaces.

Naked and Unashamed is an encouraging, edifying Bible study that focuses on what's right with God's design, why it works, and what happens when we operate both within it and outside of it. The goal of this study is to encourage women whose lives are challenged by sexual sin—others' or their own—to stand firm in Christ and to meet the challenge. It also equips mentors to come alongside those who are struggling. As with any struggle, God's heart is compassionate. True to His nature, however, His compassion lives hand in hand with His truth. This study puts forward God's truth as the route to the hope and healing that so many seek.

As you journey through this study, may God move in your heart. May He inform your beliefs about His plan for sex and sexuality. May He transform your relationships—first with Himself and then with others. And may you embrace what His divine rescue in a sexually broken world means for you so that He can work in you and through you to impact the lives of others.

A special thank you to the women who provided testimonies within this study—to their candidness as well as to the glory they give God for His faithfulness during their many and varied circumstances. Their full testimonies are located on Judy's website: www.eymministries.org.

With love and hope—always hope,

LESSON 1

In the Beginning

When you think about a particular relationship, do you conclude, *This isn't how it's supposed to be*? Humanity can't live without relationships; however, some are difficult to live with. We expect relationships to be nurturing and life-giving. But sometimes things don't turn out the way we think they should. Deep down we sense that the divine design is being violated.

No matter where the point of departure is in any relationship, once trust is broken, doubt will take its place. A host of negative emotions consumes us while loyalty, faithfulness, and reliability slowly crumble.

One of the most destructive violators of relationships is sexual immorality, which decimates even the most hallowed unions. Yet, even while it ravages relationships, our culture blames the pain on prudery rather than on poor sexual choices. What follows are examples from Christian women who have experienced the devastation of these poor choices:

"Sex before marriage didn't seem wrong; even living with him didn't seem wrong. But after the wedding, I was surprised that I was so let down on our wedding night—angry that our beginning was marred because we didn't wait until marriage to act married."

"When I discovered the affair, I was devastated. I saw the life I loved ending."

"The clinic staff was very businesslike and cold. They asked me if I was sure I wanted to go through with the abortion. What other option was there?"

"When we first learned of our youngest son's involvement with child pornography, I was bewildered, humiliated, and embarrassed. A few months later, our second son was also charged with the sin of child pornography."

"I discovered that my spouse had never been faithful, but had engaged in prostitution, massage parlors, one-night stands, and affairs. The knowledge of this betrayal was almost unbearable."

"When I was raped at age forty-one by a 'friend,' I hit a low in my life."

So he looks at dirty images on the computer when I'm not around . . . so what? I'm sure a lot of guys do that. He's not taking it any further, right? No biggie. But when

I'm smacked in the face with the reality of it, I can't help but get angry, feel hurt and know it is wrong

"My 12-year-old son came home from camp and confided in me that a sexual experience was forced on him by an older leader."

"In the early days of the affair, as I laid there in the arms of another man, I could sense the Spirit saying, "No! Get yourself out of this!""

"My husband said he had confessed to God, to the agents, and now he had to confess to me. The FBI had traced purchases of child pornography sites through PayPal to his computer."

"I found a note that revealed my husband had an affair while away on his business trip; but not just any affair—one with another man."

Do you see a loved one or yourself in any of these scenarios? They are real and reveal the evidence of a humanity that has lost its way.

Because people and relationships are the very stuff of our lives, this study is offered to sort the design from the disaster. We will also look at the disconnections so we can reconnect our dreams to God's realities. As you're moving through this study, we recommend you use a personal journal to record your more private insights.

DAY 1

THE DIVINE DESIGNER

A famous German legend tells of a place along the Rhine River where beautiful maidens cry out from the cliffs. If sailors don't cover their ears, they will be drawn to the haunting beauty of the sirens' voices and steer their boats into the rocks and to a sure death. Their demise happens something like this:

Woe to the boatman who passes the rock at the close of day! As of old, men were fascinated by the heavenly song of the Grecian hero, so was the unhappy voyager allured by this Being to sweet forgetfulness, his eyes, even his soul would be dazzled, and he could no longer steer clear of reefs and cliffs, and this beautiful siren only drew him to an early grave.

Forgetting all else, he would steer towards her, already dreaming of having reached her, but the jealous waves would round his boat and at last dash him treacherously against the rocks. The roaring waters of the Rhine would drown the cries of agony of the victim who would never be seen again.

Even today, sirens' songs beckon humanity. Why are we not covering our ears? Why are our eyes, even our souls, so dazzled that, forgetting all else, we steer toward their calls, no longer clear of the rocks and cliffs that will draw us to early graves?

What is within us that makes us willing to risk our very souls? Or should the question be, what is missing within us? In keeping with God's order, we must go back to the beginning—back to the way relationships were supposed to be and to the One who set relationships in motion with a divine design. Only the Divine Designer can fill the void in souls that would otherwise be compelled toward rocky shoals.

In the beginning, a great Creator forged the perfect Paradise in just six days. Everything He designed reflected His love, His power, His glory, and His holiness. Each new creation revealed His extraordinary genius and unveiled His incomprehensible nature.

Genesis 1 opens with the words, "*In the beginning*..." In Hebrew, *beginning* is the first word written in the Bible, meaning "the first in place, time, order, or rank. . . .[and] denotes the point in time or space at which something started"[1] (brackets ours). Consider all the theories, myths, and explanations that you've heard about the beginning of time. Is it important to know how time began? If so, why? If not, why?

The next two words in Genesis 1:1 reveal a powerful presence at work: "*In the beginning, God created*..." The Hebrew name for "God" is *Elohim*. It refers to "God as the Creator of the whole universe of people and things, and especially of the material world: he was the ruler of nature, the source of all life."[2] This tells us that from the beginning, only God had the power to create. What does Psalm 33:6–7 and 9 say about God and creation? How does this differ from what our culture teaches?

Genesis 1:2 (AMP) says that the earth was "*without form and an empty waste, and darkness was upon the face of the very great deep. The Spirit of God was moving (hovering, brooding) over the face of the waters.*" Can you picture this Creator-God manifesting His power to change what was empty, formless, and dark? "God of His own free will and by His absolute power called the whole universe into being, evoking into existence what was previously nonexistent."[3] With that in mind, read Genesis 1:1–30. Even if you've read this story many times before, ask God to give you a fresh perspective on who He is. What does this chapter reveal to you about our God as Creator?

 WORD STUDY

Whenever the Hebrew word *bara* is used in the verb form ("create, created, had created"), only God is the subject.

Author and teacher R. C. Sproul describes the Creator and the created this way: "When the Bible declares that God is the Creator of the universe, it indicates that God Himself is not created. There is a crucial distinction between the Creator and the creation. The creation bears the stamp of the Creator and witnesses to His glory."[4]

All creation "witnesses to His glory," or in the Hebrew language, to His "copious splendor." Throughout human history, God has revealed Himself by the copious splendor of creation. This is how He makes Himself known. And all creation can attest to His glory, not only to who God is but *that* God is. His glory is evident in the rolling might of a thunderhead, in the majesty of a well-muscled horse in full gallop, in the intricate design of every flower, in the perfect cycle of time, in the complex balance of systems that comprise and sustain the human body, in the perfect love of a divine relationship. And so much more.

EXTRA MILE
Psalms 93 and 104

Psalm 93 and 104 are a classic representation of the distinction between the Creator and the created. Not only do these psalms depict God's creative power at work in creation, but His care for it and its dependence on Him are evident. In what ways do these psalms affirm the creation account? What else do you discover about this distinction?

Sproul continues, "God is 'above and beyond' the universe in the sense that He is a higher order of being than other beings . . . He is called *supreme* because He has no beginning. He is supreme because all other beings owe their existence to Him, and He owes His existence to none other than Himself. He is the eternal Creator. Everything else is the work of His creation."[5]

In Isaiah 46:9 (ESV), God declares about Himself, *"I am God, and there is none like me."* Do you believe God is the ruler of nature and the source of all life, that you owe your very existence to this Creator God of the universe? If so, what does this mean for your life? If not, what does this mean for your life?

According to Genesis 1:31, how did God assess His creative genius?

God declared that everything He had made was "very good!" In the more literal texts, an additional word, *behold*, urges us to see from His perspective what He had done. His design was "appealing and pleasant to the senses . . . useful and profitable . . . abundant and plentiful . . . kind and benevolent . . . proper and becoming . . . a general state of well-being or happiness."[6] Everything God created reflected who He is. *Behold!*

What account does Genesis 2:1–2 give about the status of God's work and what He did next?

"Thus the heavens and the earth were completed" (2:1). In this verse, the Hebrew word for *completed* reflects "the awesome goodness of God's perfected and finished creation."[7] All creation and His provision for it were stunningly complete, in perfect order, mutually beneficial. It couldn't possibly get any better. No more emptiness, no more void.

God created everything that was perfect out of that which was empty and void. What do you conclude about who God is? Is your conclusion different from who you thought He was? If so, how?

Genesis 2:1 tells us that on the seventh day, a holy God "rested" (Hebrew *shabath*, from which the word *sabbath* comes). It means not only the total cessation from the work that had been done but also the celebration of a "perfected and finished creation." God ceased and celebrated—rested—totally satisfied with the work of His hands. His divine design was very good and worthy of celebration. Think about that! Does the awareness that God rested—ceased from and celebrated His work—surprise you? What further insight does this give you into our Creator God?

(i) DID YOU KNOW?

The number seven is the biblical number of completion and perfection.

This next verse in our Genesis study will reveal one of the most significant aspects of God's character even though it is only implied. Read Genesis 2:3. What did God do that made the seventh day different from the others, and why did He do it?

"So God blessed the seventh day and made it holy" (2:3 ESV). He set it apart—dedicated it— to Himself and for Himself, not because He had an immense ego but because what He did would forever reveal who He is.

Consider this: Only holiness can make something holy. If God declared the seventh day holy, then God Himself was holy. Holiness describes both "the majesty of God and the purity and moral perfection of His nature . . . All of His thoughts and actions are consistent with His holy character."[8]

Psalm 77:13 (ESV) proclaims, *"Your way, O God, is holy. What god is great like our God?"* Therefore, whatever He does is holy; wherever He is, is holy; whatever He proclaims is holy. Everything fashioned in His six days of creating then was holy.

God set the seventh day aside to celebrate all that is holy, good, complete, satisfying, and worthy of recognition and gratitude. And He will require humanity to do the same.

Holy is not a comfortable or even realistic concept in today's culture. It may have a foreign feel to most people or conjure up images of a TV program's rendition of the prudish "church lady." Say this word—*holy*—a few times to yourself—out loud. What is your response to this word?

Why is it important to remind yourself that God is holy? What does this have to do with your life, especially in today's culture?

> Prayer: In Isaiah 6:3 (ESV), angelic creatures called out, *"Holy, holy, holy is the LORD of hosts; the whole earth is full of his glory!"* They spoke of His holiness and His revealed glory throughout creation. Take a few moments now to do the same.

DAY 2

THE DIVINE RELATER

Have you ever watched a Navy ship come into port? Spouses race to sailors, children tackle fathers and mothers, and tears of joy run freely. No one can watch such a homecoming and doubt that humankind was designed for relationships.

In day 1 we talked about a holy God as Supreme Being and Divine Designer of all creation. Now let's focus on this same God as the Divine Designer of relationships.

> *"God created man in His own image, in the image of God*
> *He created him; male and female He created them."*
>
> Genesis 1:27

Compare Genesis 1:6–25 with verses 26–31. Do you see a shift in God's creation process? What is now different about God's creating?

_____

_____

_____

God made a deliberate, divine shift from creating the earth and everything in it. _"God created man in his own image, in the image of God he created him; male and female he created them"_ (1:27 ESV). Humanity was made in God's image, likeness, or resemblance, "not an exact duplicate," but the "shadow of a thing."[9] The first couple was not a physical resemblance of our Creator but a spiritual resemblance of our Creator. What do you think it meant for this first couple to resemble God?

_____

_____

_____

The shift in creation in Genesis 1:26–31 also revealed a new name for God. _Elohim_ ("God") of Genesis 1 became _Yaweh Elohim_, _"the LORD God"_ beginning in Genesis 2:4. "Yahweh is used wherever the Bible stresses God's personal relationship with his people and the ethical aspect of his nature [upright, righteous—_holy!_]"[10] (brackets ours).

Here we see the divine design of relationships not only between God and humanity but between humanity and the rest of creation. According to Genesis 1:28–30, God blessed (put an honor upon) this first male and female. What relationship did He establish between them and the rest of His creation?

_____

_____

_____

By divine decree, God initiated a foundational concept for relationships. It was trust. He entrusted His entire creation into this couple's care, and they entrusted their entire care into His hands.

By divine decree, God entrusted those He created in His image to act as His representatives on earth. Can you identify with this aspect of trust? What has God entrusted into your care? Why do you think He has done this?

_____

_____

_____

_____

By divine provision, God established His first couple's welfare and sustenance. He met and would continue to meet their every need. On whom do you depend for your every need? How does this impact your sense of security should your needs not be met?

By divine commission, the first couple was blessed and charged to *"be fruitful and multiply"* (1:28) starting with just the two of them. Up until now, only the birds of the air and living creatures were given this blessing and command (Genesis 1:22). Now the human couple was to propagate and fill the earth with their own kind. What do you think would compel them to want to? Think about that.

Just as Genesis 1 paints the big picture of creation, Genesis 2 paints a more detailed account of God's creation of the first couple. According to Genesis 2:7, God created Adam first. How did He do this?

Note that after God created the man *"out of the dust from the ground,"* He *"breathed into his nostrils the breath of life; and man became a living being."* The breath of life means "spirit" or "soul," which tells us that at that moment in time the man (and humankind in general) became not only a physical being but also a spiritual being. He had the capacity to relate to the God of the universe. How intimate a moment in creation that must have been! The created was designed to walk in fellowship with his Creator, the Author of relationships, Spirit to spirit. That would be cause for celebration! Apart from this divine design, life would not be fully life. Rather, it would be *"without form and an empty waste"* (Genesis 1:2, AMP), much like the dark earth before it was touched by God's hand.

Have you considered that the God of the universe was also the Author of relationships? What implication does this have on every relationship in your life?

Now read Genesis 2:8–14. In what ways did the Creator make it evident that He was establishing a relationship with Adam and that He cared deeply for this one created in His image?

Take a few moments to imagine God and Adam walking in the garden and talking together. Imagine the pure pleasure with which God presented this glorious Paradise. Imagine Adam's awe, wonder, and delight at the abundance of God's gift. The garden was filled with beautiful trees laden with luscious fruit. Not just one but four rivers flowed out of the garden of Eden, a land lavish with precious metals and gemstones. If we take the time to ponder the magnificence of this Paradise, our imaginations really wouldn't do justice to the garden's true beauty, riches, and satisfaction—God's perfect provision of such "copious splendors." Glory!

Can you identify with how it feels to receive just the right gift from someone you love—a gift that is not only enjoyable but which fills a need? Can you give an example?

_____

_____

God continued to affirm His relationship with Adam by entrusting him with personal responsibility over the garden. Read Genesis 2:15. What was Adam's responsibility?

_____

In Genesis 2:16–17 God entrusted Adam with the responsibility to carry out His instructions. This would be Adam's spiritual responsibility, which was critical to their relationship. What was God's message to Adam?

_____

Adam's personal responsibility was to care for his dwelling place, and his spiritual responsibility was to obey God's instructions. He was establishing Adam in his roles of leader, protector, and provider for the woman who would become his wife and for the family that would follow. How Adam discharged these responsibilities would measure his allegiance to his Maker. And it's no mistake that the woman was not yet on the scene. God was making a deliberate point: He held Adam, the man, accountable in these two areas of responsibility.

God was deliberate in all He did; therefore, each nuance of His creative hand had His divine purpose in mind for the greater good of all creation and for His glory—always for His glory.

God wasn't done with His great gift giving. What was missing from Adam's life, and how did God make this evident to Adam? Read verses 18–20.

_____

When God required Adam to name His creatures, perhaps it became apparent to Adam that he didn't have a companion according to his kind. Who would meet *his* need? Who would provide the perfect counterpart for him as was provided for each creature he named? We believe that God intentionally designed this void. Why do you think God would build a purposeful void in Adam's life?

What God had in mind for Adam was unlike any other creature He had fashioned. This *"helper suitable"* would be Adam's *ezer kenegdo*. The word *ezer* "is used only twenty places in the entire Old Testament. And in every other instance the person being described is God himself, when you need him to come through for you *desperately*."[11] This gives us insight into God's heart for Adam. He knew exactly what Adam needed. The only answer was an *ezer*, whom Hebrew scholar Robert Alter translates as "sustainer beside him."

Read Genesis 2:21–22, and describe what happened.

Why do you think God created the woman out of Adam's rib instead of out of the dust of the ground?

It would have been easy for God to create the woman the same way He created the man. But we believe He wanted to make two necessary points to Adam: First, God is the source of all provision—physical, emotional, spiritual, relational. Second, because God fashioned the woman out of Adam's own body, Adam would understand that he had a new responsibility: to lovingly lead, fearlessly protect, and faithfully provide for this one who was to be so necessary to his life.

God's counterpart (*kenegdo*) for Adam was to be the positive influence, the sustainer and support by her husband's side. Can you wrap your mind around God's concept of this counterpart? Our concept is so small, so lackluster when compared to His purposeful plan for her and for them. Think about that, especially as it relates to the many messages you write on your mental slate about being your husband's or future husband's wife. Picture being his *ezer kenegdo* as God originally intended. What would that look like?

Whether or not you're married, consider this visual: put your hands in front of you, palms toward your face. Your right hand is you, the perfect counterpart fashioned just for your husband, who is represented by your left hand. Take your right index finger and trace your left hand up alongside your little finger, down the valley and up alongside your ring finger. Continue up and down your fingers all the way to the other side of your thumb. The tips of the fingers on your left hand are your husband's (or future husband's) strengths. The valleys are his weaknesses. Now do the same with your left index finger along the fingers of your right hand. The tips of your fingers are your strengths; the valleys are your weaknesses. Now slide your fingers together with palms still facing you. Do you see that your strengths fill his valleys and his fill yours? How does this visual affirm God's divine design for marriage? What is the significance of this visual as it relates to you and your husband or future husband?

Based on what you just learned about a man's *ezer kenegdo*, assess the power and responsibility God has given this female counterpart. What blessings do you associate with her role? What can this mean for you in your own marriage?

Married or unmarried, do you understand that our holy God is the source of all provision—that only He can fill our emptiness? Our relational God desires to be the source of all provision for you. Where in your life do you need His supply right now?

God knew Adam's need, and He provided. His loving hand fashioned for Adam this exquisite feminine creature. She was the culmination of His "copious splendor." Creation was complete, and God pronounced all creation "very good"!

EXTRA MILE
Psalm 100

How does Psalm 100 describe God's relationship with those He created? What should the response of the created be?

Prayer: Do you perceive the Divine Relater working in your life, wooing you to Himself, desiring your trust in, your allegiance to, and your dependence on Him for your total provision? Whether or not you're married, do you feel alone and lonely, as if everyone else is complete but you?

Do you sense that there is more to life than what you are experiencing right now? Speak your needs to God. Even if you're not convinced, speak your trust in and dependence on Him as the ultimate provider.

DAY 3

THE DIVINE UNITER

God revealed His love, His power, His glory, and His holiness in every aspect of His creation. But the most stunning revelation of God's loving character was evident in the divine relationship He established between the first man and woman. Here the image of God in this first innocent man fused with the image of God in this first innocent woman, revealing the essence of their Creator.

Look carefully at Genesis 2:23. What was Adam's reaction when God brought the woman to him? What's significant about his response?

Adam instantly recognized and understood their oneness. His declaration was jubilant and intimate. His counterpart—bone of his bones and flesh of his flesh—was aptly named *Woman*. He professed it with the cherished language of love, as if he looked into her eyes and saw his own soul.

In that powerful moment in human history, God declared His divine design for male and female. He deliberately created "only one [woman] for Adam, not several [women] or another Adam"[12] (brackets ours). This blueprint promised them the "very good" from life and represented the immense care and concern of the Divine Relater who loved them. His design for marriage was for their good and blessing.

By today's standard, God's parameters on marriage are fast fading and in some ways considered irrelevant. But from the beginning, God lovingly established the two parameters of heterosexuality and monogamy. He sealed them with a divine, three-part command in Genesis 2:24. What was His command? What is the man's responsibility according to this command? What is the woman's responsibility?

"For this reason . . ." What reason? Adam understood that his counterpart, Woman, was now his to care for. Her welfare was in his keeping, and God would hold him accountable for this sacred trust. Adam not only understood the fact of her creation, but he also understood the sober reality of his sweet responsibility to the one who would accompany him through life in God's covenant of marriage.

*"For this reason a man shall leave his father and his mother, and
be joined to his wife; and they shall become one flesh."*

Genesis 2:24

Leaving was God's first step in the practice of marital commitment and permanence—a command given to the man. It means to "forsake, loose, leave, refuse, relinquish" dependence on father and mother in order to establish interdependence with his wife. God gave the man the responsibility to take this step first, to which his wife would respond in kind.

What does it mean to you to leave your father and mother to establish your spouse as primary? In your journal, write what you would look for in a man who left his father and mother for you. What would leaving your father and mother for him look like? If you are married, would you say that you and your husband have left your parents in order to make each other the primary relationship?

God also charged the man to *cleave* or unite to his wife—to hold her fast to himself in a way that assures her of his loving leadership, provision, and protection. She responds to his strength by cleaving to him in return as his companion, counterpart, support, and sustainer. When each cleaves, they establish mutual allegiance. *Cleaving* is God's second step in the practice of marital commitment and permanence.

Why is cleaving important in a marriage? How can you tell when spouses aren't cleaving to each other?

---

*Leaving and cleaving are strong yet tender acts of commitment.
They are also the order of commitment,
so that the third command—"become one flesh"—would be safe,
securing, and satisfying.*

Leaving and cleaving are strong yet tender acts of commitment. They are also the order of commitment, so that the third command, *"become one flesh"*, would be safe, securing, and satisfying. Becoming one flesh completes God's three-part harmony in the practice of marital oneness, commitment, and permanence. It is the ultimate act of covenant—the physical expression that ratifies a couple's commitment and affirms their permanence. This covenant sealer is sexual intercourse. God's divine design for the first couple ignited their desire for each other and drove them together as one flesh again and again. By God's deliberate intention, sex was the powerful, pleasurable, and sacred expression of their love for and commitment to each other. And each intimate encounter fostered their allegiance, secured their trust, and strengthened their oneness.

Sexual intimacy was not only the exchange of their two bodies but also the exchange of their two souls. Uniquely and purposefully fashioned into this powerful exchange was the gift of new life. It was a natural and yet miraculous phenomenon in answer to God's command to *"be fruitful and multiply, and fill the earth"* (1:28). With humanity created in God's image, the first couple would start filling the earth with people who would resemble His heart and represent Him well on the earth.

What does it mean to you to become one flesh with your husband? How does this marital act foster allegiance in your marriage? Secure trust in your marriage? Strengthen oneness in your marriage?

The first man and woman's leaving, cleaving, and becoming one set the stage for future generations to do the same. Based on what you're learning, what's right about God's divine design for a husband and wife?

Finally, read Genesis 2:25. What is the state of this couple's divine union?

To be naked was "to be or make bare." Adam and his wife were naked—vulnerable—not only to God but to each other inside and outside, fully accepting and fully acceptable, fully trusting, fully trustworthy, and fully surrendered. As a result, they were unashamed in every area— physically, emotionally, spiritually, and sexually. They didn't blush when they stared at each other in wonderment and divine awe. They had no inhibitions, no fear of rejection, no condemnation, no conditions, no selfish needs, wants, and desires being served over the other. It was innocent, beautiful, and delightful.

Security, significance, beauty, depth, soul-mate satisfaction, sexual fulfillment, and family contentment were the by-products of God's original intent for marriage, beginning with this first couple. What a beautiful picture! God's standard for marriage from the beginning was to be naked and unashamed—inside and out.

> Prayer: Perhaps you never knew that leaving, cleaving, and becoming one was God's formula for a committed and permanent marriage relationship, that they work together to foster allegiance, secure trust, and strengthen oneness. Ask God to keep His blueprint fresh in your mind so that His foundation will be established in your marriage.

DAY 4

THE DEADLY DECEIVER

Life was beautiful for Adam and his bride. We can only imagine what it must have been like for the first couple to walk hand in hand under the loving care of their God in the beauty of their divine paradise. But life quickly turned. What happened at that moment in time altered God's divine design of relationships for all generations. Let's see how.

In Genesis 3:1 a crafty serpent was in the garden with Adam and his wife. Read Revelation 12:9–10, John 8:44, and 10:10 in that order. Who was this serpent? How do these Scripture verses describe him? What was (and still is) his goal?

_____

_____

_____

_____

> *"You are of your father the devil, and you want to do the desires of*
> *your father. He was a murderer from the beginning, and does not*
> *stand in the truth because there is no truth in him.*
> *Whenever he speaks a lie, he speaks from his own nature, for he is*
> *a liar and the father of lies."*
>
> John 8:44 (NASB)

Little did this innocent pair know that Satan, hater of God and enemy of their souls, was about to poison their paradise. He would finesse the couple toward sin with a strategy that would accomplish his specific goals: separation of the man and woman from God and separation of the man and woman from each other.

Let's look at the five specific ploys that the enemy still uses today to separate relationships. They are *distraction, doubt, debate, deception*, and *desire*. Read Genesis 3:1–6, and assign each of the five ploys to its appropriate verses.

Distraction: The serpent was an added voice to this couple's otherwise intimate circle (v. 1). This distracting intruder was a deviation from their norm, but he accomplished his purpose: He attracted the woman's attention and shifted her focus away from God.

Do you recognize what distracts you away from God? How do you know when your focus is elsewhere?

_____

_____

_____

_____

Doubt: Satan used an effective question, *"Did God really say . . ?"* (3:1, NIV), to plant doubt in the woman's mind and weaken her faith. Doubt is the erosion of trust. Satan implied that God was not trustworthy.

Is Satan challenging your faith with this same strategy of doubt, attempting to erode your trust in God? In what area of your life or in what circumstance do you doubt God?

_____

_____

_____

Debate: When the serpent called God's word into question, he not only introduced doubt, but he also set the stage to debate God's lordship, His authority, and His right to rule over His creation (3:1–5). Note that the woman defended her position by exaggerating God's truth (v. 3), perhaps to magnify in her own mind what she thought she believed. We can get caught in the same deceptive web. Charles Spurgeon lends this perspective to the power of truth: "Truth is like a lion. Whoever heard of defending a lion? Turn it loose, and it will defend itself."[13]

We all question God's authority at times. We rationalize, justify, or explain away what we know to be truth by what we tell ourselves (self-talk). Or perhaps we seek out another whose counsel will support our disobedience. In what area of your life do you debate God's authority with your self-talk or another's talk?

_____

_____

Deception is about using just enough truth to make a lie believable.

Deception: Dishonest debate was the hook that reeled the woman in and prepared her for Satan's deception (3:4–5). Deception is using just enough truth to make a lie believable. Satan directly attacked God's truth, *"You will surely die"* (2:17) with a blatant lie, *"You surely will not die!"* (3:4) so that she questioned God's command. Satan also distorted God's motive, deliberately inferring that God was selfishly withholding the desirable. The implication here is that God was not trustworthy in His provision, and the woman believed the serpent.

Has someone used dishonest debate to deceive you? How did this scenario play out?

_____

_____

_____

Do you find yourself questioning God and His provision for you—that He is withholding the desirable from you? What provision is missing in your life that causes you to believe that God is not for you?

_____

_____

Desire: "When the woman saw . . ." (3:6). Can you sense the woman's discontent? Her desire was in full bloom giving rise to a previously unknown sensation—temptation. Her desire for more trumped the command of God, and disobedience was born—the deadly outcome of doing business with the devil.

Are you currently in a season of discontent? Do you wrestle with, "If only . . . ?" or "What if . . . ?" If you can finish these questions, you'll come closer to discovering the source of your discontent. What do you discover?

_____

_____

Now compare Genesis 2:9 and 3:6. What's different about the description of the tree of the knowledge of good and evil in these verses? How did Satan alter the woman's understanding of what "good" looked like? Why do you think he did this?

_____

_____

Although the tree was good for food and pleasing to the eye, God knew that if they ate they would experience not only good and blessing, but evil and death. Satan offered an alternate "truth", a counterfeit that seemed better than God's command. They chose poorly. Adam and the woman's oneness would soon be divided.

Finally, read Genesis 3:7. Something devastating happened after Adam took a bite of the fruit. What was it?

_____

_____

When *"the eyes of both of them were opened . . . "* (3:7), they experienced the sudden awakening of evil. What did they discover? What did they do?

_____

_____

Rather than uphold his leadership role. Adam listened to his wife and chose disobedience. Immediately their freedom became chains. Shame bound them, and they covered their nakedness with fig leaves. They hid from each other, and they hid from God.

When Adam and his wife chose Satan's counterfeit, their vulnerability to all that was deadly would plague them and all humanity for every generation to come. Not only had they gained nothing, but they lost everything.

Anything that God created for our good now has an evil alternative—Satan's counterfeit. Is there a counterfeit in your life to something that God created originally for your good and His glory? If so, think about that counterfeit right now. Has it altered your life? If so, for good or for evil? How do you know?

Prayer: Lord, You knew what was best for Your first couple, and You know what is best for me. Help me to discern when I'm being distracted from Your best. Help me not to doubt Your provision, debate Your goodness, be deceived by the hater of my soul, or desire what he wants for me. Help me to discern the liar's snare of *"Did God really say. . . ?"* that I may respond without doubt: *"Thus says the LORD . . ."*

DAY 5

THE DEADLY DIVIDE

The famous movie, *A Christmas Story*, describes life through the eyes of a young schoolboy in Indiana. In one scene, his official secret message decoder arrived in the mail from his favorite radio program. Scurrying to the only private place in the house—the bathroom—he rushed to open the secret instructions that he thought would reveal something powerful. With Mom and little brother banging on the door, he struggled to decode the enclosed secret message only to find that it was just an advertisement for the program's sponsor. We see the innocence wash from his face as he realized that he had been deceived.

"Things aren't always what they seem." Does this sound like a cliché? It isn't. It's a serious statement of fact. Often we're willing to trade the truly and perfectly satisfying for what seems more desirable.

God gave the first man and woman His perfect and loving best. And although what God offered them was perfectly enough, they chose to believe the lie and didn't see the "enough" in it. They chose to trust self over God and His provision for them. As a result, humanity inexhaustibly pursues the elusive "more," which will never be enough.

But that wasn't the only by-product of their disobedience. Read Genesis 3:8–10. Based on their response to God's presence in the garden, what happened to Adam and his wife's relationship with the Lord? Why did Adam say they hid from God (v. 10)?

There are two key points in verse 10: First, Adam and his wife's new knowledge of good and evil brought to them a sudden awareness of "self." As a result, their nakedness was no longer holy in their eyes, but shameful and required cover.

The second key point is that fear was introduced among a host of new and negative emotions. Adam was frightened by the very One who lovingly gave him his first breath. The relationship of trust that God had with this couple was replaced with a gulf neither could cross. It was called sin.

In Genesis 3:11, God posed an important question to Adam. Why do you think He asked him this question?

_____

_____

_____

God was giving Adam every opportunity to confess his wrongdoing. Instead, Adam chose a different route. What did he do (v. 12)?

_____

_____

_____

Adam no longer trusted God and would no longer entrust himself to God, not because God was no longer trustworthy but because Adam believed the lie. Blame now trumped confession in Adam's exchange with God. He blamed the woman for giving him the fruit, and he blamed God for giving him the woman.

Adam "threw his wife under the bus," so to speak. And God was good enough to turn to her for her side of the story. God had a different response to the woman's explanation than to Adam's. What's important about this exchange in Genesis 3:13–14?

_____

_____

_____

The woman was genuinely deceived, and God's curse on the serpent proved this point. However, because of God's holy nature, judgment was necessary. In Genesis 3:16, how did God judge the woman?

_____

_____

_____

As women, we can only imagine how childbearing and childbirth would have been different had Adam and his wife not sinned. Now every aspect associated with reproduction, every phase of childbearing (from menses to menopause) and childbirth itself would have the potential of pain and heartbreak.

And there's more. This couple's oneness radically changed. Contention replaced contentment when God told the woman, *"And you will desire to control your husband, but he will rule over you"* (3:16, NTL). She would no longer be content with her role as supporter and sustainer. Nor would she be content with her husband's role as leader in their relationship. In the same way, he would display a distorted authority over her rather than the tender role of servant/leader, protector, and provider. "Sin has turned the harmonious system of God-ordained roles into distasteful struggles of self-will."[14] This has been the state of the marital union ever since.

Did you know before now that a wife who contends for her husband's leadership role and a husband who misuses his authority are the direct result of this first couple's sin? A wife doesn't trust her husband and desires to usurp his authority, while a husband doesn't trust God and misuses his authority. Both create opposition and conflict—separation—in the marital relationship rather than the oneness God originally intended.

If you are married, is there opposition and conflict in your relationship? Is trust an issue? If so, when did this distrust begin? If you are engaged to be married, it is wise to consider these questions before you tie the knot.

_____

_____

_____

Since Genesis 2:24 is foundational to the marital commitment, everything that is right with a marriage as well as everything that is wrong with the marriage is traceable back to this one Scripture. Someone is or isn't leaving, someone is or isn't cleaving, someone is or isn't becoming one. Is this truth apparent in the opposition or conflict that exists in your relationship? If so, in what ways?

_____

_____

_____

In Genesis 3:17–19, God now addresses Adam. What were the consequences for his disobedience and why?

_____

_____

_____

Caring for the garden and providing for his family would no longer be a pleasurable endeavor for Adam. God said that Adam would work long and hard and battle the cursed ground just to put food on the table—no more plucking plentiful produce from Paradise. Why would Adam listen to his wife over God? What could the woman have said to Adam that would cause him to forego his obedience to God? Although we will never know the answers to these questions, we do know that their choices had a profound and eternal impact on all humanity.

Has your voice ever caused another to forego a conviction and choose to trade a truth for a lie? If so, what problems did that cause?

_____

_____

_____

_____

Does Adam's consequence play out in your own life? If so, in what way?

_____

_____

_____

_____

Adam's struggle would continue *"until you return to the ground"* (3:19)—a statement of limitation. Adam and all who were born after him would return to the ground in physical death.

Adam and his wife discovered that what God said was true: They would surely die. Death would have its sting by way of loss in everything that life had to offer: love, trust, oneness, and ultimately life itself. Their self-lordship led to division and death. All that was holy, moral, and securing was now profaned. All that God designed for good was now in a state of deterioration. Humanity's loss was immeasurable and irretrievable—deadly, indeed.

Read Genesis 3:20-21. Note that immediately after God pronounced His judgment, Adam renamed his wife "Eve." It means "the mother of all the living." That's the good news, since God could have ended humanity right there. The bad news is that Adam renamed her at all, signifying the shift in their marital intimacy and oneness. It reflected the shift in their relationship that God had pronounced in 3:16. "What [Adam] named her is not important. That he named her is the thing because naming is to exercise dominion, authority over her."[15]

God didn't annihilate Adam and Eve; instead, He clothed them (3:21). Why do you think He clothed them?

_____

_____

_____

_____

God was sending a spiritual message when He clothed this couple with the skins of slain animals. He was the God of provision, even in their sin; and some day He would provide the Way out of sin (v.15). What a good God.

In Genesis 3:22–24, what did God do, and why did He do it? What does this tell you about Adam and Eve's relationship with God?

_____

_____

_____

We believe that God didn't drive Adam and Eve from the garden as an act of retribution but as an act of love and protection. Had He permitted them to remain, they would have eaten from the tree of life and lived forever in sin's sting and loss. True to His nature, He was merciful. Also true to His nature, He was just. Spiritual unity with the Creator was lost to eternal separation.

And a God-shaped hole would exist in every human soul. Could Adam and Eve conceive of what their disobedience had just unleashed?

> Prayer: This week, acknowledge your Divine Designer differently. Perceive His pursuing you, calling you to embrace the divine design for which you were created. May you lean into His heart and let Him fill every void with Himself.

LESSON 2

THE DIVINE REDEMPTION

The Atlantic coast is famous for riptides, which are currents of water along the beach that run from the shore out to sea more rapidly than the surrounding surf. These strong tides can quickly pull even the most experienced swimmers far into the ocean and away from shore. Often people are caught up in riptides before they know it and must be rescued even as they deny being in trouble. Lifeguards know what swimmers have yet to discover: Riptides are almost impossible to swim against and can deplete even marathoner strength and stamina.

This is a great metaphor for a life caught up in the riptide of sin. Adam and Eve were in over their heads, caught in the current of "self," a current humanity has been riding ever since. But God . . .

DAY 1

THE ROAD TO IDOLATRY

As we learned in Lesson 1, God put purpose, pleasure, and satisfaction into everything He created. Our world is laden with "copious splendor," and we have been given the natural desire to greatly delight in it all.

One of the most beautiful expressions of God's love toward Adam and Eve was reflected in the pleasurable gift of sexual intimacy. God intended that this first couple desire and delight in each other on a regular basis with an abandonment that expressed the inexpressible. Does this surprise you? Their delight in each other was to remind them to delight in the One who is the great Giver of all things "very good."

But Satan had another plan. His deception convinced Eve that blessing from God was suspect and insufficient. When temptation was introduced, God's best for Adam and Eve was no longer good enough. They wanted what they thought God was denying them.

> *Having been exposed to nothing but God's goodness, Adam and Eve*
> *had opened the door to unimaginable evil, the greatest of which*
> *was their independence from God. Self was now the compelling*
> *focus of their everyday landscape.*

This new knowledge became a never-ending tension between the good they knew and the evil that had opened their eyes. In Genesis 3:7, the Hebrew word for *open* is *paqach*, meaning "a sudden miracle, but not a good one; a rude awakening of the conscience." They were suddenly aware of the magnitude of their poor choice, and they experienced a startling awareness of right and wrong. Having been exposed to nothing but God's goodness, they had opened the door to unimaginable evil, the greatest of which was their independence from God. Self was now the compelling focus of their everyday landscape.

Think about independence from God being the greatest of all evil. Why do you think that is?

When Adam and Eve chose to be mastered by self instead of by their Creator, everything shifted for them and for the rest of humanity. God-given desires were perverted in both concept and conduct and fostered insatiable longing. Self reigned. Lust ruled at any cost. The search and fulfillment of more desires and pleasures became a perennial pursuit. How does 1 John 2:16 describe this pursuit? Where was the shift?

Another shift was humanity's concept of self—from a God-image to a distorted self-image. No longer would the created see themselves through the loving, accepting eyes of their Creator, but through the warped lens of conditional acceptance focused on never good enough, pretty enough, smart enough, popular enough, rich enough, sexy enough, thin enough, or successful enough. We will desire more in an attempt to feel better about ourselves. According James 4:1–3, what can we resort to?

Yet another shift was humanity's concept of humanity. No longer would people see one another as created in God's image. Everyone was suspect. Fault-finding, suspicion, and blame were all by-products of Satan's plan. Evil was continually perpetrated against others in the name of "self." How did this play out in Genesis 6:5–6 and 9:6?

A final shift was humanity's concept of God-given sexuality. His paradigm was clear in Genesis 2:24 when He called the couple to leave, cleave, and become one. According to 1 Thessalonians 4:3–7, what is the evidence of this paradigm shift?

Once we made self the center of the universe, idolatry was born. We would embrace the counterfeit of all that was holy and legitimately desirable. "Forbidden fruit" would be the flavor of the day—for all our days.

DID YOU KNOW?
Is God's Jealousy Like Man's?

Because God is perfect and pure, His jealousy comes from that same place. Man's jealousy is corrupted by sin; therefore, it is self-serving. God's jealousy is "other" serving. He yearns for us to desire His best. He knows that when we give our allegiance to another, we will be at least damaged if not destroyed by what we pursue.

Let's get a perspective on this concept of idolatry. According to Exodus 20:3 and Deuteronomy 4:23–24, how would you define idolatry? What's God's warning against idolatry?

According to the Psalm 115:4–8, what happens when we put our trust in idols?

God preserved a holy lineage through Adam and Eve's third son Seth all the way to Abraham, Isaac, and Jacob generations later. He established a people to claim as His own—the nation of Israel—called to be a holy people set apart for His use, prepared and ready to represent Him and reflect His holiness to godless nations. In Isaiah 42:8 and 45:5–6, what did God assert about Himself, and why do you think He did so?

Read Isaiah 44:9–19. What did this prophet say is the folly of idolatry?

Let's focus on Isaiah 44:19 (ESV). Isaiah made a big point here about this piece of wood. He says, *"No one considers, nor is there knowledge or discernment to say, 'Half of it I burned in the fire; I also baked bread on its coals; I roasted meat and have eaten. And shall I make the rest of it an abomination? Shall I fall down before a block of wood?'"* Based on how these two halves of wood were used, what's the point?

Here is the inescapable conclusion: The problem was not with the wood, but how the wood was used—for God's intended good but also for perversity. Anything and everything that God created for good, humanity can use for evil.

The Message enhances verses 18–19: "*Pretty stupid, wouldn't you say? Don't they have eyes in their heads? Are their brains working at all? Doesn't it occur to them to say, 'Half of this tree I used for firewood: I baked bread, roasted meat, and enjoyed a good meal. And now I've used the rest to make an abominable no-god. Here I am praying to a stick of wood!'*" Can you detect the counterfeit of God's "good?"

> "He feeds on ashes; a deceived heart has turned him aside.
> And he cannot deliver himself, nor say,
> 'Is there not a lie in my right hand?'"

Isaiah 44:20

What does Isaiah 44:20 further reveal about the folly of this block of wood?

Isn't it ironic that God's people feed on ashes instead of fresh bread or a delicious steak? What makes us choose ashes rather than God's perfect good? Any time we choose to substitute anything (or any one) for God, we hold *"a lie in my right hand"* and embark on a journey toward death. Its beginnings are subtle, even seemingly innocent, but the trek is nonetheless deathward, because we cannot deliver ourselves. Riptide.

That's where idolatry will lead every time. But not all idolatry is a literal block of wood worshipped by a primitive culture. Pastor and theologian Alistair Begg talks about idolatry that "is rampant in even the most technologically advanced nations on the planet. Idolatry . . . includes the pursuit of anything other than the glory of God as one's central purpose for being. But . . . idolatry also occurs in a more subtle manner. Anytime we deny an attribute of the Lord revealed in Scripture or allow our own preferences to determine His character, we are guilty of . . . idolatry."[1] This idolatry of the heart has taken hold of societies worldwide, including our own. Sadly and predictably, it also offers only mouths full of ashes—a figurative *"lie in my right hand."*

How about you? Can you identify idols you pursue that reflect "anything other than the glory of God?" List them here or in your journal. What did you gain (or are you gaining) from this idol? What did you lose (or are you losing) from this idol?

What attributes of God might you deny or ignore in pursuit of these idols?

When was the last time you had a mouthful of ashes? What did those ashes represent? What do you think God's provision was for you?

These questions may be difficult and even unnerving because our answers may reveal idolatrous hearts—hearts that are more faithful to something or someone other than God. And that's the point. Every one of us at some time or other will choose the idol instead of what God offers. We choose our own pursuits over God's perfect provision for us, and we wade right into the riptide. Are you there?

> Prayer: Lord, at times I feel like an Israelite. I know there is no other God besides You, but I sometimes search for more apart from You. I don't want to be a fraud, Lord, or desire the fraudulent. I want the real thing. Show me when I hold *"a lie in my right hand."*

DAY 2

THE ROAD TO DEATH

The death toll was staggering. Here lay a marriage ripped apart by deceit, a sacred relationship cut in two by hurt, anger, and distrust. A husband's reputation and integrity crushed; a wife's security and dreams shattered; their children's innocence and stability shaken—all casualties of a broken covenant. How did this happen? How did something that began so well end so tragically?

Read Romans 5:12. What did Adam's disobedience introduce into the world, and how did it affect us all?

Romans 1:18–32 illuminates humanity's road map to death after the fall. In verses 18–20, what's the problem and why?

Look carefully at verses 21–22. How are the ungodly characterized?

_____

_____

Humanity ceased to be thankful to its Creator God even though *"that which is known about God is evident within them; for God made it evident to them"* (1:19). As a result, their thought lives became futile, their foolish hearts were darkened (v. 22), and an exchange was made: the incorruptible and immortal for the corruptible and mortal (our idol of choice). Today's idols don't look like the ones of old. They are "often mental rather than metal. But people still devote their lives to, and trust in, many things other than God."[2]

What was God's response to humanity's misbehavior (sin) in verses 24, 26, and 28?

_____

_____

_____

He *"gave them up"* (KJV), *"abandoned"* (NLT), *"gave them over"* (NASB), to themselves (1:24). According to verse 23, why was that?

_____

_____

_____

With each giving over, humanity's sin became darker. According to verses 24, 26–28, how did sin progress?

_____

_____

Why did this happen? The answer is in Romans 1:25. Write it here:

_____

_____

> *"For they exchanged the truth of God for a lie,*
> *and worshiped and served the creature rather than the Creator,*
> *who is blessed forever. Amen."*
>
> Romans 1:25 (NASB)

Even today we exchange the true God for idols. And God will let us. Doesn't that scare you—even just a little? Paul makes a compelling case. Who in their right mind would choose to be given over to self? Self should be the last place we want to be, and yet it's right where unregenerate humanity is—in the center of self.

How has *"that which is known about God"* (1:19) been made evident to you? In other words, how do you know God is real?

_____

In what ways has our culture exchanged *"the truth of God for a lie"* (1:25)? Has this exchange affected how you view God? If so, in what way? If not, why not?

Why won't God let us off the hook even today (v. 20)?

Humanity believes God is not good enough, big enough, giving enough, fun enough. He does not satisfy and is not satisfying. He is not fulfilling, and He will not fulfill us. The lies start small, almost imperceptibly subtle, adding lie upon lie to establish a mind-set that prefers independence over God-dependence.

Here's the truth about the lie: The minute we choose to step away from God for another thing, we don't have that thing. That thing has us. Idolatry takes over any time the truth is traded for a lie, and eventually it takes us where we never intended to go.

The Message (1:25) puts humanity's dilemma this way: *"They traded the true God for a fake god, and worshiped the god they made instead of the God who made them—the God we bless, the God who blesses us."*

It bears repeating: The truth versus the lie has always been, is, and will always be the stuff of idolatry. "No one should complain that God has left insufficient evidence of his existence and character; the fault is with those who reject the evidence."[3] Even in the garden of Eden, God made His existence and character clear to Adam and Eve. However, the enemy was also at work in the garden to alter their perceptions of God's character—and the more warped their perceptions, the darker their sin. Satan strives to do the same today.

According to Romans 1:29–31, what sins other than sexual sins result from turning away from God?

If all the sins in this Romans passage (vv. 24–31) are the outflow of turning from God, is any sin worse than the other? If yes, what makes it worse? If no, what makes them all the same?

Paul makes a final, startling declaration in Romans 1:32. What is he saying, and what do you think he means?

_____

_____

_____

In light of verse 32, revisit this question: If all the sins in this Romans passage (vv. 24–31) are the outflow of turning from God, is any sin worse than the other? If yes, what makes it worse? If no, what makes them all the same?

_____

_____

_____

All unrighteousness is sin (1 John 5:17), and all sin results from turning away from God, which is the ultimate sin.

When you practice any behavior, whether righteous or unrighteous, it becomes your habit and eventually your lifestyle. Are you currently practicing any of the behaviors in this Romans passage (vv. 18–32)? If so, has it become your lifestyle? If yes, what truth have you exchanged for the lie? How has this practice impacted your life? Others' lives?

_____

_____

_____

EXTRA MILE
Desperate for a Redeemer

Read Romans 3:9–20 and reflect on why all humanity is desperate for a Redeemer, whether we admit it or not. Then continue with Romans 3:21–28 to discover how God met us in our desperation and why. Look closely at verses 23–25. Read these verses slowly and out loud so that you can sense the many short, almost step-by-step phrases of what God did for us through Jesus Christ. Each phrase illuminates the beauty of the gospel and the amazing love of our gracious God.

If all wrongdoing (unrighteousness) is sin, then unless we're perfect, we are all sinners. Now go to Romans 3:23. What's the message to all humanity even in this twenty-first century? What do you think of this message?

_____

_____

_____

Romans 6:23 says that *"the wages of sin is death."* Think about this! God has relegated all humanity to death. This is not just the physical, wasting-away kind of death. It is spiritual death. We are separated from God—even while very much alive physically. And when physical death comes, unless our sins are forgiven we are forever separated from God to a place of eternal torment and everlasting punishment (Mark 9:48–49). We will either live eternally in heaven with God or in hell without Him.

 EXTRA MILE
What Is Hell?

Hell is a bold, biblical reality. We give it little personal consideration, and it gets even less press from the pulpit. But God wants us to take hell very seriously. What does Scripture say about hell in Matthew 3:12; 10:28; 25:41; Mark 8:35–37; 9:43, 47–48; 2 Peter 2:4; Revelation 20:10. Now really, who would want to go there?

Yet, we may be arrogant enough to believe that we can secure our own good, eternal outcome, so we try different roads to save or redeem ourselves. We may gather more knowledge, major in theology, keep moral principles (be "good"), and rack up more good works. We may give more generously and try more earnestly to hit the mark. Somewhere in our souls is the compulsion to be redeemed by somebody. But we can only be redeemed by the One in whose image we were created. We are powerless to deliver ourselves from death.

How can we get back on course? How can we get back into a relationship with God the way it was before the fall? What is our hope?

It's not what; it's Who?

> Prayer: Lord, I thank You for the hope You provide in the midst of deception, darkness, and death. Nothing in my right hand will save me. May I set You continually before me.

DAY 3

THE ROAD TO REDEMPTION

Have you ever been in a relationship that was as close to perfect as you could imagine? Life was good and joyful. You were loved, accepted, and satisfied. And you loved, accepted, and satisfied in return. You both were mutually vulnerable and yet safe and secure.

And then something went wrong. Doubt supplanted trust. Hearts closed and grew cold. The relationship was dying. It was painful; it was personal. Who would step out and initiate the healing, reconciliation, and redemption that could resurrect this relationship?

This is what happened between God and us. And whether we realize it or not, it's still painful and it's still personal. Redemption is still required.

The problem is we don't have what we need to redeem ourselves. According to Romans 5:12, why is that?

Based on Romans 6:23, Who is humanity's hope and what does He offer?

Second Corinthians 5:21 is one of the most revealing Scriptures in the Bible. Read it carefully. What qualifies Jesus Christ to save us from our sin and why? What Great Exchange took place?

Jesus Christ, who was pure, holy, and sinless, traded our sin for His righteousness. He was the only One through whom our sins could be forgiven. He was the only One who could restore us to God for all eternity.

Consider this: If we have all sinned and fallen short of God's holy standard (Romans 3:23), then our sin can be forgiven only when the One who had no sin becomes sin for us *personally*. For the whole picture, read Romans 3:21–26. How can we be made right with God?

Love compelled God to offer His great gift of salvation to anyone who will receive it through faith in Jesus Christ. It is for all who believe (Greek, *pisteuo*), who "cleave to, rely on, trust in, and have faith in" Jesus in a way that "creates complete dependence upon the Lord and not independence."[5]

But Jesus paid a brutal ransom for what we owed. And because the stakes were so high—our eternal destiny—it wasn't a cheap ransom. According to Isaiah 53:1–12, Matthew 26:28, and Hebrews 9:22, what was required for the forgiveness of our sins?

Betrayed and sold (Matthew 26:14–16)

Treated with contempt (Luke 23:11)

Wrongly accused (Matthew 27:12)

Scourged, flogged, whipped (John 19:1)

Struck on the head again and again (Matthew 27:30; John 18:22; 19:3)

Blindfolded, beaten, spat upon, slapped in the face (Mark 14:65; 15:19)

Crowned with a laurel of 3-inch thorns (Matthew 27:29)

Mocked and reviled (Matthew 27:39-44; Luke 23:35)

Stripped (lots cast for clothes) (Matthew 27:28; Luke 23:34)

Offered sour wine (Luke 23:36)

Bore His own cross (John 19:17)

Crucified (Matthew 27:35)

Denied by those He loved (Mark 14:66–71)

His disciples left Him in His time of need (John 16:32)

Forsaken by His Father (Matthew 27:46)

Died (Luke 23:46)

Pierced with a spear to prove He had died (John 19:34)

He was buried (Luke 23:50–54)

According to 1 Corinthians 15:21–22, what did Christ's sacrifice on our behalf accomplish?

Do you see that Great Exchange again in this scripture? Christ's death brought about our resurrection. We are not only alive in Christ but eternally so. What final declaration is made in John 19:30 and what do you think it means?

Here's the bottom line: if we don't believe in the death and resurrection of Jesus Christ on our behalf, there is no Great Exchange for us. Instead, we remain separated from God because our sins haven't been forgiven. We remain eternally and internally impoverished by our sin debt.

Read the following steps in the redemption process and consider where you.

The Poverty: Oswald Chambers puts redemption (salvation) into perspective: "The knowledge of our own poverty is what brings us to the proper place where Jesus Christ accomplishes His work ..."[4] We must recognize our poverty and then acknowledge our need of the Savior. Where is your poverty evident?

The Personal: The Great Exchange—trading our sin for His righteousness—is captured in the most famous verse in the Bible: *"For God so loved the world that he gave his one and only Son, that whoever believes in him shall not perish but have eternal life"* (John 3:16 NIV).

If you were the only one in the world, this promise would stand. What does this mean for you *personally*?

The Prayer: Have you made the Great Exchange with Jesus—your sin for His righteousness? Have you accepted His payment for the debt you owe? Second Corinthians 6:2 (NLT) says, *"the 'right time' is now. Today is the day of salvation."* Jesus said, *"Yes, I am the gate. Those who come in through me will be saved"* (John 10:9, NLT). You can enter in with a simple prayer:

> Lord God, I acknowledge my sin to You, recognizing that You alone can set me free from the sentence of death. I gratefully receive Jesus' payment for the forgiveness of my sin, confident that I am no longer under condemnation. I am righteous in Your eyes. Thank You for so great an exchange. In the name of my Savior, Jesus Christ, Amen.

The Party! Luke 15:10 says that *"there is joy in the presence of the angels of God over one sinner who repents."* Repentance is not a work; it is a response to God's call to return to Himself. To repent simply means "to change the mind...It involves regret or sorrow, accompanied by a true change of heart toward God."[6] Repentance allows us to take hold of God's grace at the point of salvation as well as throughout our lives. Heaven throws a party at your redemption. What does that tell you about your value?

The New Position! As a believer in Jesus Christ, you are a child of God (John 1:12) and a resident in His kingdom (Colossians 1:13–14), permanently redeemed (Hebrews 10:12). Nothing can separate you from His love (Romans 8:38–39). Your salvation is secure! What does this mean for you personally?

EXTRA MILE
The New Covenant

The New Covenant provided complete atonement (total amends) for all believers' sins— past, present, and future. Examine 2 Corinthians 3–4:6 and Hebrews 8–10 in order to fully understand how great a gift!

The Pledge: If you are already a Christian, would you say that you are living in honor of the debt that Christ paid for you? Is your life committed to His lordship? It's one thing to acknowledge Jesus Christ as your Savior. It's quite another to acknowledge Him as your Lord. Will you recommit to Him now as Lord of your life with this simple prayer?

> Lord, it's always tempting to be my own master, but I know that as Your child, I do not have the right to myself anymore. I have been bought with a price, and I am no longer my own (1 Corinthians 6:19). I am Yours, and. I recommit my life to You now. In the mighty name of Jesus—Amen.

It is finished!

DAY 4

THE ROAD TO TRANSFORMATION

The beauty and the certainty of responding yes to God's gift of salvation is that we now have the capacity to live a different life, a life that responds to God's love, a life that desires to please Him. This is evidence of a transformed heart! We become aware of God's presence with us in our places of pleasure as well as our places of pain, in our understanding of life's blessings as well as its trials and tragedies, in the joy of our relationships as well as in the fear of where they're heading.

Christian author John Eldredge wrote, "The redemptive work of Jesus Christ reaches the depths of the human heart. This is absolutely essential for us to believe. For one thing, a good part of Christendom doesn't understand that this is true; they have been told that their heart is still the disaster it was before Jesus found them. Not so."[7]

The New Living Translation puts this passage this way: "Then I will sprinkle clean water on you, and you will be clean. Your filth will be washed away, and you will no longer worship idols. And I will give you a new heart with new and right desires, and I will put a new spirit in you. I will take out your stony heart of sin and give you a new, obedient heart. And I will put my Spirit in you so you will obey my laws and do whatever I command."

So how do we know our hearts can change? The prophet Ezekiel foretold a prophecy that was fulfilled through Jesus Christ. According to Ezekiel 36:25–27 what was promised in every new believer and for what purpose? What is God's part? What is the believer's part?

> *"Then I will sprinkle clean water on you, and you will be clean. Your filth will be washed away, and you will no longer worship idols. And I will give you a new heart, and I will put a new spirit in you. I will take out your stony, stubborn heart and give you a tender, responsive heart. And I will put my Spirit in you so that you will follow my decrees and be careful to obey my regulations."*
>
> Ezekiel 36:25–27 (NLT)

According to 2 Corinthians 5:17, how was the Ezekiel prophecy fulfilled in Christ?

Eldredge continues, "God went for the jugular when he set about our transformation in Jesus Christ. He knows the human heart is the source of our iniquities; he knows that to leave the heart untouched would sabotage his redemptive mission. He promised a new heart; he has given us a new heart."[8]

Even when we don't "feel" like we've been given a new heart, the facts are the facts. Something dramatic happens when one becomes a believer. God infuses His "super" into a new believer's "natural"—that spiritual miracle which converts us from death (the sin nature) to life (the nature of Christ), from old creature to new.

If you've ever rescued a puppy from an animal shelter, you will understand where redemption leads. That puppy was destined for death. You, however, bought him out of his captivity and death sentence and brought him into your "kingdom," your home. He learns that mastery isn't an evil thing when the heart of the master is good. It is from his new master that he receives love in the form of provisions, nurture, training, and discipline. His tail wags every time he's in your presence. His eyes are eager to communicate with you. He willingly responds to your love with loyalty and faithfulness and is totally yielded to you.

This is analogous to our lives in Christ, who rescued us from certain death, removing our chains, and canceling our death sentences. God has delivered us *"from the domain of darkness, and transferred us to the kingdom of His beloved Son"* (Colossians 1:13)

Understanding Ephesians 2:1–10 illuminates the heart of God toward us. This is key to our transformation as well as to how we respond to life's circumstances. According to verses 1–3, what was our condition, and who were we following when God saved us?

_____

_____

In most translations, this next verse begins, *"But God. . . ."* Those two words should always trigger awareness in our minds that power is being enacted on our behalf. In verses 4–5, *"But God"* introduces yet another miraculous exchange. What is it? Why did He do it? How did He do it?

_____

_____

_____

Dead in our sins and alive to Christ. Why? Because of His great love for us. How did He do it? By His grace. What a transaction! He exchanged our chains of death for His newness of life.

Do you find it difficult to believe that you are new because of this exchange? If so, why? What does *"made us alive together with Christ"* mean to you? What can it mean for you right now as you deal with challenging circumstances in your life?

_____

_____

_____

When we least deserved it, God pursued us, drew us, captured our hearts, and restored us to Himself by His grace. What wonderful promises do you discover in Ephesians 2:6–10?

What does verse 10 say is prepared for us and why?

_____

_____

_____

God's grace unfolded His divine plan. We are not only saved by God's grace, but we are secure in it. We are not saved by our works, but we're saved for His works, because there are no good works apart from Christ. And His works in us and through us are necessary in the difficult stuff of life that you may currently be facing.

Understand this: God's grace saved us and not our own goodness. God did not use condemnation or force or coercion or trickery or manipulation. Nor did He wait for us to be better, do better, or do more. The grace that lovingly drew us to Himself is the same grace that lovingly transforms us. By His grace, God drew us and brought us to Himself and by that same grace is transforming us into the image of His Son.

Why do you think God uses grace to transform you rather than moral law, moral code, self-determination, or dutiful rituals?

_____

_____

_____

Think in terms of what you are responsive to when it comes to transforming a negative character trait in yourself. How would you respond to condemnation? To force? To coercion? To trickery? To manipulation? To grace?

_____

_____

_____

Trying to change someone by means of condemnation yields destructive shame and inner defeat. Coercion yields rebellion (either inward or outward). Force yields bitter resentment. Trickery or manipulation yields mistrust. Grace yields reception and responsiveness. God uses grace to divinely influence our hearts. Through grace He reveals Himself and extends His love so that our worst can be influenced by His best. And His grace is His pattern for us as we learn to deal with the worst in ourselves and in others. Grace secures us since it brings about His good and perfect results, both in us and through us. We all need this same grace, especially in life's relational challenges.

> _God's grace is His pattern for us as we learn to deal with the worst in ourselves or even in others._

Let's get a biblical perspective on how grace works in the conversion/transformation process. According to Romans 6:5–7 what happens to us when we are united with Christ? For what purpose? What point is Paul making to a new believer?

_____

_____

_____

_____

Paul doesn't say that believers will never sin again. He says that they are no longer enslaved to sin, that they are set free from sin's power over them. Think about what that means for your life or another's.

Prayerfully consider: Is there something to which you are enslaved? For example: food, Internet, computer time, gossip, television, alcohol, self pity, anger, shopping, lusty books, sexual sin, other? Write it here or in your journal.

_____

_____

Reread Romans 6:6–7 and apply it to what enslaves you. According to these verses, what happened in you?

_____

_____

What do you think *"for he who has died"* (v. 7) means? Died to what?

_____

_____

Now fill in the following blanks with whatever ensnares you: *"We know that our old self was crucified with him in order that the body of sin might be brought to nothing, so that we would no longer be enslaved to _____. For one who has died has been set free from _____"* (Romans 6:6–7 ESV).

How does this apply to your struggle?

_____

_____

_____

Do you grasp the hope that Christ brings to your life or to another's life? We don't have to be enslaved to any of our idols. We can be free in Christ! That's what He came to do for us, and that's what He will accomplish in us—in His way and in His timing. Let's continue:

Read Roman 6:8–11. How should we now view ourselves?

_____

_____

_____

In Romans 6:12–13, a tension rises between God's grace and a believer's response.

According to these verses, what do we stop doing? What do we start doing?

_____

_____

_____

> *"For sin shall not be master over you, for you are not under law but under grace."*
>
> Romans 6:14 (NASB)

This is not just about staying away from something that draws you into sin; it's about turning toward God, presenting yourself to Him, and practicing the righteous thing. These verses are gracious entreaties for our allegiance to a loving Master rather than to the tyrannical mastery of idolatry. Gratitude for so great an exchange—*"dead to sin, but alive to God in Christ Jesus"*—can have but one response: *"not My will, but Yours be done"*—just like Jesus (Luke 22:42).

Finally, according to Romans 6:14, why will sin have no dominion over a believer?

_____

_____

How can being under God's grace cause the power of sin to diminish in your life?

_____

_____

_____

What is it about grace that can compel you to respond to God with, *"not My will, but Yours be done"?"* How can understanding God's grace compel you to pray for a loved one caught up in sexual sin?

_____

_____

Grace is God's lifelong gift of transforming love. Thank You, Lord!

> Prayer: Lord, I thank You that I have been crucified with Christ; and it is no longer I who live, but Christ lives in me; and the *life* which I now live in the flesh I live by faith in the Son of God, who loved me and gave Himself up for me (Galatians 2:20). Because of Your grace, I yield.

DAY 5

FOLLOWING THE HOLY SPIRIT'S LEAD

A young couple took a vacation to Maine's beautiful northern woods. One morning they set out for the state park. They climbed in the car with coffee mugs and maps in hand. By the afternoon, they were seriously lost. They knew where we were. They know where they wanted to go, but after repeated dead-ends, confusing signs, and considerable backtracking, they had made little progress. Frustrated, they asked a local gentleman for directions. As he leaned into the husband's window, a languid smile broke over his face, and he said, "You can't get there from here." It seemed that the road that went directly through on the map did not exist on the ground. Isn't that often the way tests and trials feel in our lives?

> *"I will ask the Father, and He will give you another Helper, that He may be with you forever; that is the Spirit of truth."*
>
> JOHN 14:16-17 (NASB)

What does Scripture say about our tests and trials? What do James 1:2–4 and 1 Peter 1:3–7 say are the purposes of the challenges we face in life?

We want to meet these challenges. We want to pass the tests and trials and prove that our faith is genuine. And we set out on that road every day with a new resolve to face the painful things and people in our lives only to find ourselves hopelessly lost and dead-ended. We can't seem "to get there from here."

But God made the perfect provision available to us when we became believers. That provision is the Holy Spirit. A believer's transformation in Christ is totally dependent on the Holy Spirit who resides in us from the point of conversion until we join Jesus in Glory! He will daily impart God's Word to us and help us apply it to our circumstances.

According to Ephesians 1:13, how do we believers know that we have the Holy Spirit?

Based on the Scriptures that follow, who is the Holy Spirit, and how does He work?

John 14:16–17

John 14:26

John 15:26–27

John 16:13

Jesus assures us that we would not be left alone but that He will give us a Helper. Billy Graham adds to this assurance: "When we come to Christ, the Spirit comes to dwell within us—whether we are aware of His presence or not."[9]

Different Bible translations and versions may refer to the Holy Spirit with different names, such as Helper, Comforter, Counselor, Intercessor, Advocate, Strengthener. In John 14:16, how is He named in your Bible version or translation? Write His name here: _____. What does this tell you about how He can work in your life?

Always remember that transformation is a process. It's a little by little, degree by degree, day by day transaction of Holy Spirit teaching and training. Let's personalize the Scriptures that follow. Based on what you learn from each one, how can the Holy Spirit's power work in you and in your circumstances?

Romans 5:3–5

Romans 8:26–27

2 Corinthians 3:17–18

Galatians 5:22–23

Ephesians 3:20

Titus 3:3–7 (This one's huge!)

What do you conclude about the Holy Spirit's life in you?

_____

_____

_____

_____

Read 2 Peter 1:3. What does this mean for a Christian's life every day?

_____

_____

_____

_____

If we are children of God, we have His divine power in us. Therefore, we have the capacity to respond in a godly way to whatever happens on any given day. It takes ears that can hear the Spirit's promptings.

Here's the bottom line about the Holy Spirit in us: Forgetting, misunderstanding, or ignoring Him in our lives is like having all the conveniences in our homes—heat, telephone, water, electricity—and not using them. Then we wonder why we're cold, lonely, thirsty, dirty, and sitting in the dark. By the power of the Holy Spirit, God works His plans for us, His nature in us, and His purpose through us. It is a divine process, a supernatural process, a Holy Spirit process that continues until we join Jesus in our heavenly home. That's transformation!

Oswald Chambers tells us that God

> "will not allow you to escape from the scrutiny of the Holy Spirit for even one moment…He wants you to recognize the nature you were exhibiting—the nature of demanding your right to yourself. The moment you are willing for God to change your nature, His recreating forces begin to work. And the moment you realize that God's purpose is to get you into the right relationship with Himself and then with others, He will reach to the very limits of the universe to help you take the right road."[10]

You can get there from here!

> Prayer: Lord, may Your Holy Spirit rule in my heart.[11] Rule in my heart, Lord—one day or even one moment at a time.

LESSON 3

DESIGNED TO TRUST

W e all long for someone we can trust.

DAY 1

TRUSTING GOD'S LOVE

At the heart of most great movies is a great love—a love that can be trusted. Whether driven by love of mother, apple pie, a nation, fellow warriors, or the man or woman of one's dreams, what brings out the best in us is a reflection of love.

What brings out the best in the worst of us? What drives epic courage? What makes an individual trustworthy? Scripture tells us love is the power behind all good. There is a love worth dying for, a "perfect love" that casts out fear. Today's lesson looks at this love.

The New American Standard Bible uses the word *love* over three hundred times. However, where the English language has one word for love, the Greek and Hebrew languages combined have several different words that express various aspects of love.

Superseding them all is the Greek word *agape*. "[*Agape*] is a deep, incomprehensible passion for those who are totally undeserving of love."[1] *Agape* is an unconditional, unselfish, totally accepting, sacrificial love with the capacity to give without expecting in return. It is a benevolent goodwill toward others which values and serves; a voluntary decision of the will; a love of action and not of emotion, based on decision and commitment rather than performance, attributes, or worthiness.[2] It isn't given to get; it is merely given. It cannot be manipulated, defiled, or diminished. Its supply is inexhaustible and unalterable. It is an others-oriented love. This is the stuff of committed, courageous, covenant love. This is God's love for humanity. And because this love is not based on changeable emotions or performance, this is the love that is faithful in all circumstances. This is the love of Christ for you and me—while we were yet sinners—and it cost Him His life. This love can be trusted! However, trust means many different things to people. Write your definition of trust here:

WORD STUDY
Trust

The thesaurus adds the following words to illuminate the characteristics of *trust* (noun): "faith, belief, hope, conviction, confidence, expectation (to hope before), reliance, dependence." The verb *to trust* means "to have faith, to have faith in, to believe, rely on, depend on, confide in, have confidence in, count on, bank on, be sure about." Of these words, underline the ones that speak to you most about trust.

Clinical therapists Rory C. Reid and Dan Gray describe trust this way: "Trust represents confidence in a person's predictability. It is more than hoping a person will act a certain way. It is a firm belief that in a given circumstance a person *will* act a particular way again and again. It is the extent to which outcomes of a person's choices are predictable and reliable."[3]

Reliable. Predictable. Someone we can count on. Someone we can believe in. Someone we can be sure about in any and all circumstances. Sounds like a trustworthy hero!

Turn to Luke 12:6–7 and 22–32. Make a list of the ways God loves us with a trustworthy love.

We read this list and understand that God provides great love for our most basic physical needs. Loving us when our needs go far beyond the basics, when we have needs of the soul, is another thought to grasp altogether.

In order to truly understand how trustworthy God's incomprehensible *agape* is, let's look at how God's *agape* meets the needs of the soul in Psalm 107. For what do the people give thanks (v. 1)?

What has God's love accomplished according verses 2–3?

> *"Oh give thanks to the Lord, FOR HE IS GOOD, for His lovingkindness is everlasting."*
>
> Psalm 107:1 (NASB)

There are four accounts of God's trustworthy love in Psalm 107:

THE FIRST ACCOUNT

In verses 4–5, what is the nature of the people's distress, and who caused it?

What did the people do next, and what was God's response (v. 6)?

How did God deliver the people from their distress (v. 7)?

How did the wanderers respond to God's rescue (v. 8)?

According to verse 9, what will God do for those who are *"hungry and thirsty; their soul fainted within them"*?

From this scenario of distress, what do you conclude about God's love?

These are lost, lonely people who couldn't be satiated but instead were wasting away. Desperately isolated, they realized that only God could fill their empty souls.

Have you ever *"wandered in desert wastelands"* (v. 4 NIV)? Much like a desert wasteland, how is sexual brokenness a physical manifestation of the hungry, thirsty soul? Is there evidence of this in your life or the life of a specific loved one?

THE SECOND ACCOUNT

In verses 10–11, describe the people's distress. Who caused it and how?

What was God's response to their rebellion, and how did that impact the people (v.12)?

_____

_____

What did the people do next, and what was God's response (v. 13)?

_____

_____

How did God deliver the people from their distress (v. 14)?

_____

_____

How did the prisoners respond to God's rescue (v. 15)?

_____

_____

According to verse 16, what will God do for those who are *"prisoners in misery and chains"*?

_____

_____

From this scenario of distress, what do you conclude about God's love?

_____

_____

The cause of the people's distress was rebellion against the words of God. They not only chafed against God's Word but also spurned His counsel, rejecting it with contempt. This reveals their disdain for the One who formerly received their favorable attention. Their rebellion resulted in bondage of the mind, which was symbolized by darkness. The bondage of the physical body was symbolized by iron, and the bondage of the heart resulted in their hard labor. However, "just as man cannot be his own savior, neither can he find any other man to save him. But no bondage proves too hard for the Lord who can *shatter* even *bronze* and *iron*."[4]

Have you ever *"sat in darkness and the deepest gloom"* (v. 10 NIV)—perhaps about your own sexual sin? Or perhaps it was the sexual sin of a loved one who has you in this place? Have you ever considered a rebellious response? After reading this passage, do you know why you are in this place? How do you think God's love could shatter your gates of bronze and cut through your bars of iron (v. 16 NIV)?

_____

_____

_____

_____

THE THIRD ACCOUNT

What was the nature of the people's distress in verses 17–18, and who caused it?

How did God respond to their plea for help (vv. 19–20)?

How did these people respond to God's rescue (vv. 21–22)?

From this scenario of distress, what do you conclude about God's love?

Verse 18 reads, *"Their soul abhorred all kinds of food"* This was a thankless attitude that despised God's nourishing provisions for body and soul.

Are there areas in your life in which you are never satisfied? Have you spurned, abhorred, or despised God's provision? What part has thanklessness played? As it relates to sex, how have you or a loved one stepped outside of God's best and encountered the consequence of affliction? Are you or a loved one headed for destruction? Do you understand why? What is trustworthy about God's Word, and how will it deliver you from destruction? What part does thanksgiving to God play?

THE FOURTH ACCOUNT

In verses 23–24, how are these people different from those in the first three scenarios?

What was the sailors' distress, and from whom did it come (v. 25)?

How did this distress impact the sailors (vv. 26–27)?

_____

_____

What did the people do next, and what was God's response (vv. 28–30)?

_____

_____

How did the sailors respond to God's rescue (vv. 31–32)?

_____

_____

From this scenario of distress, what do you conclude about God's love?

_____

_____

Although these sailors and merchants were going about their daily business, they acknowledged the God of their success. However, this did not exempt them from distress or the fear that it generated.

Why do you think God commanded this violent storm? What could be trustworthy about God's love during a time like this? What about the storms in your own life? Do you think God's love is trustworthy in them? Do you trust that in due time He will cause your storm to be still and guide you to where you need to be?

_____

_____

_____

_____

_____

Because He is God and we are not, we can trust His command in our situations.

God will cause or allow storms in our lives for reasons known only to Him and He will not let us navigate them alone. He knows precisely what we need to develop trust in Him. No matter what our circumstance, when we call on Him, He will provide the help we need.

Would (or do) storms in your life cause you to walk away from God? If so, why? How can storms in your life deepen your trust in God? If your circumstance isn't good, is God still good? Is His love still trustworthy? Think about your answers. What do you conclude and why?

_____

_____

What is your response to a loving God in your distress?

What is your response to a loving God who delivers you out of your distress?

Are you willing to give God thanks and praise whether or not He immediately delivers you? If yes, why? If no, why not? (revisit vv. 1–2.)

These four scenarios challenge our notions about trusting God's love. Do we tend to make God's love smaller than it really is? Do we believe He is worthy of our trust? His love is an unconditional, overcoming, trustworthy love that we *can* rely on no matter what. But will we? Whether we find ourselves in situations of our own making or those outside our control, God is there with His lovingkindness, and it will not fail us. Thank You, Lord!

> Prayer: Lord, I know that You will not always keep me free from trials but perhaps even bring them. Whatever the cause, let me cry out to You. Let me trust Your saving love in the midst of my trials, and let me be thankful for what You are doing. Teach me to trust Your love in the midst of painful places.

DAY 2

TRUSTING GOD'S FAITHFULNESS

We all long for someone who is faithful—a faithful friend, a faithful spouse. There's something sacred about knowing you can count on, rely on, trust someone to share your greatest joys, your deepest confidences, or your darkest hours.

We all long for someone who is faithful.

It's easy to question whether or not God is faithful when faced with circumstances that seem overwhelming. Such was the case with Elisha's servant. Read 2 Kings 6:8–17. Verses 8–12 build the story. What's happening?

What did the king of Syria determine to do to Elisha, and how did he do it (vv. 13–14)?

What alarmed Elisha's servant the next morning (v. 15)?

What did Elisha's answer reveal about God? What does Elisha's answer reveal about himself (v. 16)?

Elisha did more than just calm his servant verbally. He called on the Lord—in other words, he prayed. What did he pray (v. 17), and how did God answer?

Based on this passage, what was it about God's character that Elisha trusted?

What impact do you think this experience had on Elisha's servant?

What the servant originally saw was the Syrian army surrounding the city. What Elisha saw was the faithfulness of God, and he wanted his servant to see what he knew—that the army of God was *"more than those who are with [the enemy]"* (brackets ours) (v. 16). God's army so closely surrounded them that it stood between them and the enemy. The enemy had no access.

No matter what our circumstances look like "out there," the faithfulness of God's presence "close in" is always greater. Can we trust that God is doing battle on our behalf? When our circumstance seems to loom larger than our hope, how can we be assured that this same protection is available to us today? How do Romans 8:31 and 1 John 4:4 answer this question? Based on the lesson thus far, what have you learned about His faithfulness?

"If God is for us, who is against us?"

Romans 8:31

Do you believe God is faithful to you—all the time? What experience have you had that supports your answer?

_____

_____

_____

_____

In the verses that follow, what are the benefits of entrusting ourselves to a faithful God?

Scripture Passage	Benefits	Our Part	God's Part
Psalm 18:1–3			
Psalm 46:1–3, 10–11			
Psalm 56:3–4, 9–11			
Psalm 62:8			
Psalm 125:1–2			
Proverbs 3:5–8			
Isaiah 26:3–4			

In these passages, we see a common denominator on our part. It is to trust God. We also see a common denominator on God's part. It is to show Himself trustworthy through His faithfulness. But we may not often give God that opportunity. When we truly trust His faithfulness, we are protected, defended, and helped in our trouble. Moreover, we are unafraid, forever secure, and perfectly peaceful. Even when we make a mess of things or when our circumstances make a mess of our lives, He never stops being faithful. He never gives up on us and never stops being for us.

How important is it for you to trust God's faithfulness in your circumstances?

In the chart, which benefits are you most in need of right now?

What's difficult about doing your part?

How might trusting God's faithfulness alter your response to your circumstances? How might that alter your circumstances?

> Prayer: *"I will sing of the lovingkindness of the Lord forever; to all genera-tions I will make known Your faithfulness with my mouth. For I have said, 'Lovingkindness will be built up forever; In the heavens You will establish Your faithfulness.'" "O Lord God of hosts, who is like You, O mighty Lord? Your faithfulness also surrounds You."* Remind me daily, Lord, that You are faithful in all my circumstances. (*see* Psalm 89:1–2, 8).

DAY 3

TRUSTING GOD'S MERCY AND GRACE

We all long for someone who shows us mercy when we deserve it least and grace when we need it most. God's trustworthy grace and mercy are sometimes found in surprising circumstances.

 DID YOU KNOW?

The Hebrew name *Yo'el* (Joel) means, "Yahweh is God."

IN PLACES OF MISERY DESERVED

Joel, a minor prophet and contemporary of Elisha, called the leaders of God's people to repent, return to, and trust in the God of Israel again after their nation suffered great calamity. Let's venture into this time in history for a glimpse of God's grace and mercy in Joel 1:1–15. Read verses 1–5. What has happened?

When the Scripture talks about destruction in fours such as it does in verse 4, it is a way of emphasizing a complete and total devastation. This is not an annoyance or a small difficulty but utter destruction. We can see that four successive waves of locusts decimated every form of plant life in their paths throughout Judah.

In verse 6 the swarm of locusts is likened to an invading nation's great army. Describe them.

In verses 7–12, describe their destruction and how the people responded.

God's people were in misery, suffering the consequences of their faithlessness.

What specific things did He require of the priests and why (vv. 13–14)?

Yes, God destroyed the very things that the people failed to offer back to Him. He called the priests to put on sackcloth (the garment of mourning, repentance, or fasting) because there was nothing now to offer to the Lord by way of sacrifice.

Verse 15 is pivotal, so pay attention. What's the message?

"The day of the Lord" indicates a time "when the presence of the Lord brings judgment and/or deliverance and blessing, depending on the circumstances."[6] Where there is repentance, there is hope for restoration. Where there is rebellion, there is only judgment.

But a greater desolation awaited the people if they refused to repent and return to the Lord. He would send an army to come against them: "The LORD utters His voice before His army; surely His camp is very great, for strong is he who carries out His word. The day of the LORD is indeed great and very awesome, and who can endure it?" (Joel 2:11).

In Joel 2:12, what does God want from His people? How? Why (v. 13)?

_____

_____

God calls His people back from their sins because of His grace and mercy. This has always been who God is, and they knew it. This was evident in the earliest days of Israel's history. Exodus 34:6–7 (ESV) says, *"The LORD, the LORD, a God merciful and gracious, slow to anger [mercy—withholding what we deserve], and abounding in steadfast love and faithfulness [grace—extending to us what we don't deserve], keeping steadfast love for thousands, forgiving iniquity and transgression and sin"* (brackets ours).

God wanted them to mourn their neglect and repent of their cold indifference, to course-correct while they still had the opportunity. God called them to return with their whole hearts. And the only way back was for the people to repent with fasting, weeping, and mourning. He also called them to rend (rip) their hearts rather than their garments. Rending garments was their outer expression of their inner anguish. Rending their hearts would express whole hearts yielded to God.

When hearts are genuinely repentant and wholly turned over to God, His blessing and purpose for them will unfold. Let's see how God responds to His people's repentance and return.

Read Joel 2:21, 24–26, and answer the questions that follow: What has replaced their mourning and why (v. 21)?

_____

_____

What did God promise in verses 24–26?

_____

> *"Then I will make up to you for the years that the swarming locust has eaten, the creeping locust, the stripping locust and the gnawing locust, my great army which I sent among you."*
>
> Joel 2:25 (NASB)

Returning and repentance leads to restoration. God's grace and mercy are woven throughout the process. He uses all necessary means to encourage our return, even when it hurts. That's mercy. However, when we refuse to return, the place apart from Him will be worse than the first. When He calls us to repentance, He meets us there with all available grace. With this in mind, how does verse 26 depict God's grace and mercy?

_____

_____

Now think about this next question as it relates to all of the passages we've read in Joel: What necessary means did God use in order to restore His people?

God's great army of locusts—which He sent among His people in order to restore them—was how He dealt wondrously with them (v. 26). It was a surprising place of His mercy and grace.

Finally, read Joel 2:27. God's mercy and grace are intended to accomplish His goal for His people. What is His goal?

"God never gives up on us . . . While some consequences from the past may remain, we can be confident that God has a good and glorious future for those who trust in Him!"[7]

It took four progressive waves of locusts to totally decimate everything that brought the nation of Judah comfort, sustenance, productivity, provision, and even indulgences. As Christians we can get pretty complacent with what we have and choose not to offer everything back to God as our great provider. Our neglect can be costly.

It's fair to do a little self-examination. Not every calamitous event in Christians' lives is because we've neglected God. But some are. In either case, our challenges should draw us close to God in trust, to seek His grace in each painful circumstance and His mercy throughout. He will waste nothing that we experience. Is there something in your life that the "locusts" have eaten? What is it?

When we are in sin, God is gracious and merciful to call us back, and yes, we may still have to deal with the consequences associated with our sin. If you have already experienced consequences what are they, and how have you responded to them? What would it take to restore what the locusts have eaten?

If a loved one has sinned and you are experiencing consequences, how have you responded to them?

If you or a loved one is experiencing a calamity or a potential calamity right now, what do you think God's goal is for you and/or your loved one?

Prayer: Lord, sometimes I don't know how to respond to Your mercy and grace. But *"who is a God like you, who pardons sin? . . .You do not stay angry forever but delight to show mercy"* (Micah 7:18 NIV). Out of gratitude, Lord, may I repent and return in any areas where I have kept my distance from You. May I yield to You as I face my own sin. And may I yield to you as I face another's sin.

DAY 4

TRUSTING GOD'S GRACE AND POWER

When suffering for something undeserved or unwarranted, we all long for someone who gives grace in our weakness and strengthening power in our struggles.

IN PLACES OF MISERY UNDESERVED

Following Christ's death and resurrection, Scripture gives us a clear picture of another who endured unmerited suffering. In his writings, the apostle Paul reveals the grace and power with which God sustained him throughout his daring ministry. About twenty years into his ministry, Paul wrote his second letter to the believers in Corinth. In this letter Paul disclosed the scope of his perils, sufferings, and afflictions for the sake of the gospel and what kept him going—God's faithful supply of grace and power.

To gather insight on what and how much Paul endured, read, 2 Corinthians 11:22–30. In this passage, he lays out the scope of his hardships. He found himself *"in far more labors, in far more imprisonments, beaten times without number, often in danger of death"* (v. 23). Read the rest of this passage carefully. Try to imagine each experience from a personal perspective. List all of Paul's perils (vv. 24–27).

According to verses 28–29, what else was Paul concerned about?

What was Paul's "boast" in verse 30?

_____

_____

Paul not only endured personal hardships and physical harm, but he also endured relentless persecution from both Jews and Gentiles (non-Jews). His physical safety and state of mind were severely taxed. And yet he never gave up on his mission to advance the ministry of the gospel and represent Christ well.

According to 2 Corinthians 1:1–10, in what ways did Paul's suffering deepen his relationship with the Lord?

_____

_____

_____

How did Paul's suffering benefit him? How did Paul's suffering benefit others (vv. 1–7)?

_____

_____

_____

Paul and Timothy were _"burdened excessively, beyond our strength, so that we despaired even of life"_ (v. 8). According to Paul, what was the purpose of this oppressing distress (v. 9)?

_____

_____

What did God's grace grant Paul, and what was Paul's confidence for his future (v. 10)? What does this mean for all Christians?

_____

_____

_____

Paul didn't want the Corinthians to underestimate the excessive hardships that he and his co-workers experienced. And nor should we. _Wycliffe Bible Commentary_ tells us that the language Paul uses in verse 8 counts this trial among the "most excruciating of human experiences,"[8] but what a beautiful outcome to his suffering. God didn't waste Paul's enormous burdens, and He won't waste ours. Instead, He equips us to touch the suffering of another "with the comfort with which we ourselves are comforted by God" (1:4) It is worth noting that our comfort and our ability to comfort others are only possible when we rely on God rather than on ourselves.

> _God didn't waste Paul's enormous burdens,_
> _and He won't waste ours._

Up to this point, how have you viewed your suffering? How have you understood its origin and its outcome? Have you seen a purpose in it?

Who has comforted you in your suffering? How did you respond? How have you comforted another in a similar circumstance?

In 2 Corinthians 4:7–18, Paul's perspective on his suffering shifts a bit. In verse 7 he said they *"possess this precious treasure (the divine Light of the gospel)"* (AMP) in *"jars of clay"* (NIV) or *"earthen vessels"* (KJV), which is meant to depict their frail human weaknesses. For what reason?

Read verses 8–9 and 16–17. How has Paul's perspective on his hardships shifted in these verses from that of chapter 1:8–9? Why do you think it has changed from when they *"despaired even of life"*?

On what is Paul now focusing as it relates to his suffering (vv. 11–12 and 17–18)?

Depending on the power of God can keep us from losing heart once we view our suffering from a spiritual perspective: Do I suffer in such a way that Christ and His eternity is seen in me?

Have you ever been (or are you) in a situation that you thought would be the end of you? Where did you (or do you) place your hope? Why?

_____

_____

_____

Read 2 Corinthians 12:1–10. In verses 2–6, Paul is apparently reluctant to boast about himself, so he boasts on behalf of "a man" who was *"caught up* ['raptured'] *to the third heaven...into Paradise...and heard inexpressible words, which a man is not permitted to speak"* (brackets ours). He himself refrained from boasting about these extraordinary revelations given to him *"so that no one will credit me with more than he sees in me or hears from me."* What do you think Paul meant by this statement?

_____

_____

_____

Apparently Paul's attitude had been important to God too. How do we know (v. 7)?

_____

_____

Paul described the affliction "given" to him as a *"thorn in the flesh."* Who gave it to him? For what purpose?

_____

_____

_____

"The magnitude of Paul's revelations caused the Lord to give to him a divine deterrent (a thorn) in order to deflate any tendency toward exaltation and pride. Paul needed some reminder that, in spite of his rapture to heaven, he still was a man among men."[9] We can be given those same divine deterrents in order to thwart Satan's mission and accomplish God's. (A prideful believer is totally useless to God.) When we trust Him more than we fear Satan, His grace and power can work in and through us to accomplish His mission. Note that Paul's thorn was not specifically identified, and we believe for good reason. If Paul's thorn was specified, and it wasn't like our thorns, we would reject his experience and its application to our own thorns and its impact on our lives.

How did Paul petition God about his thorn (v. 8)? How did God answer Paul's plea (v. 9)?

_____

_____

_____

_____

Why do you think it was more important for Paul to operate under God's grace rather than have the thorn removed?

_____

_____

_____

The Amplified Bible puts the beginning of verse 9 this way: *"But He said to me, My grace— My favor and loving-kindness and mercy—is enough for you, [that is, sufficient against any danger and to enable you to bear the trouble manfully]."* Based on this insight, how would *"My grace is sufficient for you"* speak to a trial or affliction in your life or that of a loved one?

_____

_____

_____

James MacDonald writes that in the Greek, the word order of "My grace is sufficient for you" is "Sufficient for you is the grace of Me."[10] This is so clarifying! We yield to the sufficiency of His grace—to Jesus Himself. His grace covers us in our trials and thorns. This is the means by which we grow, mature, heal, and most important, come to understand God's love more deeply so that others may benefit.

Second Corinthians 12:9 (AMP) says, *"For My strength and power are made perfect—(fulfilled and completed) and show themselves most effective—in [your] weakness."* Why do you think Christ's power is made perfect in Paul's weakness and not in Paul's strength?

_____

_____

_____

How would God's answer apply to every believer's "thorn?"

_____

_____

_____

> *"For My strength and power are made perfect—fulfilled and completed) and show themselves most effective—in [your] weakness."*
>
> 2 Corinthians 12:9 (AMP)

Can you identify with Paul's predicament? What is your "thorn?" Define it here.

_____

_____

_____

_____

After begging three times for release from this affliction, Paul didn't just resign himself to his new reality; he embraced it! First, Paul chose to boast about his thorn and did so most gladly." Why (v. 9)?

_____

_____

The Amplified Bible says (12:9), *"Therefore, I will all the more gladly glory in my weaknesses and infirmities, that the strength and power of Christ, the Messiah, may rest—yes, may pitch a tent [over] and dwell—upon me."*

To *boast* means to "glory, exult, both in a good and bad sense."[11] In Paul's case, it was a good kind of boasting because doing so exalted God. He gloried in his weaknesses and infirmities with gladness because he knew that *"the strength and power of Christ"* was working in him, through him, and for him as his circumstances unfolded—guaranteed. Paul was boasting out of gratitude to God for what would be the outcome of his thorn and his trials. For all believers, this boasting—or glorifying God—invites the power of Christ to move in us, in our trials, and in others as we testify about what God is doing with our trials and not what our trials are doing with us. This is the difference between being victors through our trials (glorifying God) or victims in our trials (glorifying ourselves).

 IN THEIR SHOES
Humble Boasting?

When one boasts as Paul did, his boasting was about what God's power did for him in his weakness, not what he did for God. We can boast about what God has done for us—with the intent to draw attention to ourselves, our accomplishments, our victories, our worthiness. Paul's boasting was born out of his firsthand experience with God's grace and power in every aspect of his ministry. We know his boasts were from a godly motive because he was not deterred from what other suffering lay ahead. His boasting was utterly humble; therefore, it was utterly glorifying to God.

In 2 Corinthians 12:10, Paul chose to be "content" with his *"weaknesses, with insults, with distresses, with persecutions, with difficulties."* Why?

_____

_____

_____

What do you think it means to be content *"with weaknesses, with insults, with distresses, with persecutions, with difficulties, for Christ's sake"* (v. 10)? How does this apply to you right now?

_____

_____

_____

_____

Paul chose to be content in every category of human suffering, "to view with favor":

His weaknesses—his want of strength

His insults—overbearing insolence, harm, hurt, or reproach from others

His distresses—unavoidable calamities

His persecutions—pursuit, particularly of enemies, hostile prosecution

His difficulties—the distress that arises from within such as anguish, worry, or discomfort[12]

Think about this: Paul, the apostle was supernaturally visited by Jesus Christ and commissioned to take the gospel to the world. And although he was made privy to great revelations, he was not exempt from physical, mental, and emotional suffering.[13] He willingly embraced his trials because he knew *"for when I am weak (in human strength), then am I [truly] strong—able, powerful in divine strength"* (12:10 AMP).

In the categories of Paul's trials, where does your trial fit? What is your struggle? What is your response to your trial?

How could you or do you boast about your trial in a "good sense?" How could you or do you boast about your trial in a bad sense?

Could you, like Paul, embrace your trial and learn to be content with it "for the sake of Christ?" What would (or does) being content in your trial for the sake of Christ look like?

This is not to say that you embrace sexual sin (yours or a loved one's) for the sake of Christ. This is to say, I will accept with peace my current circumstance so that Christ can give me the grace and power to deal with it righteously. What would that take?

Consider this: Why is it that we humans think we can get through our tough times on our own as if getting on the other side of difficulties were the only purpose? Why won't (not can't) believers trust God's grace to get us through and His power to work out the details while we're being His credible witnesses?

Read Ephesians 3:20 (also written by Paul!). What empowered Paul to embrace his trials God's way?

There are no limits to what God can accomplish through our limitations when we yield to His grace and power. Both are always available to every believer at any time in every circumstance. His grace will never be too little or too much, too soon or too late, but always just enough and just in time to remind us of Who sustains us and by Whose power we are able to righteously respond in weaknesses, insults, distresses, persecutions, and difficulties. Will you believe this?

> Prayer: Lord, You said that Your strength and power show themselves most effective in my weakness. Therefore, it's enough to get me through this tough season. You promised grace and power as I maneuver through this affliction. I surrender all of my weak self to You. Lord, I come.

DAY 5

TRUSTING GOD'S SOVEREIGNTY

Do you know that woman who likes to take control? She's in every church, every PTA, every neighborhood. She's everywhere! Don't we all like to be in control? And don't we all bristle even just a little bit when someone tries to usurp our control?

We see the controller quickly in others but not so quickly in ourselves. Yet, God sees it in us. It's glaring to Him because it competes with His sovereignty—that holy attribute of His that gives Him the prerogative to control all things. Note that within the word "sovereign" is the word "reign"—a right of His that He will neither give up nor give over. Pastor John Piper says, "God is in ultimate control of the world, from the largest international intrigue to the smallest bird-fall in the forest. Here is how the Bible puts it: 'I am God and there is no other...my counsel shall stand and I will accomplish all my purpose'" (Isaiah 46:9–10, author's translation).[14] Therefore, nothing will happen to us that doesn't pass before our sovereign God first. Nothing. And even when it doesn't feel like it, God is in its operation for our highest good.

Consider Job. He believed that God was sovereign, that He ruled and reigned. And yet things still careened out of Job's control. But they weren't out of God's!

Read Job 1:1–5. What kind of man was Job?

Continue with Job 1:6–12. In all of Job's goodness, like Paul, he wasn't exempt from trials. What transpired between Satan and—are you ready for this?—God (vv. 6–12)?

How did the Lord describe Job to Satan (v. 8)? Why do you think God drew Satan's attention to Job?

Does it surprise you that Satan was in God's presence? Does it surprise you that God brought Job to Satan's attention? Although this makes no sense to our finite minds, our Sovereign God had His reasons. Let's continue...

According to Job 1:9–11, what was Satan's accusation and challenge in response to God's mention of Job?

In verse 12, what was God's limitation to Satan's activity? What do you think about God giving Satan a "green light" in Job's life?

We remember from Paul's experiences that testing comes through weaknesses, insults, distresses, persecutions, and difficulties. Job's first test was in the form of great distress: actual, unavoidable calamity! What calamity befell Job in 1:13–19?

What was Job's response to this test (1:20–22)?

Where is God's sovereignty evident in this account?

Job's trial was not over yet. The second conversation between God and Satan was much like the first, only with a different outcome. Read Job 2:1–10. God praised Job. Why (v. 3)?

What was Satan's slanderous retort (vv. 4–5)?

Again, God permits Satan to put Job to the test. What was His limitation on Satan this time (v. 6)?

What was Job's second test (v. 7)?

What was the contrast between how Job and his wife responded to his affliction (vv. 8–10)?

Satan spared no tactic in his effort to separate Job from God. He even used Job's wife. And yet, *"Job did not sin with his lips"* (verse 10). You can bet Satan wasn't pleased about that!

Here's a complex truth: Although God does not commit evil, He does permit it, as in Job's case. Until Christ returns and defeats our enemy, evil will continue to exist in our lives; however, it (and Satan) will always be on God's tether, within His boundaries, and used for His greater purposes.

What is your response to God allowing evil in your life or that of a loved one?

 IN THEIR SHOES
Among the Ashes

To sit among the ashes not only symbolized Job's mourning but gives the vision of one who was formerly revered by all to one who was relegated to utter desolation, an outcast.

Further complicating Job's trial, three friends came by to weep with, console, and "comfort" him (chapters 3–37); however everything his friends assessed about Job, about his circumstances, and about God's involvement was wrong. All their "blather" didn't meet Job in his deepest need. In his misery Job laments, *"My days are swifter than a weaver's shuttle, and come to an end without hope* (v. 7:6). "What appeared to Job and his friends as evidence that God had turned against him was just the opposite. God was so confident of Job's integrity that He trusted him in this battle with Satan. Later, Job's hope and life were renewed."[15]

Few of us can truly fathom or identify with Job's heartbreak and his incalculable losses. But some can. Are you one? What was your initial response to your loss? What is your current response to your loss?

Whatever your struggle, do you trust God, or do you go to your friends? If you go to your friends, what do you think you'll gain from them that you don't believe you will receive from God? Do they lead you back to Him or away from Him? How do you know when you are being drawn further away from God by a friend?

We cannot fathom God's infinite mind. What does God have to say about His sovereignty, and why in Isaiah 55:8–11? What's the bottom line in everything He does (v. 11)?

 EXTRA MILE
Job 38-42

'For the total picture of how God addressed Job, read Job 38–42. If you have any doubt about God's sovereignty and sufficiency, settle it here. And while you're reading, discover everything over which God claims sovereignty in His omniscience (all-knowing), His omnipresence (everywhere at one time), and His omnipotence (all-power).

Along the course of Job's great travail, he reminds himself and his friends of what he believes about trusting God. Read Job 13:14–16. What does he believe? How can that apply to believers today?

Don't we all want that safe access to our Sovereign God? We can always appeal to God on the basis of Christ. How does Hebrews 4:14–16 affirm this?

Have you ever argued your case with God? On what basis? What were you hoping to receive from Him?

EXTRA MILE
Joseph

For another astounding example of God's sovereignty in the life of an "innocent," read about Joseph in Genesis 17–50. How did he respond to attempted murder, being sold into slavery, being falsely accused of a sex crime, being unjustly imprisoned, and then years later facing the family members who meant him harm? Only God . . .

Finally, Job got an audience with God, who spoke for Himself and made His character very clear. Read Job 38:1–4; 40:1–14; 41:11. What were the points that God made to Job?

What two things did Job come to know about God in Job 42:2?

According to Job 42:3–6, how did this knowledge change Job's perspective?

Theologian Oswald Chambers says, "God frequently has to knock the bottom out of your experience as His saint to get you in direct contact with Himself... And the real trial of faith is not that we find it difficult to trust God, but that God's character must be proven as trustworthy in our own minds."[16]

Job repented from his lack of faith in God's sovereignty. Now read Job 42:7–10. What occurred after Job prayed for his friends (verse 10)? What does this imply for a believer today?

_____

_____

_____

In every case for the believer, what the enemy would use to destroy us, God would use to mature our faith as well as our Christ-like character (Romans 8:28–29). And in His sovereignty, He knows the perfect conditions to make that happen. Charles Spurgeon once said, "If you could have chosen your own circumstances and condition in life, you could not have made so wise a choice as God has made for you."

Because God is trustworthy, our hope is in His sovereignty. If you are in a painful circumstance, how does God's sovereignty give you hope?

_____

_____

_____

Oswald Chambers writes, "A saint's life is in the hands of God like a bow and arrow in the hands of an archer. God is aiming at something the saint cannot see, but our Lord continues to stretch and strain, and every once in a while the saint says, 'I can't take any more.' Yet God pays no attention; He goes on stretching until His purpose is in sight, and then He lets the arrow fly. Entrust yourself to God's hand."[17]

> Prayer: If your trust in God's sovereign nature is weak, appeal to Him now for courage and perseverance with a steadfast confidence that what you know about God will transcend how you feel about your circumstances. Though He slay you, will you still trust Him?

LESSON 4

In an age of sound bites, media frenzies, and image managers, it is difficult to know the truth about life, our world, and people. A clear example is the recent story of a college football player and his "dying" girlfriend that generated large interest because the player was a Heisman trophy contender. Sympathetic people began searching for details about this player's now deceased girlfriend. The truth they discovered was stranger than fiction. Having never met the girl in question, the football player had carried on the relationship through the Internet and texting. Stranger still, after she reportedly died, it was discovered that the girl never existed at all, that she was actually a man deceiving the athlete.

Sometimes we think that knowing spiritual truth is equally suspect. Scripture tells us otherwise. The Bible reveals truth and the Author of truth. We can only know truth when we know the One who is truth. In truth, He is the difference between life and death, both here on earth and for eternity. The power of truth is this week's lesson.

DAY 1

WHOSE TRUTH OR WHO'S TRUTH?: UNDERSTANDING THE INFLUENCE

Who or what influences your thinking? Have you ever thought about that? On any given topic or issue, you have an opinion.

Our opinions are formed over time by any number of influences, such as childhood upbringing, church dogma, leaders' opinions, and peer influences. For example, think about your morning so far. Did you have the TV, radio, or Internet on? What kind of messages did you hear? Or as you drove this week, what advertising did you see? What messages did you receive from these various media?

How you would define *truth* (not a dictionary definition but your own definition). Write your definition here:

_____

_____

_____

Pastor and author, J. D. "Doc" Watson writes, "The English words *truth* and *true* speak of what is real, what really is, what is factual. It's not opinion, it's not conjecture, it's not hypothesis or theory. . . The Greek *aletheia* means basically . . .'nonconcealment'. . . The fundamental concept to understand about truth is that it is that which is absolute, that which is incontrovertible, irrefutable, incontestable, unarguable, and unchanging. If something is true, it's *always* true and can *never* be untrue, no matter what the circumstances."[1]

Scripture asserts that God is the Author of truth (Exodus 34:6; 2 Samuel 7:28). Doesn't this make sense, since God is the Author of everything? As its Author, God's divine truth is fundamental to righteous living. Because truth is unconcealed but open and known, God freely reveals it to us by His Word and in His Word. His truth is ever faithful, firm, and stable. And because God doesn't change, His truth doesn't change. "God and truth are inseparable. Every thought about the essence of truth—what it is, what makes it 'true,' and how we can possibly know anything for sure, quickly moves us back to God."[2]

Compare what you have just discovered about truth with your previous definition of truth. Are any parts similar? Would you change anything or add anything to your definition based on what you have just learned? Write those changes here:

_____

_____

_____

Who does John 1:1, 14 and 14:6 say is the source of all truth and why?

_____

_____

We can look for truth in the same way we look for knowledge—by canvassing opinions, by searching authoritative books, or by our own reasoning. Scripture tells us that Jesus Christ is truth. He is the Word of God and the only authoritative "book" for every Christian.

Read John 14:26. Who is the imparter of all truth? How does He do it?

_____

_____

> "When He, the Spirit of truth, comes,
> He will guide you into all the truth."
>
> John 16:13 (NASB)

The Holy Spirit, who is in you, imparts all truth to you. You have the capacity to receive it and understand it as He reveals it to you. Do you have any other source of truth? Is it your feelings? Your friends? Your fantasies? Your intuition? Your selftalk? When your world is shaken, from where do you derive truth to make sense of your circumstances?

Three enemies work separately or all together to establish themselves against the truth of God—the world, the flesh, and the devil. Each can have a powerful impact on the directions our lives take. Let's examine them a little more closely.

THE WORLD

In today's secular culture, truth is fluid rather than absolute. Instead of standing firmly regardless of influences or circumstances, it goes with the flow of the cultural agenda and associated pressures. A common term for this is *relativism*. Fluid truth morphs according to individual or group desires. Absolute truth never changes but is perpetual and permanent.

Let's get a biblical perspective on relativism. You may recall that God established the nation of Israel through Abraham. Under the leadership of Joshua, the Israelites conquered the land of Canaan and were establishing their territory for each tribe. After the death of Joshua, Israel was without leadership and "repeatedly fell into idolatry, foreign political domination, intermarriage with pagans, and other major sins. They were in a general state of spiritual confusion."[3] Bad things happen to God's people when they turn their backs on Him and His truth. Read Judges 2:11–23. What happened to Israel?

In Judges 2:16, what was God's response to their distress?

In this context, judges served not only in judicial positions. Many were national rulers and in many cases military leaders.

What pattern do you detect in Israel in Judges 2:17–19?

Judges 2:20–23 summarizes the rest of the story. What does God do and why?

At the end of the book of Judges, we see the final state of Israel. According to Judges 21:25, what is it?

"Everyone did what was right in his own eyes." This is moral relativism. And this results when people turn their backs on God. They are in chaos; they reject God's faithful, firm, perpetual, and stable truth. The by-product of their rebellion is instability. And it always will be.

> *"Every man did what was right in his own eyes."*
>
> Judges 17:6

The prophet Isaiah whipped some woes on Israel. Read Isaiah 5:20. From this perspective, how has God's truth morphed into worldly relativism?

_____

_____

Finally, read 1 John 2:15–17. What does it say about loving the world?

_____

_____

What is the promise for those who reject the world?

_____

_____

"The Bible teaches that worldliness is a force, a spirit, an atmosphere of the cosmos that is in opposition and in contradiction to all that is godly and Christian. Its goal is selfish pleasure, material success, and the pride of life. It is ambitious, self-centered. God is not necessarily denied; He is just ignored and forgotten."[4] The world's compelling call draws us to everything destructive, much like the sirens' calls draw us toward the rocky shoals. God calls us toward everything that is good because He is good.

If truth is not absolutely God's truth, then it is relative to whatever is morally suitable at the time. Think of moral issues where you might argue absolute truth over relative truth or relative truth over absolute truth? Which truth do you use to argue sexual issues?

_____

_____

_____

THE FLESH

What is "the flesh?" In his New Testament writings, Paul uses the Greek word, *sarx*, to "depict sinful impulses and carnal cravings."[5] Our flesh is all of our "self"—our selfishness, self-centeredness, self-absorption in constant search of self-satisfaction and self-gratification. The flesh goes after whatever we want for ourselves, and it's typically what God would not want for us.

In Romans 7:15–20, Paul lamented about the influence of the flesh in his own life. In what areas of your life can you identify with Paul's lament?

_____

_____

_____

Galatians 5:16–17 describes the tension that believers have between the flesh and the Spirit within. In what areas of your life can you identify with this tension?

_____

_____

According to Galatians 5:19–21, what behaviors or deeds can result if the believer gives way to the flesh? Which deeds can you identify with?

Verse 19 says that the *"deeds of the flesh are evident."* This means "to appear, to manifest, to become visible, to become apparent, to become seen or be well known, or to become conspicuous."[6] Even though we may try to hide these deeds, there will be evidence of their existence in our lives (1 Corinthians 4:5). Greek linguist Rick Renner maintains that "a life dominated by the flesh is a hard life. It is filled with excess, imbalance, extremity, laziness, self-abuse, hatred, strife, bitterness, irresponsibility, and neglect. The way of the flesh is the hardest route for any individual to take; yet the flesh cries out to be in charge, screaming to have its own way, demanding to be the boss. Unless you take your flesh to the Cross and mortify it by the power of God, it will keep screaming until you finally surrender to it and allow it to produce its ruinous effects in your life."[7] If permitted, our flesh will drive us toward the very behaviors that are described in verses 19–21.

All of these fleshly sins can still beset us after we become believers and will work in our minds to convince us that we are powerless against them. But Romans 8:1–14 gives a freeing truth for the believer. What has the Holy Spirit accomplished so believers can be assured that they will win the war with their flesh (vv. 1–4, 10–11, 14)?

What is our responsibility (vv. 4–9, 12–13)?

Pastor J. D. Watson encourages us with, "Ponder this: We do not have the inability to sin, but we do have the ability not to sin. Did you get it?. . .No longer can we say, 'I just couldn't help it.' Yes, we can 'help it' because of the Holy Spirit. Even though our passions and impulses are strong, we can still claim victory. Again, we are not sinless, but we do 'sin *less*.' "[8]

If by the power of the Holy Spirit we are not *"dead to sin and alive to God in Christ Jesus"* (Romans 6:11), then we will forever be fooled by our flesh. We will also be forever ruled by our flesh.

What thoughts has this section on the flesh stirred in you? Is there a sin, sexual or otherwise, that you have been excusing or living out as if it were acceptable to God? If so, based on what you have just learned, what is the truth of your matter?

_____

_____

_____

_____

Is there something that must change? Write what that is here:

_____

_____

_____

_____

THE DEVIL

Do you recall how Jesus described Satan? He called him a liar and the father of lies (John 8:44–45). Satan's career with humanity began in the first garden with the infamous words, "Did God really say…?" He operates in the same way today. Not only does Satan lie to us by distorting God's truth, but he also spends day and night accusing believers before God (Revelation 12:10). All lies!

In the following passages, what do you learn about this enemy, Satan?

Matthew 4:1–4

_____

_____

2 Corinthians 11:14

_____

_____

Ephesians 2:1–2

_____

_____

Ephesians 6:11–12

_____

_____

1 Peter 5:8

_____

_____

For now, *"the whole world lies in the power of the evil one"* (1 John 5:19). But it won't always be that way because he is a defeated foe. Read 1 John 2:14. What overcomes the evil one and why?

_____

_____

Just like in the first garden, the enemy uses the same hook, "Did God really say . . . ?" If you're not battling this question <u>every day</u> with God's truth, then you're losing the battle. In what areas of your life, to include your sex life, are you believing the enemy's, "Did God really say . . . ?" instead of the Father's, "Thus said the Lord . . . "?

_____

_____

_____

Here's the bottom line: As Christians, we have the Source of all truth that the Holy Spirit uses to combat the world, the flesh, and the devil. His name is Jesus (Revelation 19:13). He is the standard we should use to assess all input regarding every circumstance in our lives. And until He returns, we will have battles. We must fight each battle—one lie at a time—with the truth of God.

> Prayer: Lord Jesus, You are the Word, and Your Word is truth. Show me when something or someone other than Your Word influences me so that it is You who sets my course and not the world, the flesh, or the enemy.

DAY 2

CRAFTING OUR OWN "TRUTH": UNDERSTANDING DECEPTION

Sometimes truth is tough to take. Sometimes truth hurts. And when it does, we want to change it, rearrange it, rationalize it, or downright deny it in order to fit our own thoughts, emotions, or expectations. Do you remember Isaiah 44:20 from lesson 2? It stated, *"He feeds on ashes; a deceived heart has turned him aside. And he cannot deliver himself, nor say, 'Is there not a lie in my right hand?'"* We can be fooled into thinking that whatever we pursue has no consequence.

We see a perfect example in King David, who rationalized, even denied his sin of taking Bathsheba for himself. He then arranged the murder of her husband when she told David she was pregnant. Let's take a closer look at this amazing exposure of the man who crafted his own truth. Read 2 Samuel 11:1–25. There are a number of deceptions in this passage. What are they?

_____

_____

_____

DID YOU KNOW?

Adultery was not a prerogative of any king. Even heathen kings knew that taking another man's wife would bring judgment on them (Genesis 20:1–3).

David crafted his own truth (self-deception) when he told himself he didn't need to be at war with the rest of his nation. Kings take their nations to battle. David rationalized that he didn't need to be where he belonged. That was his first mistake (or sin). Let's track the rest of them: In his leisure, perhaps he went looking. Having found what his eyes should not have seen, he didn't turn away. He made inquiries, he sent for the one on whom his desire was set (even when he discovered that she was the wife of one of his thirty mighty men), he took her and lay with her.

You would think that once the lust was satisfied, that would be that. *Au contraire!* Let's continue to track the progression of deception:

- Bathsheba conceived David's child.
- David conceived a plan of perception. If he could get Uriah to sleep with his wife, everyone would think that the child was Uriah's, and David was off the hook.
- David called Uriah out of battle and sent him home for the night.
- David's plans failed because Uriah's integrity wouldn't allow the luxury that the rest of the troops didn't have—being at home sleeping with their wives.
- David sent a desperate and deadly missive to his commander, Joab, regarding Uriah, "Get him killed!"
- David and Joab spun the truth in order to deceive others and cover their murderous sin.

Now read 2 Samuel 11:26–27. What was Bathsheba's response to her husband's death? What was God's response to what David had done?

WORD STUDY
Mourned

David and Bathsheba's encounter was not a sappy soap opera. David "took" Bathsheba. His was a grievous act! We know this in part because of how Bathsheba mourned or lamented her husband's death. In the Hebrew, "to mourn" is the word *saphad*, which means "to tear the hair and beat the breast...to lament, to wail." Is there any question?

We might think that David and Bathsheba planned their tryst while Uriah was at war. But this passage gives us the impression that Bathsheba mourned (lamented, wailed) deeply for her dead husband.

Self-deception weaves an ever-larger web that ensnares others. Have you ever deceived yourself? If so, what was the circumstance, and how did you realize that you were deceiving yourself? Were any others affected by your self-deception? If so, how?

_____

_____

_____

We do know, however, when we calculate to deceive others. Have you ever deceived another or others for selfish gain? What was the outcome?

_____

_____

_____

Or perhaps another person has deceived you. How was the deception discovered? What was the outcome of that deception?

_____

_____

_____

Here's a tough truth: When we don't want to deal with God's truth, we will craft our own.

God can penetrate the deceptive heart. God got David to see truth by exposing David's departure from truth. Read 2 Samuel 12:1–10. How did God use Nathan to appeal to David's heart (vv. 1–4)?

_____

_____

What was David's response (vv. 5–6)?

_____

_____

What led David to do evil in God's sight (v. 9)?

_____

_____

What was God's response to David's sin and deception (vv. 7–10?)

_____

_____

_____

Note that in verses 9–10, the Lord said to David, *"Why have you despised the word of the* *LORD by doing evil in His sight? . . . Now therefore, the sword shall never depart from your* *house, because you have despised Me and have taken the wife of Uriah the Hittite to be your* *wife."* God used the word *despise*, meaning "to disesteem or disdain." It is significant that God equated despising His Word with despising Him. And yet, would any of us ever consider that choosing not to "esteem" God's Word was the same as despising God?

Consider this perspective from pastor/author Jonathan Leeman: "To hear [God's] words that comprise the whole Bible is to hear Him. To obey His words is to obey Him. To ignore His words is to ignore Him . . . God so identifies Himself with His words that our response to His words is our response to Him."[9]

How about you? What do you think of Dr. Leeman's statement? Are there places in your life where you're not "esteeming" God's Word? How does this reflect your viewpoint of God?

Revisiting 2 Samuel 12, what consequences followed in verses 10–13?

What is God's indictment in verse 12?

God exposed what David plotted in secret. Proverbs 10:9 says, *"Whoever walks in integrity* *walks securely, but he who makes his ways crooked will be found out"* (ESV). Our sins may be hidden for a season, but in God's perfect timing, He will "out" us and our sins.

Why do you think God's Word (truth) spoke to David and rendered a repentant response?

God's mercy sent the truth to David and brought his sin to light. That is always God's goal—bringing sin to light so that we can repent and be restored to Him. What was David's response in Psalm 51:1–4?

David responded in a way that was to his credit (v. 13). He owned up to his sin and repented. He chose to recognize God's truth and yield to it. This is why David was *"a man after God's own heart"* (Acts 13:22).

Only the Word of God can effectively confront sin. Whether we're self-deceived, deceived by another, excuse another's deceptions, or deceive others, only God's truth can conquer deception.

Can you remember a time in your life when your self-deception was exposed? What did it take to break through your deception?

When you don't want to face truth, what do you do to avoid it?

What compels you to avoid truth?

> *"Whoever walks in integrity walks securely, but he who makes his ways crooked will be found out."*
>
> Proverbs 10:9 (ESV)

When it comes to crafting our own truth, can we ever look back on all that it alters and say, *It was worth it?*

> Prayer: Lord, when I violate Your Word by crafting my own deception, expose me, *"see if there be any hurtful way in me, and lead me in the ever-lasting way"* (Psalm 139:24).

DAY 3

KNOWING ABOUT OR TRULY KNOWING: UNDERSTANDING THE DIFFERENCE

Jesus. Do you know about Him, or do you truly know Him? Does it matter? The Pharisees knew about Him, but they didn't truly know Him. Did it matter? Pontius Pilate knew about Him, but he didn't truly know Him. Did it matter? Saul knew about Him, but he didn't truly know Him. Did it matter? Then Saul knew Jesus and became known as Paul. Paul truly knew Jesus. And it mattered. Let's see how that came about.

Saul came on the scene shortly after Jesus' death and resurrection. He is the perfect example of knowing about Jesus but not truly knowing Jesus. He claimed of himself: *"If anyone else has a mind to put confidence in the flesh, I far more: circumcised the eighth day, of the nation of Israel, of the tribe of Benjamin, a Hebrew of Hebrews; as to the Law, a Pharisee; as to zeal, a persecutor of the church; as to the righteousness which is in the Law, found blameless"* (Philippians 3:4–6) On fire for his Jewish faith, Saul agreed with the Jewish religious leaders that Jesus was a subversive whose followers deserved death. Saul's obsession caused him to breathe *"threats and murder against the disciples of the Lord"* (Acts 9:1).

While Saul was persecuting followers of Jesus, Jesus was pursuing Saul. Read Acts 9:1–9. What specific means did Jesus use to get Saul's attention? What were Jesus' instructions (v. 6)?

Saul just met the living Christ who turned his life upside down. In Acts 9:10–14, Jesus chose a man named Ananias to contribute to the next step in Saul's transformation. What was required of Ananias, and what was his response to Jesus' instruction?

In Acts 9:15–16, God reveals His plans for Saul. What were they, and how would they be accomplished?

EXTRA MILE
What Does It Mean to Know Jesus?

To know Jesus is to "become more deeply and intimately acquainted with Him, perceiving and recognizing and understanding [the wonders of His Person] more strongly and more clearly" (Philippians 3:10 AMP). How will you become more deeply and intimately acquainted with Jesus? How will you perceive and recognize Him on a daily basis? How will you understand the wonders of who He is more strongly and more clearly, especially in your times of trial?

Ananias was afraid of Saul and rightly so. But the Lord encouraged him with the assurance that Saul would prove himself faithful in the trials he would face for Jesus' sake.

According to Acts 9:17–22, How did Paul's encounter with Christ change his life?

Consider this: Paul persecuted believers based on what he knew about Jesus. Only after his encounter with the living Christ did he know Jesus.

Think about all the things you know about Jesus. How do these differ from how you know Jesus? What's the evidence that you know Jesus?

_____

_____

_____

In our religiosity, we, like Saul, may not see the truth for what it really is. Instead, we can live our lives in a way that has little to do with truth and righteousness because we "know about" rather than "know" Jesus.

Something powerful compelled Paul to give up everything he was and had. Remember, his pedigree set him among the ruling elite. It came with education. It came with dedication. It came with adulation. He had power. He had influence. And he gave it all up for Jesus.

Let's journey with Paul from his self-righteous heart to his heart's new purpose. The pursuit of Christ, the power of His resurrection and the pain of His suffering all helped Paul to know Jesus more intimately. Read Philippians 3:7–9. What did Paul give up to pursue Christ? What did Paul gain by his pursuit of Christ?

_____

_____

_____

Philippians 3:10 is powerfully stated in the _Amplified Bible_: "[For my determined purpose is] _that I may know Him [that I may progressively become more deeply and intimately acquainted with Him, perceiving and recognizing and understanding the wonders of His Person more strongly and more clearly], and that I may in that same way come to know the power outflowing from His resurrection [which it exerts over believers], and that I may so share His sufferings as to be continually transformed [in spirit into His likeness even] to His death..."_

This is not an easy verse to unpack, so let's apply it personally: What does "determined purpose" mean to you?

_____

_____

_____

_____

What would you do or are you doing to pursue Christ with Paul's determined purpose in order to _"become more deeply and intimately acquainted with Him, perceiving and recognizing and understanding [the wonders of His Person] more strongly and more clearly"_?

_____

_____

_____

_____

Paul also talked about the power of Jesus' resurrection. It is the same power that raised Jesus from the dead and now operates in you to resist and reject sin and overcome death. Why is understanding and personally taking hold of the resurrection power central to knowing Christ?

_____

_____

_____

How does the pain of sharing in Christ's sufferings help you to know Jesus?

_____

_____

_____

Paul truly knew Jesus, and it mattered. He discovered what eludes many of us; that nothing matters more than knowing Jesus. Knowing Jesus changed how Paul measured his worth from having it all to counting all loss as gain. It changed what he influenced as a stately Pharisee to a lowly, persecuted believer. It changed what and whom he influenced—From his place as a stately Pharisee to a lowly, persecuted believer. It changed what influenced him—From Jewish law and tradition to Jesus Christ and His Holy Spirit. It also changed how he viewed suffering, from causing it to welcoming it. Paul considered _"everything as loss compared to the priceless privilege (the overwhelming preciousness, the surpassing worth, and supreme advantage) of knowing Christ Jesus my Lord"_ (3:8 AMP). And the power of Paul's faith walk was totally dependent on the depth of his intimate knowledge of his Savior.

Let _us_ not stop short of the transforming power of knowing Jesus Christ. That's gain!

> Prayer: Lord, may my determined purpose be to truly know Jesus and the power of His resurrection so that my sufferings will transform me into His likeness. Lord, I want to know You.

DAY 4

PURSUING TRUTH: UNDERSTANDING THE POWER

Have you ever told a true story only to have the listeners look at you and say, "Really?" Although you may not have considered their responses from this perspective, what they're saying is, "No! We don't believe that!" We can have that response to God's truth: "No! I don't believe that for myself, for my life" and on and on.

What truths from God's Word are you struggling to believe or are you disregarding for your particular circumstances?

_____

_____

_____

What we tell ourselves has power. We will either tell ourselves the truth as God gives it, or we will tell ourselves a lie as the world, our flesh, or the enemy gives it. Little white lies, rationalizations, justifications, deceptions—all have deadly consequences.

God will not let us get away with living a false and hollow existence. If we're in a scenario where we are being lied to and deceived or where we ourselves are lying and being deceptive, we can trust that God will still be true to His Word because of who He is. How can we be sure? Because He said so. Read Psalm 18:25–36. What do you learn about God, and how can this truth about Him impact your personal situation?

We want to give you a qualifier about God's truth: We can't pick and choose from the Bible what we believe. Either all of it is true, or none of it is true. Do you believe this? If so, how do you know? If not, how do you know?

As women we are more likely to interpret our circumstances with our feelings rather than with the facts. Sometimes we believe that our feelings are the facts. Can our feelings be trusted if they stand in opposition to God's truth? Do you remember when Satan caused Eve to doubt God's truth with just four little words, *"Did God really say...?"* The only effective counter to that question is and always will be, *"Thus says the Lord..."* Regardless of our circumstances, doubting that God's Word is truth will be as disastrous for us as the siren's call that dashed ships against the rocks. God's truth will always direct us safely through dangerous passages.

Let's take a look at what God's truth says about God's truth. Read Psalm 19:7–14, and answer the questions that follow. In verse 7–9, the Word of God is described by a variety of nouns and adjectives. What are they? (For example, in verse 7, God's Word is called the *"law"* and is described as *"perfect."* List the rest below.

Returning to verses 7–9, what does it have the power to do in our lives?

Based on verse 10, what should our attitude be toward God's truth?

Verse 11 says, *"Moreover, by them Your servant is warned; in keeping them there is great reward."* Warning and reward are two assurances we receive from God's Word. What do you think is the benefit of warning? How will keeping God's Word reward us?

Verses 12–13 describe two types of moral failings. What are they, and what do you think they mean? How did the psalmist feel about the presence of these sins in his life?

Hidden sins are those that we don't remember or those we commit out of ignorance. They are stuffed in an unknown darkness. The psalmist asked to be cleared of unintentional sins. Presumptuous sins are deliberate sins "committed in arrogant disregard of divine commands."[10] They are intentionally nurtured in a deliberate darkness. The psalmist realized how powerful these sins were. They were "great transgressions" that revealed a heart of rebellion, a heart enslaved. They were sins that needed to be exposed. And he pleaded with God, "Keep me from them; don't let them control me!" He understood that pursuing God and His truth were the only remedies for sin.

Pursuing God and His truth are the only remedies for sin.

EXTRA MILE
Micah 7:8–9 and 18–20

We are going to fail God, perhaps on regular occasions. How do these verses say God responds to us when we fail Him? How does His response influence your growth as a Christian?

Have you ever asked the Lord to acquit you of those sins in your life that you weren't even aware of—sins stuffed in an unknown darkness? If so, what prompted you to do that?

Have you ever caught yourself "in arrogant disregard of divine commands"—sins nurtured in a deliberate darkness? Has God been speaking to you about a specific command to which you refuse to yield? Write it here:

Let's talk about the "disregard of divine commands" in light of sexual sin. There is nothing hidden about deliberate sin. And if it's sexual sin, it is a dangerous choice with dire consequences. If you are currently involved in sexual sin, what dire consequences can it have or has it already had on your life or that of others?

_____

_____

_____

If a loved one is involved in sexual sin, what have been the resulting consequences? What consequences do you yet fear?

_____

_____

_____

How have you responded to this loved one involved in sexual sin? What kind of response to this sin would be "in arrogant disregard of divine commands?" For example, has anger expressed itself as malicious, explosive condemnation rather than genuine, heartfelt yet resolute confrontation? Others?

_____

_____

_____

_____

Perhaps we have behaviors we think God would overlook because He is a good God and He loves us. This is dangerous thinking and the ultimate deception. "Not being reconciled to the fact of sin—not recognizing it and refusing to deal with it—produces all the disasters in life."[11]

Returning to Psalm 19, why would the psalmist end the way he did in verse 14?

_____

_____

The psalmist knew and understood the power of God's truth. He depended on the truth of God to keep him from deception, and he acted on it. As with the psalmist, the power that God's truth can have in our lives will only come as we use it and obey it.

Hebrews 4:12 talks specifically about the capability of God's Word. From the *Amplified Bible* that follows, underline all that God's Word is, and circle all that it will do: *"For the Word that God speaks is alive and full of power [making it active, operative, energizing, and effective]; it is sharper than any two-edged sword, penetrating to the dividing line of the breath of life (soul) and [the immortal] spirit, and of joints and marrow [of the deepest parts of our nature], exposing and sifting and analyzing and judging the very thoughts and purposes of the heart."*

Based on this verse, what does the Word of God mean for a believer's life?

_____

_____

What is your response to the power that the Word of God can have in *your* life? Are you willing to let it expose, sift, analyze, and judge the very thoughts and purposes of your heart? Carefully and prayerfully answer the following questions as they relate to sexual sin (yours or your response to another's sin against you or a loved one):

Has the Word of God *exposed* the thoughts and purposes of your heart? If so, in what way? Have you been willing to receive it? If yes, why? If no, why not?

_____

_____

_____

Has the Word of God *sifted* the thoughts and purposes of your heart? If so, in what way? How have you responded?

_____

_____

Has the Word of God *analyzed* the thoughts and purposes of your heart? If so, is God requiring something from you? If yes, what?

_____

_____

_____

Has the Word of God *judged* the thoughts and purposes of your heart? If so, how do you know and what is your response?

_____

_____

_____

Based on your answers to these questions, how powerful would you say the Word of God is in your life?

_____

_____

_____

Only God's truth has the power to expose the deepest, darkest, most deceptive, and most deceived parts of ourselves. We must believe in its power for ourselves, embracing it for our lives and for all the stuff of life. What do the following Scriptures say about God's truth and its power in your life?

Scripture	What Scripture Says about God's Truth	The Power of God's Truth in My Life
John 17:17		
John 8:31–32		
2 Timothy 3:16–17		

"Sanctify them in the truth; your word is truth."

John 17:17 (NASB)

 WORD STUDY
What Does *Sanctify* Mean?

From the Greek, *hagiozo*, *sanctify* means "to make holy, to purify, to render clean in a moral sense." Sanctification is an ongoing process of growth in the believer by the power, influence, and teaching of the indwelling Holy Spirit. Read the following Scriptures, and record any insights: 1 Corinthians 6:11; 1 Thessalonians 5:23; Hebrews 10:10, 14; Revelation 22:11.

Wherever we are stuck in life, we are impotent and powerless. Life seems dark. Only the Word of God will move us out of our impotent darkness into the realm of the supernatural light where it will sanctify us, free us, teach us, rebuke us, correct us, and train us in righteousness. If we want the power of God to work in our circumstances, then we must bring the power of His truth into them. Then we will be adequate for what we face. Then we will be equipped for every good work. Will it change our circumstances? Perhaps, perhaps not. But it will change us!

Prayer: Father, Your Word is alive and full of power. I want it to be active, operative, energizing, and effective in my life. Because it's sharp and penetrating, send it to the deepest places of my nature. Use it to expose my erroneous, ungodly thoughts and deceptive motives. Sift my inner thoughts and motives until only what is pure is left. Let me yield to Your standard that my life may please You, O Lord, my Rock and my Redeemer.

DAY 5

WALKING IN TRUTH

As toddlers learning to walk we didn't stand one day and run a marathon the next. To develop the right muscles for the job, we began with rolling over, then crawling, then pulling ourselves to a standing position, then taking those first wobbly steps. After those steps, it took practice, practice, practice. And now walking is second nature to us.

The apostle John said in his third letter, *"I have no greater joy than this, to hear of my children walking in the truth"* (3 John 4). We have to learn to walk as Jesus did—and then practice, practice, practice until it becomes second nature to us. However, what we don't use, we lose.

When we walk in the truth, we're applying the Word of God to our lives and living it. The ability to do so effectively is called the wisdom of God. God takes this walk seriously, and He wants us to take Him seriously. According to Proverbs 9:9–11, where does wisdom begin, and what impact will it have on our lives?

 EXTRA MILE:
Job 28:20–28; Proverbs 1–9.

Wisdom is about knowing God's truth, understanding its intent for us, and applying it effectively to our lives and circumstances. What was Job's understanding of wisdom? According to these chapters, what are the characteristics of wisdom? How does wisdom benefit a life? (Note that wisdom is personified in Proverbs as "she.")

According to the following Scriptures, how should we walk as Christians and why? In your journal, write how each Scripture speaks to your struggle with sexual sin or that of a loved one, or with your response to sexual sin against you or against a loved one.

John 12:35–36

Galatians 5:16

Ephesians 4:1–3

Ephesians 5:2

_____

_____

Ephesians 5:8–10

_____

_____

Some of these passages have spoken specifically to your current circumstances. Which ones have you found encouraging and why? Which have you found convicting and why?

_____

_____

_____

Read 1 John 2:1–6. What's the evidence that one is not walking in God's truth? What is the evidence that one is walking in God's truth?

_____

_____

_____

> _"So Jesus said to them, 'For a little while longer the Light_
> _is among you. Walk while you have the Light,_
> _so that darkness will not overtake you; he who walks in the dark-_
> _ness does not know where he goes.'"_
>
> John 12:35–36 (NASB)

Perhaps today's verses seem overwhelming in terms of how we're to walk. We can obsess about every detail, or we can depend on the source—the Holy Spirit— who will ensure that we will have all we need to walk in a manner worthy, no matter what the situation. Remember that our painful places require action—not to fix our circumstances but to walk with God in them so that He can influence and impact them and us. And when we fail to _"walk in a manner worthy"_ (Ephesians 4:1), we have _"an Advocate with the Father"_ (1 John 2:1).

Learning to walk in truth is a process. In order to begin this process, we must have a plan. The following exercise can create your own personal "walking-out-what-Jesus-is-working-in" plan. Write in your journal those insights and Scriptures that speak to you and to your circumstances on this joyful walk with God. Let's begin with fifteen suggestions that can turn your life around. Find one today that will help you walk in the truth more consistently, then gradually add a new step daily or weekly until walking in the truth becomes an established habit.

Make your life about Jesus Christ! He's already made His life about you. Read Colossians 3:1–4. What is the encouragement in this passage? What will you do to make your life more about Jesus Christ?

_____

_____

_____

Acknowledge God every day. Read Psalm 118:24. How do you or will you acknowledge God every day in your home?

_____

_____

_____

Anticipate His Spirit working in your life every day. Read 2 Corinthians 3:17–18. Where in your life today do you need His Spirit working?

_____

_____

_____

Be faithful with daily Bible reading and quiet time with the Lord. Read Deuteronomy 8:3 and Psalm 27:8. What do you have in place to meet with the Lord daily? If you're new to Bible reading, here are two great starting points: Read a psalm daily and think about it along with a few verses in the Gospel of John. Ask God to give you insight. Write your plan for a daily quiet time in your journal.

Fill your mind with God's promises so that you have them when you need them. Read Psalm 119:105 and 2 Corinthians 1:20. When a verse seems to be meant for you, write it on a Post-It note, 3x5 card, or in your journal, and read it regularly. Keep a collection. When tough times come, the Holy Spirit will remind you of the specific truth that applies to your situation. What do you do or will you do to record those promises meant just for you?

_____

_____

_____

Fill your children's minds with God's promises! Read Deuteronomy 6:7. This is like double-dipping for moms and grandmoms and has an exponential return. For example, you can share His answers to your prayers, do a daily devotional with them, memorize Scripture with them, or buy them a book specific to God's promises for them. What do you do or will you do to encourage your children or grandchildren with God's truth?

_____

_____

Worship and praise God on a daily basis. Read Psalm 59:16–17 and 103. We worship and praise God for Who He is and what He's done. Words of adoration lift us up out of the darkest places and remind us that God is still sovereign and in command. That's truth. Pick an attribute of God, and praise Him for it right now. Then do this each day. This reminds us of who He is. How will doing this help you in your deepest times of trouble?

Be thankful in every circumstance. Daily express gratitude to God, even in the difficult places. This reminds us that He is good and He is with us. Read 1 Thessalonians 5:18, and learn why we're to be thankful. Note how many times in one day can you express this thanks, starting today—and write them in your journal.

Be willing to wait on God in your circumstance and let Him walk you forward. Read Psalm 40:1–5. Where would you say you are in this passage? What is your hope while you wait?

Play and sing praise/worship music. This is another way to saturate your mind with truth about God and His heart for you. You'll find yourself awakening with praise songs in your mind. It's like praying twice! Read Psalm 150. Which songs make an impression in your heart and speak to your circumstance? Write their titles and key messages in your journal.

Listen to tapes of encouraging sermons or radio programs. Read Hebrews 13:17. In your journal, write the big idea from each sermon you hear and its personal application to your life. Then ask God to help you live it.

Be a hearer and a doer of God's Word. Read James 1:22–25. This is the practice, practice, practice of walking as Jesus walked. What have you recently heard that you now know you must do, especially as it relates to your circumstance?

Seek a biblically grounded female friend to counsel you when you're stuck, if the Lord prompts you. Read Proverbs 27:5–6. And ladies, if you're that friend, have the courage to ask hard questions and give clear biblical answers. Are you willing to hear the hard biblical truths from a well-grounded friend? And friend, are you willing to speak God's truth lovingly, not your own truth or opinions, to a friend who needs to hear it?

Pray intercessory prayers for those who hurt you. Read Matthew 5:44–45 and 1 Timothy 2:1. How would doing so begin to transform your heart about both the people and the circumstance?

> *"The one who says he abides in Him ought himself to walk in the same manner as He walked."*
>
> 1 John 2:6 (NASB)

Walk as Jesus walked! Read Acts 17:28 and 1 John 2:5–6. Each day we get to choose how we'll walk the path we're on. Walking in the truth is living it day by day. Would you say that you are walking in the truth? If yes, what is the evidence? If no, how do you know?

Prayer: Lord, sometimes I still feel brand-new in my walk with You as if I've taken only baby steps. May Your Spirit strengthen my gait for this journey by bringing to mind Your truth and to practice, practice, practice that truth. After all, practice makes permanent.

LESSON 5

So far what you've learned in this study may seem to have little to say about sex. In fact, what you've learned has everything to do with sex because understanding and believing who God is and what He says as truth prepares us to navigate the rough waters of unhealthy sexual messages and practices.

The truths in this chapter are contrary to what the world teaches, what the flesh responds to, and what the enemy offers. We can't fix what is wrong in sexual thinking or resolve sexual struggles unless we embrace sexuality as God intended. These next five days will teach you about God's design for sex, His standard, and His specific intent so that you will know what safe, holy, healthy, and pleasurable sex was always intended by God to be.

DAY 1

DESIGNED FOR SEX SPIRITUALLY: TRUE SACRED SEX

When God made light, the angels
drew near to let the refractions roll
over their faces like a symphony.

When God made earth, they poked
their fingers into its moistness;
they put a fleck to their nose and smiled.

When God made the sea, they kicked
at the foam and sat in its cool
till their bones laughed.

When God made a rose, they parted
its petals and passed it among
themselves, saying, "So fragile,
yet how it grasps the soul."

When God made a giraffe,
they touched the strange hide

and murmured to themselves that God
was up to something magnificent.

When God made man, each one
retired to his chamber and peered
into the writings, looking for some
clue to the mystery.

When God made woman, they came
back out of their chambers and gazed,
their jaws slack with awe.

When God joined man to woman
and said, "Let them become one flesh,"
everything suddenly made sense.
The cheering still shakes
the galaxies.[1]

Mark Littleton
(used with permission)

Together this first man and woman reflected the fullness of their Creator. Together their touches introduced the intimacy of sexual love and ushered in a new and holy realm of relationship—oneness—their two separate and distinct souls now fused in a powerful act that ratified their covenant. Together they were in union with each other, much like they were in union with their God. Together as one entity—fully male and fully female—they represented the full image of God. Together they were an inseparable partnership that would carry out God's plan on earth. Is it any wonder that the galaxies still rejoice?

In his book, *Sacred Sex: A Spiritual Celebration of Oneness in Marriage*, pastor and counselor Tim Alan Gardner asked questions that few of us ever think to ask ourselves: "What do I really believe about sex? 'How do the things I think and feel affect my sex life?' 'What were God's original intentions when He created sex?' In sum, 'Why sex?'"[2]

God's command to Adam and Eve in Genesis 2:24 to leave, cleave, and become one flesh established marriage as a covenant relationship—a holy, unbreakable, indissoluble commitment that is continually ratified by the one-flesh sexual experience. Have you ever considered that sex was God's design to "seal the deal" of the marriage covenant? What do you think about that?

Have you ever considered that sex was God's design to "seal the
deal" of the marriage covenant? Because the marriage covenant is
sacred, then the sealing of that covenant is sacred.

Because the marriage covenant is sacred, then the sealing of that covenant is sacred. The Bible has no greater example of this sacred seal than in the Song of Solomon (also called the Song of Songs). Read Song of Solomon 4:1–15. A new bridegroom is verbally caressing his bride on their wedding night. What is sacred about his expression?

_____

_____

_____

Read Song of Solomon 4:16. What is his bride's response? What is she inviting? What is sacred about this?

_____

_____

_____

In Song of Solomon 5:1, two people are speaking. In the first part, it's the bridegroom. What conclusion do you draw from his statements in the first half of verse 1?

_____

_____

The bridegroom and his bride are in the presence of another at the end of Song of Solomon 5:1. What does this person say to the couple?

_____

_____

> *"Eat, friends; drink and imbibe deeply, O lovers."*
>
> Song of Solomon 5:1 (NASB)

Many Bible scholars believe that it was God who spoke to this couple at the end of their lovemaking and that He heartily approved. Gardner emphasizes that sex is "a beautiful, holy act that invites the presence of God...It is in sex, in the full unity of both male and female, that the full image of God is represented."[3] That is the "sacred" in the sex. What a wedding gift!

Prior to this lesson, did you consider marital sex as sacred? If so, how did you arrive at that? If not, how do you view sex?

_____

_____

_____

Have you ever considered sacred sex as God's protection? Protection from what?

_____

_____

_____

Why is it important, as well as beneficial, for marital sex to be as God originally intended? How does this awareness influence your attitude toward sexual intimacy with your husband or future husband?

The angels in the poem at the beginning of this day's lesson understood that the sexual union of Adam and Eve also united their souls. Sexual intercourse completed not only the creation picture but revealed the awesome character of our God, who, out of love, sealed the covenant of marriage with this incomparable expression. It was a union designed, instituted, and applauded by the Creator Himself and one that reflected their relationship with Him. It was true, sacred sex!

Gardner also emphasizes that "sexual intimacy, as experienced in and by God's design, is certainly an undeserved journey into the treasure house of the divine. It is a sacred reminder of our vertical relationship with Christ and His church as celebrated in the horizontal intimacy of a husband and a wife, fellow heirs of God's grace."[4]

There is a "90-Degree Dynamic" between the covenant of marriage and the covenant with Jesus. How is this described in Ephesians 5:31–32?

 EXTRA MILE
What Is the 90-Degree Dynamic?

The 90-Degree Dynamic reveals how our vertical relationships with Jesus Christ influence our horizontal relationships with others, such as our spouses or potential spouses as well as others with whom we're in relationship. The degree to which we are in right relationships with Jesus is the degree to which we can be in right relationships with others. Specific Scriptures that illuminate the 90-Degree Dynamic include John 13:34 (love), Romans 15:7 (acceptance), and Matthew 6:14–15 (forgiveness). How can awareness of this dynamic change how we relate to others?

Let's review these two covenants from the perspective of the 90-Degree Dynamic:

COVENANT WITH YOUR SPOUSE	COVENANT WITH YOUR LORD
Leave: Your husband leaves the establishment of his youth (a home with mother and father in the parent-child relationship) to establish a home with you, his bride who is now his priority human relationship. In response, you leave your father and mother and follow him to establish your new home with him, your priority human relationship.	**Leave:** The Bridegroom (Jesus) leaves the establishment of His heavenly realm (dwelling with His Father) to establish a relationship with you, His Bride (all believers) (See John 1:1–2 and 14.). In response, you leave all other "loves", anything or anyone that vies for His place in your heart, which is where He establishes His home.
Cleave: As his expression of loyalty and devotion, your husband inseparably and actively joins himself to you as your leader, protector, and provider. His sacrificial love holds you to him, securing you. In response, you faithfully cleave to him.	**Cleave:** Nothing can separate you from the love of your Bridegroom (Christ); no one can remove you from His hand. He is forever with you, and He will neither leave nor forsake you. In response, you cleave to Him by faith. (See Romans 8:35–39; 1 John 4:19.)
Two Become One: Sexual intercourse is God's divine wedding gift that seals the marriage covenant between you and your husband until death parts you. Because this act unites your very souls, it serves to enhance every area of marital intimacy (physical, mental, emotional, sexual, spiritual). This act of oneness not only makes the two of you into a new entity (creation), but can also result in new little biological creations.	**Two Become One:** When Christ enters your heart by the power of His Holy Spirit, your covenant with Him is established (1 Corinthians 6:17) and sealed forever (Ephesians 1:13). You offer your body (physical, mental, emotional, sexual, spiritual faculties) to Him as a living sacrifice, holy and acceptable (Romans 12:1). Oneness with your Bridegroom (Jesus Christ) results in a brand new you (2 Corinthians 5:17).

Can you see the spiritual 90-Degree Dynamic of leaving, cleaving, and becoming one with Jesus Christ as well as with your spouse? What is sacred about leaving all others for a spouse? What should that look like in a marriage?

What is sacred about cleaving to a spouse and no other? What should that look like in a marriage?

What is sacred about becoming one flesh with a spouse and no other? What should that look like before marriage? What should that look that like in a marriage?

EXTRA MILE
What about Divorce and Remarriage?

Will God bless your marriage if one or both of you have been divorced? If you have been married, divorced, and are now remarried or desire to remarry, God will meet you right where you are now. You serve a forgiving, forward-moving God, one who doesn't want you stuck in past sins and mistakes (yours or your husband's). Do you have something from your former marriage that needs to be reconciled with God? If so, do it now. He desires to bless you when you ask His forgiveness. Then you are free to follow Him in your current or future marriage. Keep your eyes fixed on the Author and Finisher of your faith, and let Him move where you are now. You can glorify Him there.

There is a purposeful you-and-you-alone directive to spouses in marriage as well as those in covenant with Christ (Genesis 2:24 and Ephesians 5:31–32). It goes like this: "I leave all others for you and you alone; I cleave to no other but to you and you alone; I become one with only one other—you and you alone—until death do us part."

> Prayer: God, it is hard to imagine that this powerful, intimate, sacred act of covenant was divinely designed not only for our pleasure but also for our protection. May I begin to see sex through Your eyes. Please put the sacred into my sex life today—that which is a tender, holy, beautiful, and protected covenant between bride and bridegroom and between Christ and me.

DAY 2

DESIGNED FOR SEX PHYSIOLOGICALLY: A PERFECT FIT

God designed the human male and female for sex. He confined this act to marriage alone and proclaimed it very good! In this beautiful fusion, God ensured that the physical construction, chemistry, and hormones of the male and female bodies would result in the perfect fit to be cultivated for a lifetime.

Before the fall, sex was all good because it was all God. However, after the fall, the enemy counterfeited both the meaning and purpose of sex. Our understanding of what God originally intended for masculine and feminine sexuality became distorted.

How would you define a healthy sexual relationship?

Recall that Genesis 1:27 states, *"God created man in His own image, in the image of God He created him; male and female He created them."* God created two distinct humans, each in His own image but different nonetheless. These differences are real and compelling.

Our design is not accidental. What does Psalm 139:13–15 say about our design? How does this relate to our design for sex?

In his book, *Wired for Intimacy*, William Struthers writes: "It is important to understand that there are significant differences between men and women that are rooted [in] our wiring, our neurological and physiological makeup. Men and women image God both independently and together in distinct ways influenced by God's intentional design of their physical bodies"[5] (brackets ours).

Although the obvious differences between male and female are physical, few understand the intricacy of God's sexual design. Counselor Harry Schaumburg instructs, "First, we must marvel at God's design and second, with gratitude, be amazed at the Father's heart for sex. God has placed more nerve endings in the penis and clitoris than any other part of the body except the tongue. Clearly, God wants us to enjoy the pleasure of good food and holy sex."[6]

 DID YOU KNOW?
Do You Know the Difference?

Testosterone and the Male (in concert with less dominant hormones):

- Turns energy to muscle to support the work/defend requirement
- Produces large, strong, hard muscles (to work the ground and defend the family/ community)
- Contributes to his more physical nature (he's a doer)
- Contributes to a practical/logical approach to life; a concrete thinker (doesn't let his emotions think for him)
- Contributes to well-developed spacial skills (he's sports/action-oriented)
- Contributes to a competitive/aggressive nature (Is paint ball an Olympic sport?)
- Contributes to risky behavior as well as a sense of duty (what heroes are made of)
- Motivates the natural instinct to lead, protect, and provide (he will die for his wife, his family, and yes, his country, if necessary)
- Motivates his sex drive (Did we say "drive?" Yup, God put that stuff in him.)

Estrogen and the Female (in concert with less dominant hormones):

- Turns energy to fat to support pregnancy (What was God thinking?)
- Produces a "gentler" musculature; rounder, softer physique (for nurturing, comforting, and tender nuzzlings)
- Contributes to her more relational ties (yes, we're girls!)
- Contributes to a more emotional approach to life; she thinks intuitively (her feelings rather than facts can influence her decisions)
- Contributes to well-developed verbal skills ('nuff said)

- Contributes to a reflexive/cautious nature (what mommies are made of)
- Contributes to a compassionate heart (what heroines are made of)
- Motivates support and nurturance (will give her best to husband, family, friends, community)
- Assists in fueling her sexual desire (More testosterone anyone?)

Significant hormonal differences influence male and female sexuality and are helpful to understand if we want to have a healthy sexual relationship in our marriages. Testosterone is the stuff of sexual response for both male and female, although its production in the male is approximately twenty times that of the female each day. It "remains at a steady level within the male body . . . and creates a fairly consistent desire"[7] for sex until later adulthood when the amount steadily decreases.

In the female, testosterone is cyclically produced in small amounts in her ovaries and serves to enhance her sexual response, her muscle mass, bone density, energy level, and sense of well-being. As the amount of testosterone in her body increases during her cycle, sexual desire increases, enhancing sensitivity to arousal and orgasm. And although many women experience a desire for sex regularly, a woman's desire for sex doesn't typically rival the male sex drive. The female's testosterone level, along with estrogen and progesterone levels, also begins to abate in later adulthood.

It's necessary to address a common misunderstanding about the typical male. He is not sex-crazed. He has a physiological drive for sex that God put in him. Now before your head explodes, let's share some further evidence: Depending on his age, the average man is capable of two to six ejaculations daily with millions of sperm at the ready in each firing. Without release, semen is built up every forty-eight to seventy-two hours during which time there can be an associated physiological pressure.[8] If a man is stressed, busy, or well-disciplined, he may not be distracted by the buildup, and it will dissipate. However, if he's in a more relaxed mode, the sexual pressure is more likely to become a distraction. And if the pressure is unreleased, a man can experience both physical discomfort and emotional frustration. In young boys and men, nocturnal emission, also known as wet dreams, is one of two ways God provides for young men to physically release this sexual pressure. The other is sex in marriage, which is intended to be God's primary way of release.

How might this knowledge challenge your opinion about men and their sexuality?

From the point of arousal, God beautifully designed the male and female sexual organs to lubricate and engorge in preparation for intercourse. Arousal and orgasm were designed by God to be involuntary reflexive responses for both men and women. They were meant to move us from arousal to orgasm "automagically"—a biological miracle that fulfills and satisfies and perpetuates its repetition. But because of the fall, negative emotions, fears, inhibitions, distractions, physiological and sexual dysfunction, and other performance issues often get in the way.

Orgasm, however, wasn't God's finish line. By divine design, a husband and wife selflessly recreate this beautiful bonding experience throughout their lives together. Doing so is an intentional mutual invitation as well as an intentional mutual response that God designed to secure the great big O—oneness. He accomplished this oneness through some amazing chemistry. He concocted a chemical trio within each human brain that triggers bonding during togetherness, romance, and lovemaking. The first of the trio, dopamine, flushes our brains with a feel-good reward whenever we do something thrilling. From warm eye contact to handholding to the urgent embrace that culminates in the full-out perfect fit of lovemaking, dopamine serves to stimulate, attain, and maintain bonding. Said another way, the better sex makes us feel, the more we want to experience it. This bonding experience is also reinforced by the joy we feel when we please our spouses sexually. It is both mutually gratifying and gratifyingly mutual.

Oxytocin is the second of the trio. This powerful neurochemical is most active in the female, securing healthy sexual bonding and creating trust in her mate when engaging in intimate touching and sexual intercourse. Neuropsychiatrist Dr. Louann Brizendine explains that the female gets the feeling of closeness when oxytocin floods her brain. Oxytocin is the bonding chemical that keeps couples pursuing each other, and the more they pursue and connect, the stronger, longer, and more durable their bond. Over time in a marriage, the dopamine rush associated with their intense sexual pursuit settles down to create a more comfortable pace. Brizendine explains, "It's not a sign of love grown cold, it's a sign of love moving into a new, more sustainable phase for the long term, with bonds forged by two neuro-hormones, vasopressin and oxytocin."[9]

Vasopressin, the final neurochemical, is more active in males and is known as the monogamy molecule. It generates bonding, attachment, and commitment between a male and his mate. In their book, *Hooked*, Joe McIlhaney and Freda Bush describe it this way:

> The relationship that continues long-term experiences a bonding that, in a sense, glues the two people together for life. This bonding, as we have examined, is due in part to the oxytocin and vasopressin secreted into the woman's and the man's brains [respectively] as a result of their contact with each other. This is the deep, abiding love of a mature relationship. One long-term result of the mature love relationship that stays intact… is a relaxed, trusting, loving, rewarding, faithful, sexual relationship (brackets ours).[10]

Keep in mind that this is the way God designed it to be even if it's not your current experience. What is your response to God's physiological design for sex?

_____

_____

_____

_____

Let's see how Scripture advises us to handle our chemistry. Before marriage, when romance kicks in, unless discipline kicks in along with it, liberties may be taken that jeopardizes a couple's future oneness. What is Paul's wise counsel in 1 Corinthians 7:1–2?

Paul is not anti-sex in this passage. He understood that sex sprang from God's divine and holy inspiration and that a couple's love-relationship required the proper restraint before marriage in order to thrive. Their powerful emotions were to lead them to the altar and *then* to their marriage bed.

The physiology of sex beautifully contributes to God's securing goal of oneness for a married couple. It is not the "accidental by-product of evolution that helps us pass on our genes to the next generation. It is the purposeful creation of a loving God who has set out the guidelines through which it is best experienced."[11] The true, perfect fit!

> Prayer: *"O Lord, Thank You for making me so wonderfully complex! Your workmanship is marvelous—how well I know it"* (Psalm 139:13–14 NLT). May I truly embrace the precision of its performance, the power of its protection, and purity of its purpose. You are God, and Your way works. Show me Your way, Lord.

DAY 3

DESIGNED FOR SEX EMOTIONALLY: TRUE SAFE SEX

The biblical phrase *"two become one flesh"* conveys the sexual bond that ratifies the marital covenant between a man and a woman. It also conveys the beautifully intimate and deeply emotional connection that blends their two souls over time.

According to Genesis 2:25, what indicates that Adam and Eve were emotionally close? What do you think this meant for them?

Imagine the first virgin male and the first virgin female gazing at each other, tenderly exploring each other's bodies without shame. The Hebrew word for *shame* is *bosh*, which means "to become pale or to blush." They didn't blush when they stared in wonderment and divine awe. There was no shame associated with their personal sexuality or the sexuality of their mate. They had no inhibition, no hesitation, no disgrace, no disgust, no guilt, no disappointment. They were totally acceptable to themselves, acceptable to the other, and accepting of the other. They experienced unabashed, exquisite freedom physically, sexually, emotionally, and spiritually. Naked and unashamed! They must have reveled in the "wow!" of their intimate and sacred experience—not just the "wow" of their orgasm, but the "wow" of their oneness.

"The man and his wife were both naked and were not ashamed."

Genesis 2:25 (NASB)

Although orgasm was not the ultimate goal in the first married couple's lovemaking, it was the divine expression of God's inexpressible—the beautiful physical climax to their shared emotional vulnerability and abandon. Tim Alan Gardner writes, "It is in that gift of abandoning control to our mates and trusting them in our most vulnerable state that the full union of physical oneness is most deeply experienced. It is there that we find sacred sex at its most powerful manifestation. The extreme intensity of the orgasmic experience is due to the fact that it is had with our God-given mate."[12]

Being naked (vulnerable) and unashamed (abandoned) in marriage, physically and emotionally, is the evidence of a couple's mutual acceptance and trust. Each is safe with the other: free to share tender thoughts, fresh wounds, lofty dreams; free to kindly and respectfully communicate anything forthrightly and honestly without fear; free to express sexual needs and desires; free to occupy the same bed and feel peace and comfort; free to speak words of passion while in passionate embrace. And surrender is sweet.

Do you remember the three bio-buddies from day 2—dopamine, oxytocin, and vasopressin? The emotional side of intimacy is reinforced by these "biochemicals of connection." They bathe the brains of both genders with the chemicals that cause us to desire emotional intimacy along with sexual intimacy. And although sexual intimacy reinforces "an intense experience in the mind—an experience of deep connection,"[13] emotional intimacy reinforces an intense experience of the heart, further enhancing the sexual connection. The Divine Designer wired us so that emotional intimacy and sexual intimacy are mutually reinforcing.

Let's get a biblical perspective from the Song of Solomon. Before their marriage, it's easy to pick up on the sexual tension between them. Let's see how they handled it. Revisit the Song of Solomon 1:15 and 2:2. How did the groom laud his beloved bride-to-be?

In Song of Solomon 2:3–6, the bride fantasized about her beloved. What words and phrases did she use to describe how she felt about him? How would you qualify her love for her betrothed?

In Song of Solomon 2:7, she spoke a caution. What was it, and what do you think it means? How did this caution foster trust in their relationship?

This couple didn't succumb to passions that would sabotage their relationship. They rightly channeled their God-given, God-driven emotions in order to protect and preserve their mutual trust. One can sense the fragile handling of this relationship in order to "allow their love to proceed at its proper pace, which includes waiting until the right time to consummate it (in marriage)."[14]

 EXTRA MILE
Banner of Love

The banner of love is yet another example of the 90-Degree Dynamic. What do Exodus 17:15, Numbers 2:2, and Song of Solomon 2:4 say about this banner? What does each banner indicate? Just as the earthly Bride is under the banner of love and protection by her heavenly Bridegroom, Jesus Christ, the bride is under the loving protection of her earthly husband. The banner indicates a name, a covering, the indication of belonging and commitment as well as protection.

Let's revisit their wedding night from the perspective of emotional security. In Song of Solomon 4:1–11, the groom tenderly wooed his bride. How can his approach encourage, develop, and help to seal emotional intimacy in the relationship?

In Song of Solomon 4:12–15, note that the word *garden* is often used. In the Hebrew, a garden or garden of spices often referred to a place of refreshment. This man's place of sexual delight and refreshment was in his wife's private garden. What do you deduce about his wife's garden in verse 12? Verse 15?

The bride responded positively to her husband's foreplay. (Although we are reading his verbal foreplay, we must assume that he wasn't sitting on his hands.) Read Song of Solomon 4:16. What do you think enabled her to surrender so completely to her husband?

Finally, in Song of Solomon 5:1, what was the groom's response to his wife's total surrender to him?

Can you sense this bridegroom's fulfillment? It's not just physiological. He is emotionally satiated with his wife's passionate response to him, her passion no longer bridled but unreservedly given.

> *Here's a truth worth noting: A man is more emotionally responsive*
> *when he is sexually fulfilled. A woman is more sexually responsive*
> *when she is emotionally fulfilled.*

In the passages that follow, you'll see emotional intimacy growing as their marriage unfolds over the years. Read Song of Solomon 5:10–16. How does his wife's regard for him continue to build trust and intimacy?

In Song of Solomon 7:1–9, the couple had been married awhile. Unlike in chapter 4, the husband praised his wife differently. What was different? What did his praise reveal about her beauty, value, and worth?

What was her response in Song of Solomon 7:10, and what makes her response so meaningful after years of marriage?

According to Song of Solomon 7:11–13, where did their emotional intimacy take them?

This wife's continued respect and admiration throughout their marriage knit her husband's heart to hers. He freely expressed his love for her, and she freely received it. Mutual trust had secured each in the other. Vulnerable (naked). Abandoned (unashamed) How safe is that! How intimate!

How does trust create and foster emotional intimacy? If you are married, are you naked (emotionally vulnerable) and unashamed (willingly abandoned) with your spouse? If yes, to what do you attribute that? If no, to what do you attribute that?

_____

_____

_____

What part does trust play in being naked and unashamed before God? How would this affect your being naked and unashamed with your husband or future husband?

_____

_____

_____

From the beginning, being naked and unashamed in our marriages was God's divine design for sex. When we know that we are emotionally secure, we will be able to surrender ourselves to our husbands inside and out. Vulnerable (naked). Abandoned (unashamed). This is true safe sex!

> Prayer: Lord, help me understand how to be emotionally vulnerable (naked) and freely abandoned (unashamed) with my husband. Help me to delight in You and the "very good" of us.

DAY 4

DESIGNED FOR SEX RELATIONALLY: TRUE SEX GOD'S WAY

God knows what makes for good sex in a marriage, but most of us today would be hard pressed to articulate what that is. We are not the first people to have this problem. Let's turn back to 1 Corinthians 7.

Recall that in 1 Corinthians 7, Paul addressed a problem in the church of Corinth. Not only did he address sexual immorality outside of marriage, but apparently some believers were under the impression that sexual relations should be avoided even in marriage. They wrote that *"it is good for a man not to have sexual relations with a woman"* (7:1 ESV). How did Paul's response address their problem in verse 2?

_____

_____

_____

Isn't that just like the enemy to so skew God's beautiful and intentional design that Paul needed to remind believers of the importance and sanctity of sex within marriage? In the three simple verses that follow, he laid out foundational principles (actually, they're commands) that reaffirm God's relational design for sex in marriage.

> *The Principle of Need.* "The husband must fulfill his duty to his wife, and likewise also the wife to her husband."
>
> 1 Corinthians 7:3 (NASB)

The first is found in 1 Corinthians 7:3, which expresses the Principle of Need. How does this verse address each spouse's sexual needs?

_____

_____

Why do you think God would have to instruct (command) spouses to meet each other's needs?

_____

_____

It's no mistake that God first addressed the husband to *"fulfill his to duty to his wife."* The word for *duty* in the Greek is not as we understand it in English. In the Greek, *eunoia* calls a husband to meet his wife's sexual needs as an act of benevolence and kindness, to be well-intentioned toward her, to treat her with good thoughts, blessing, grace, acceptance, and pleasure.[15] *"And likewise"* or *"in the same way,"* the wife is to be benevolent, kind, and well-intentioned toward her husband and his sexual needs. What an amazing, relationship-building concept!

Does this concept of *eunoia* contradict what you think about meeting a spouse's sexual needs? If so, in what way? If you're married, would you say that you and your husband meet the standard set in this verse? If yes, how do you know? If no, how do you know? How should benevolent, kind, and well-intentioned conduct toward one another enhance, build, and deepen your sex life? What can get in the way of meeting each other's needs?

_____

_____

_____

_____

Although we are sexual creatures, we are also selfish creatures. The important message of this verse affirms that both husbands and wives have sexual needs that are tied to how we treat each other throughout the relationship. Therefore, each is to meet the other's sexual needs with *eunoia*, even though we rarely have the same needs at the same time or with the same frequency. Verse 3 is the way it's *supposed* to be, and through our relationship with Jesus Christ, we can rise to His standard.

Emotional fulfillment secures wives and prepares their hearts, attitudes, and bodies for sexual intimacy. Wives seek "to experience life with their men in a deep intimate, never-ending way. There's no particular goal in mind; they just want to cherish the experience of the relationship." [16]

Sexual fulfillment secures husbands and prepares their hearts and attitudes for emotional intimacy. Robert Lewis and William Hendricks, authors of *Rocking the Roles*, explain: "Few things affirm a man in his masculinity as does his wife's sexual responsiveness. Spontaneous hugs, kisses, and other demonstrations of affection, as well as intercourse, do more than the relationship."[16] These actions meet a much deeper need. They reassure a man. They confirm him in his masculinity! . . . *Sexually interested*—I wish I could burn those words into the soul of every wife. It makes a man feel like a man!"[17] According to Lewis and Hendricks, specific questions are ever on a man's mind because they are so linked to his identity: " 'Am I performing well? Because of how I perform sexually, do you feel drawn to me?' [and] 'Do I give my wife pleasure?' "[18] (brackets ours). Yes, a man derives emotional fulfillment from the pleasure he gives his wife. It affirms him as her man, which meets a deep need in him. This is where the emotional need and the sexual need are inexorably linked. When these needs are met, then sex is more than just sex to him. It becomes sexual fulfillment, and it is truly a tie that binds him to his wife.

In his book *Sexual Detox*, author Tim Challies explains, "Sex is intended to be a means of mutual fulfillment, an expression of love in which a husband thinks foremost of his wife, and the wife thinks foremost of her husband. It is a uniquely powerful means by which husband and wife can fulfill the Lord's command to esteem another higher than oneself. As they fulfill each other's needs, they also have their own needs fulfilled. It is a beautiful picture of intimacy . . . The more selfless the sex, the better the sex becomes . . . the more fulfilling, gratifying, and beautiful the experience."[19]

> *The Principle of Authority: "The wife does not have authority over her own body, but the husband does; and likewise also the husband does not have authority over his own body, but the wife does."*
>
> 1 Corinthians 7:4 (NASB)

First Corinthians 7:4 gives us the Principle of Authority. What insights do you glean for a couple's sexual intimacy? What part would *eunoia* play in this principle?

Having authority over each other's bodies is a gift that God grants as a marital honor, privilege, and responsibility. He calls us to selflessly share ourselves even when we might not feel like it—to initiate tenderly and to respond positively in a manner that honors our mates. This authority doesn't force, misuse, reject, neglect, or abuse. When exercised with *eunoia*, each is protecting the other and their relationship. Rightly used, this authority is a powerful expression of selfless, sacrificial, serving love—an opportunity to bless our mates. And one that God will bless.

Have you associated this principle of mutual sexual authority with permission and freedom? How can this authority enhance, build, and deepen your relationship in general?

In what manner has your husband exercised authority over your body? How do you respond when he initiates sex? In what manner have you exercised authority over your husband's body? How does he respond when you initiate? What, if anything, impedes your mutual authority?

The Principle of Habit: "Stop depriving one another, except by agreement for a time, so that you may devote yourselves to prayer, and come together again so that Satan will not tempt you because of your lack of self-control."

1 Corinthians 7:5 (NASB)

Finally, read 1 Corinthians 7:5. This verse conveys the essence of our sexual commitment. What is the Principle of Habit, and what do you think it means? What's the exception to God's command for consistent sexual intimacy?

The Amplified Bible puts verse 5 this way: *"Do not refuse and deprive and defraud each other (of your due marital rights), except perhaps by mutual consent for a time, that you may devote yourselves unhindered to prayer. But afterwards resume marital relations, lest Satan tempt you [to sin] through your lack of restraint of sexual desire."* To *refuse* means "to reject, rebuff, or turn down, with or without words." To *deprive* means "to rob, leave without, withhold." And to *defraud* means "to rob, despoil, cheat, or deceive." If you are married and one or more of these words speaks to your sexual response to your husband or his to you, circle it.

Intimacy with our spouse is interrupted when *"both agree to refrain from sexual intimacy for a limited time so you can give yourselves more completely to prayers"* (NLT). And although there may be other reasons to temporarily abstain from sexual relations, such as geographical separation, recovery from illness, childbirth, or extreme fatigue, these don't fall under the guise of refusing, depriving, and defrauding our spouses in which there is deliberate intent to withhold or avoid sex. When we regard each other as more important than ourselves, we will not merely look out for our own personal interests but also for the interests of our spouses (Philippians 2:3–4).

If you are married, would you say that you are habitual in your sexual intimacy? If yes, how does that impact your relationship? If not, how does that impact your relationship? How would consistency enhance, build and deepen your relationship with your husband?

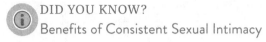
DID YOU KNOW?
Benefits of Consistent Sexual Intimacy

Here are some of God's intended benefits resulting from consistent marital sexual intimacy. It...

- affirms his manhood
- secures a wife emotionally, relationally
- shores up mutual trust
- realigns hearts toward each other
- protects marriage from intruders
- shores up marriage as weaker areas are addressed
- comforts when life is tragic or tough
- deepens devotion for later years

Based on today's lesson, what should healthy sexual intimacy look like in a marriage?

How would it benefit oneness in a marriage?

Prayer: God's protection and blessing are imbedded in His principles of need, authority, and habit. But because of the fall, exercising them in your marriage won't come naturally. This is why God commanded them. He knows the benefit they bring to marriages, even difficult ones. And He knows you'll need His help. Ask Him for it. Let Him chart a new beginning in your heart for your sexual relationship with your husband. Thank Him for designing sex to be an intimate pursuit within marriage— not a duty but a blessing.

DAY 5

EMBRACING THE DESIGN

Leading and following ensure success in any endeavor if done correctly. However, in most cases they must be learned. For example, in the art of ballroom dancing, the man learns to lead with his whole self—his chest first, then his feet and arms as he tenderly, yet firmly, guides his partner. He learns to protect their space, secure her in his hold, steady her with his strength, and provide the energy and momentum behind their more dramatic moves.

But their dance would not be fluid without the woman's active participation as a follower. She applies positive tension through her arms to his—muscle to muscle—as if interconnected. Her applied tension is such that "she strengthens the strength she receives, and . . . refines and extends the leadership she looks for."[20] On the floor, she doesn't move independently of him or compete for control, but responds to his lead, yielding to his forward motion, trusting their fluid oneness through the dance to completion. As a result, the man is made extraordinary as he leads, and the woman is made beautiful as she follows. The dance is incredible to behold.

As with the art of ballroom dancing, learning to lead and follow appropriately is also essential to the art of marriage. A husband who decisively and tenderly leads his wife (headship) and a wife who willingly and respectfully adapts to his leadership (submission) is its own beautiful dance to behold.

Headship and submission are not words most women want to hear because of the negative connotations associated with them. God didn't design a husband and wife to be independent of each other—rather, interdependent. And if we are truly honest with ourselves, we "secretly yearn for the very thing our independence has destroyed—strong, confident men. There is something wonderful and even erotic about trusting the strength of a man who can provide, protect, and lead. So women are caught in the crossroads of wanting the strength of a man, but not wanting to be controlled."[21]

We hope this lesson will clear up the many misunderstandings of God's original intent for a husband's headship and a wife's submission in the marriage relationship. Neither is about control.

> *Marriage and Dancing: A husband who decisively and tenderly leads his wife (headship) and a wife who willingly and respectfully adapts to his leadership (submission) is its own beautiful dance to behold.*

BIBLICAL HEADSHIP ~ LOVING LEADERSHIP, PROTECTION, AND PROVISION

According to Ephesians 5:25–33, in what ways should a husband love his wife? What should this look like in today's marriages?

Biblically, *"the husband is the head of the wife, as Christ also is the head of the church"* (5:23); therefore, a man's leadership in his family is called headship. "Head" is used metaphorically and refers to "the husband in relation to his wife . . . insofar as they are one body and one body can have only one head to direct it."[22] How does this quote help to explain God's order within a marriage?

"Husbands, love your wives, just as Christ also loved the church and gave Himself up for her."

Ephesians 5:25 (NASB)

According to Matthew 20:28 and John 10:4, 11, 14, and 27, what are the attributes of Christ's headship? What is it about Christ's headship that makes the believer want to follow?

How should a husband's headship compare with Christ's? What is it about a husband's headship that would make a wife want to follow?

Read 2 Corinthians 5:15. What gives Jesus Christ the right to be in the center of a marriage?

Author Stu Weber offers this perspective on responsible headship: "Why, in our culture, do so many discussions of male/female roles seem so painful, unfair, unreal, unfunny, and even preposterous? Because of men who demand submission from their wives but in turn submit themselves to no one, including God. We men truncate the divine process by our arrogant, foolish, egocentric, SELFishness. We cannot blame women for being frustrated because they fear the injustice of being under headship that itself is not accountable... Yes, God has given men a certain amount of authority. But they are first and foremost men under authority."[23]

As Head of the body, Christ not only led His flock, but He loved, served, and died for them out of obedience to God. Christ is the ultimate example of what a servant-leader husband should be like.

Biblical headship enhances *all* areas of God's divine design for the marriage relationship. Look carefully at this role through His eyes and answer the following questions.

BIBLICAL HEADSHIP IS *NOT...*

Harsh or domineering, physically or emotionally abusive. Read Colossians 3:19. With Christ, a husband's authority is "not the self-centered exercise of power but leadership that takes care to serve the spiritual, emotional, and physical needs of the wife."[24] Describe what you think it means to feel safe under a husband's authority.

Demeaning to a wife's value. Read Galatians 3:28. How does being one with Christ impact a wife's value?

Foregoing his convictions to keep her happy or to keep the peace. Read Genesis 3:17. How can a wife derail her husband's responsibility to God and to her?

Optional for the husband. Read Genesis 2:18, 3:16, and Ephesians 5:25–33.[25] What does this mean for the husband? For the wife?

BIBLICAL HEADSHIP IS ...

Loving sacrifice, just like Jesus. Read Ephesians 5:25. According to this verse, to what end? What response should this elicit from his wife?

Loving servant leadership, just like Jesus. Read Matthew 20:25–28. What benefit would this bring to the marriage relationship?

Loving spiritual leadership, just like Jesus. Read Ephesians 5:26–27. He is not the spiritual "heavy" but the spiritual example. How would the marriage relationship benefit?

_____

_____

_____

Loving care, just like Jesus. Read Ephesians 5:28–33. What should that care look like to a wife?

_____

_____

Loving honor, consideration, and understanding, just like Jesus. Read 1 Peter 3:7. Insights?

_____

_____

Married or not, what does it mean to you to have Christ in the center of your husband's or future husband's headship? How can loving leadership, provision, and protection (headship) enhance God's Principle of Need in the sexual relationship? The Principle of Authority? The Principle of Habit?

_____

_____

_____

_____

BIBLICAL SUBMISSION ~ RESPECTFUL RESPONSIVENESS

Submission is an attitude of the heart. In the Greek, the word *submission* means "to voluntarily place oneself under another's authority"—in this case, a wife under her husband's God-ordained leadership. Ephesians 5:22–24 and 33 unfold powerful truths behind God's principle of submission in marriage. How is a wife to respond to her husband's leadership? Based on verse 33, what word is used that links submission to the attitude of the heart?

_____

_____

Under what circumstances are wives to submit to (respect) their husbands (vv. 22–24)? Why do you think this matters? Why *"in everything"* and not only in those things that you know will succeed?

_____

_____

_____

What do you think it means to submit *"as to the Lord"* (v. 22)?

_____

_____

To lend perspective, read 1 Peter 3:1–2. How does respectful submission apply in these verses and to what benefit?

_____

_____

_____

True biblical submission is first yielding our wills to the will of God. It is a voluntary act, and its foundation is faith. Contrast this with doormat submission, typically an involuntary act. Its foundation is fear. The former exhibits strength and dignity, the latter only weakness. As with headship, submission comes with responsibility.

Biblical submission enhances *all* areas of God's divine design for the marriage relationship, so let's look carefully at this role through His eyes. **(Important note**: God's principle of submission may not be applicable if a husband has a serious psychological problem or area of bondage. Professional biblical counsel is necessary to determine what a wife's response to her husband's behavior should entail.)

BIBLICAL SUBMISSION IS *NOT* . . .

About status but about function. Read 1 Corinthians 11:3. Submission falls within God's established order with God as the final authority. What is the difference between status and function? How can understanding this difference change one's perspective on the roles in marriage?

_____

_____

_____

Depending on our husbands to meet all of our emotional needs. Read 2 Peter 1:3. Ultimately, we depend on Christ with courage and conviction. Why is this important in a marriage?

_____

_____

Permitting a husband's abuse (physical, emotional, spiritual, or sexual). Read 1 Peter 3:7. Insights?

_____

_____

Being afraid to be a positive influence on her husband, which is different from nagging or controlling him. Read Genesis 2:18. Wives can respectfully discuss needs, problems, concerns, insights, and associated thoughts and feelings. This is what a helpmate does. Insights?

Covering or making excuses for (enabling) her husband's sin or irresponsible behavior, such as abuse of alcohol, drugs, or finances. Read Proverbs 27:5. A helpmate doesn't call in "sick" for him, doesn't get a job to support his gambling debts, doesn't turn a blind eye to his pornography habit, or does not defend his angry outbursts. (More in later lessons.) Insights?

📖 Does Forgiving Sin Enable Sin?

There is a difference between enabling sin and forgiving sin. Although God does call us to love in a way that "covers a multitude of sins" (1 Peter 4:8), this love (*agape*) forgives and doesn't hold sin against another. Instead, it addresses the sin forthrightly and lovingly so that the loved one will have the opportunity to choose change. Forgiving sin does not sanction sin. It frees us to address sin in love without being encumbered by the emotions that hinder love and continue to foster unforgiveness.

Owning a husband's bad behavior, guilt, or shame. Read John 14:26–27. Submission is not giving a husband permission to make her responsible for his choices. Insights?

Joining her husband in his sin. Read Proverbs 31:25–26, 30. Pastor and author John Piper writes, "The husband does not replace Christ as the woman's supreme authority. She must never follow her husband's leadership into sin. She will not steal with him or get drunk with him or savor pornography with him or develop deceptive schemes with him. But even where a Christian wife may have to stand with Christ against the sinful will of her husband, she can still have a spirit of submission—a disposition to yield. She can show by her attitude and behavior that she does not like resisting his will and that she longs for him to forsake sin and lead in righteousness so that her disposition to honor him as head can again produce harmony."[26] Insights?

Fearing a husband's decisions and where they'll lead. Read 1 Peter 3:3–6. Submission is about faith in the One who has ultimate authority over her husband, whether or not he's a believer. Only then can she do the right thing without giving way to fear. How can trusting God and entrusting her husband to God, help a wife deal with her fear of decisions and outcomes?

Being a doormat who, out of fear, meets a husband's every demand, no matter how sick or sinful. That's blind obedience. Read Proverbs 3:21–23. How can blind obedience damage the marriage relationship?

BIBLICAL SUBMISSION IS . . .

Voluntary, first to Christ, then she will know how to voluntarily adapt to her husband's leadership. Read Colossians 3:18, 23–24. She can be who she is and still function within God's paradigm as a matter of obedience to God's truth. How would an attitude of voluntary biblical submission benefit the marriage relationship?

An attitude of respect (honor) that affirms a husband as a man, husband, lover, father, leader, protector, and provider. She doesn't marginalize him in any of these capacities. Read Proverbs 12:4. What makes a wife "excellent?" Why is this important to God?

An inner peace that affirms her trust in God as her husband leads. Read Proverbs 3:5–6. How can this peace benefit the marriage relationship?

Trustworthy to bring good to the marital team. Read Proverbs 31:10-12. She has a positive influence on her husband by respectfully discussing needs, problems, concerns, insights, thoughts, and feelings. This is what a helpmate does. Insights?

Positive, strong, dignified, effective, and motivating. She respects who he is and supports what he does. Read Proverbs 31:25–29. How will respect motivate a husband?

_____

_____

Glorifying to God. A wife's attitude of godly submission would make Christ credible in her. Read Proverbs 31:30 and Titus 2:3–5. Insights?

_____

_____

_____

Respectful biblical submission is to the husband what loving biblical headship is to the wife.

Married or not, what does it mean to have Christ in the center of your response as a wife?

_____

_____

How can a respectful attitude of submission enhance God's Principle of Need in the sexual relationship? The Principle of Authority? The Principle of Habit?

_____

_____

_____

Submission and headship are not about who gets to take the lead but about how we spur each other on toward Christ, often without words, always with action. It's living our one-Spirit relationship with Jesus Christ through our one-flesh relationship with our spouse. And if we're not rightly relating with Jesus Christ, it will impact our relationship with our spouses. Conversely, if we are not rightly relating with our spouses, it will impact our relationship with Christ.

Submission and headship create every good thing in a marriage and are the most effective means by which a husband and wife become one in Christ since *"they who live might no longer live for themselves, but for Him who died and rose again on their behalf"* (2 Corinthians 5:15). When it comes to biblical headship and biblical submission, God will not absolve us from doing our part, even if we're doing it alone. However, He will always do His part. He will ever be with us, cling to us, pursue oneness with us, and spur us on toward oneness with our spouse.

> Prayer: Lord, help me to be respectful of and responsive to my husband's leadership. May I be responsive to You so that I am the follower You want me to become. Protect him as he leads, protects, and provides. Encourage him to draw closer to You, making him the servant leader You want him to become.

LESSON 6

COUNTERFEIT SEX

"As it is written: 'None is righteous, no, not one; no one understands; no one seeks
for God. All have turned aside; together they have become worthless; no one does
good, not even one. Their throat is an open grave; they use their tongues to deceive.
The venom of asps is under their lips. Their mouth is full of curses and bitterness.
Their feet are swift to shed blood; in their paths are ruin and misery, and the way of
peace they have not known. There is no fear of God before their eyes'"
(Romans 3:10–18 ESV).

In this passage, Paul laid out why humanity is so captured by the counterfeit. At the root of sin is *"no fear of God before their eyes."* They have no "deep and reverential sense of accountability to God or Christ."[1] They do not recognize the sacred. Do we?

In the next five days, we will study the impact that *"no fear of God before their eyes"* has had on our current American culture—a culture that worships the counterfeit.

DAY 1

FROM SACRED TO PROFANE

In most societies, people consider certain acts so vile, so offensive that those who do them are penalized by a legal system. This is humanity's tacit admission that life and relationships are sacred. Even godless cultures recognize that the sacred should not be profaned. And yet it often is.

We used the word *profane* from which the word *profanity* comes. In the Hebrew, the word is *chalal*, meaning to "'defile, pollute; to prostitute; to make common; to loose; to break. Originally, the word was used to refer to sexual defilement . . . Generally speaking, *chalal* refers to doing violence to the established law of God . . . It is a desecration of something which is holy."[2] When we violate God's divine design for sex, we profane what is and always will be holy and sacred.

Why would we choose the sacred for the profane—the substitute? Perhaps we are deceived; perhaps God isn't real enough to us; perhaps we would rather do what we want. In every case, we have an enemy who wants to separate us from the Designer of the sacred, and he uses deception and the counterfeit in order to do so.

Satan's most brazen and effective deception is his counterfeit of God's divine design for sex. His substitute cuts the heart out of relationships, not only with others but also with God.

Counterfeit sex is "every kind of sexual activity outside of marriage."[3] It trades the hallowed for the hollow. The Greeks refer to it as *porneia*, also called "sexual immorality" or "fornication." What do you think qualifies as sexual immorality?

_____

_____

Scripture reveals what constitutes sexual immorality. What sexual behaviors are exposed in the following passages?

Matthew 5:27–28

_____

John 4:16–18

_____

John 8:4–11

_____

Romans 1:26–27

_____

1 Corinthians 5:1

_____

1 Corinthians 6:9 and 1 Timothy 1:10

_____

1 Corinthians 7:1–2

_____

1 Thessalonians 4:5–6

_____

Lust and impure thoughts (both fed and fostered today by pornography), premarital sex, extramarital sex (adultery), incest (sexual relations with a relative), cohabitation (living together outside of marriage), and homosexuality (same-sex relationships) are all passions that try to supplant the sacred. Do some of these descriptions of sexual immorality surprise you? Which ones didn't make your list? Do any of them seem acceptable to you? Which ones?

_____

_____

_____

Has a counterfeit been tempting you to give up the real thing for what you perceive as more satisfying or more fulfilling? Identify it.

_____

_____

_____

Sexual lust is to false intimacy what agape love is to true intimacy.

Although we typically associate lust with sex, it is a powerful, greedy, inordinate desire for anything. Sexual lust is false intimacy. It is an insatiable longing or drive to selfishly satisfy our sexual urges by any means, even within the legitimate means of marriage, and always at the expense of the well-being of another human being. Replacing true intimacy with the false will never fulfill. And yet many pursue it as if it eventually will.

Job 31:11–12 (NLT) describes lust and its goal: *"For lust is a shameful sin, a crime that should be punished. It is a fire that burns all the way to hell. It would wipe out everything I own."*

> *"For lust is ...a fire that burns all the way to hell.*
> *It would wipe out everything I own."*
>
> Job 31:11–12 (NLT)

Proverbs 7:1–27 powerfully depicts how lust coupled with deception warps God's original design for sex and where both will lead. In verses 1–5, what is the father's appeal and why?

_____

_____

_____

This parent was no slouch. He knew what was out there that could endanger his children. What did he observe about the adulteress in (vv. 6–10)?

_____

_____

_____

How does Dad describe the adulteress in verses 11–12?

_____

_____

This woman was not only seeking attention, but she was everywhere, eagerly waiting for her clueless victim. Doesn't this caution you about what's out there eagerly waiting for you, your husband, your son, or your daughter—the one who lies in wait to entrap any of you, whether the man or woman on the prowl or the lurid and alluring images on the Internet? Think about the seriousness with which this father addressed his responsibility to prepare himself (vv. 1–9) in order to prepare his sons (and daughters). He was an involved parent who kept up with what was going on around him so that neither he nor his children would get caught with their "pants down," so to speak.

How have you (or how will you) teach and warn your children about that which lies in wait for them *"in the street, now in the market, and at every corner"* (7:12 ESV).

_____

_____

_____

Back to Proverbs 7. In verses 13–20, what methods of persuasion did this woman use to lure her unguarded prey? (Look very carefully. She uses many different attractions.)

_____

_____

_____

Living a lifestyle that contradicted her religious practices (v. 14), this woman stopped at nothing to snare her prey. She caught him off guard with a bold kiss (v. 13); appealed to his ego with disingenuous words (v. 15); charmed his senses with sight and smell (vv. 16–17); tempted and enticed with words that ignited lust (v. 18); and calmed his fear of discovery with assurances of her husband's long absence (vv.19–20). This woman had practice.

Consider her persuasive speech in Proverbs 7:21. What did she do, and how did she do it?

_____

_____

This guy had just been had! How do we know? Read verses 22–23. What do you conclude about this man's future?

_____

_____

_____

What is this father's final appeal to his sons, and on what did he base it (vv. 24–27)?

_____

_____

_____

You can imagine one of these sons saying to himself, *That would never happen to me!* not really fully embracing the fact that this adulteress was an accomplished deceiver.

What's out there today that's waiting to pounce on you or an unguarded loved one? How are you protecting yourself? If applicable, how are you protecting your children?

_____

_____

_____

_____

How would you recognize an accomplished deceiver?

_____

_____

_____

In your past, have you ignored a similar warning about persuasive men or women? If so, what happened?

_____

_____

_____

Have you (or a loved one) ever rationalized that sexual immorality was right for you? If so, what happened?

_____

_____

_____

Other dangers and losses are associated with counterfeit sex. According to this same father's teaching, what do Proverbs 5:7–14 and Proverbs 6:27–35 say they are? What do you think this means for someone who gets caught up in this deception today?

_____

_____

_____

_____

One last point. According to 1 Corinthians 6:15–18, how do sexual relationships outside of marriage affect a relationship with Christ?

_____

_____

_____

These verses speak of a harlot or prostitute, but "because sexual union has a spiritual component, sexual activity outside marriage is a unique sin both against Christ and one's own body."[4] That's the victory of the counterfeit.

> Prayer: Lord, You designed sex to be a sacred, spiritual act within marriage. Pretending it's not sacred doesn't remove this reality. It's still sacred because it's Yours. Keep me from being deceived into believing otherwise.

DAY 2

THE ANATOMY OF BONDAGE

Many people use the term *addiction* when they talk about the enslaving properties of sexual compulsions (or any compulsion). We prefer the word *bondage* because Scripture says that humanity is *"of flesh, sold into bondage to sin"* (Romans 7:14). Bondage is enslavement. It is cruel; it is subjugating. No one wakes up one morning and says, *Today I think I will sell myself into bondage.* However, we can make choices that will lead us one step at a time into that ultimate "hell."

A futuristic movie comes to mind as we consider the power of lust and how it tempts us. In *Minority Report*, a regional police force has the ability to detect murders before they happen. While in a state of suspended animation, three "readers" foresee future violence and mentally translate their foreshadowing onto police computer screens. The police identify and arrest the guilty party before the crime is ever committed. However, when the readers finger the program's chief for murder, he sets out to prove them wrong. When he comes face-to-face with his son's alleged killer, he knows the readers are right; he is going to kill this man. His lust for revenge will see to it—until one of the readers whispers hauntingly into him: "You . . . have . . . a . . . choice." Over and over and ever more urgently she whispers, "You . . . have . . . a . . . choice!" Yes, he did. We all do, no matter what our lusts tempt us toward. We. . . .have . . .a. . .choice.

When faced with sexual temptation, we can choose poorly. Whatever the reasons, we find ourselves in a swamp of emotions, cravings, and behaviors that most would give anything to be free of. But we have a cruel enemy who today has pulled out all the stops in his effort to *"steal, kill, and destroy"* individuals, marriages, and families. Try as many do to fight his onslaught of sexual counterfeits, *"The spirit is willing, but the flesh is weak"* (Matthew 26:41).

As we read some of the reasons why so many are caught in sexual bondage, please engage a compassionate heart. God's goal is always redemption.

 IN HER SHOES

"My husband had been turning to sexual arousal and climax to deal with depression (and whatever stress came along) from the time he was very young, as early as nine years of age. It had become a lifelong habit to which he had turned almost daily for relief. [As a boy] he discovered the sexual arousal that came from looking at the girls in underwear in the *Sears* catalog. He began using them to fantasize at that early age. *National Geographic* magazine played into that pattern too. Once the Internet came into our home, he quickly succumbed to the temptation to find new images, and the bondage grew."

Some discover the counterfeit accidentally at a very early age (both boys and girls) and are enticed into it by exposure to pornography, unguarded, salacious television programming, and other media (even catalogs and store fliers), which lead to curiosity, early sexual experimentation, and masturbation.

Some live the counterfeit because they don't know how to escape it. Those who have been sexually abused, exploited, or raped may live the counterfeit—some because they don't know how to resolve or escape the situations they *were* in, and some because they can't or don't know how to escape the situations they *are* in.

Some turn to the counterfeit for escape, solace, and comfort. The issues are many and inter-related: some to escape shame, some to relieve depression, some because of a low sense of self-worth, some because of rejection or neglect, some because of loneliness and isolation, some because of physical or emotional abuse by domineering, dysfunctional people, or some because they became victims of another's lust for money, power and sexual dominance.

 IN HER SHOES

"Molestation and pornography gave me a sexual education beyond my years. I quickly realized that boys my age were very happy to find me. What I misinterpreted as their love would temporarily fill all the empty places in my soul. It also provided me that rush of adrenaline that allowed me to escape, at least until the feelings of that relationship would go away. And then it was time to find another boy."

Some seek the counterfeit due to an inability or fear of developing healthy intimacy. They desire to be wanted or validated, so they seek the counterfeit rather than investing in relationships.

Some default to counterfeit intimacy in order to avoid the hard work that true intimacy requires. To these, true intimacy is exhausting. It requires them to slog through fields of emotions, feelings, needs, and desires in order to develop, nurture, and sustain intimate personal relationships. They prefer the counterfeit since it requires nothing from them emotionally and they think they will owe it nothing when they're done.

Some deliberately seek the counterfeit out of boredom or curiosity. They seek pleasure, excitement, risk, and escape for gratification's sake. Although they are aware of their wrongdoing, they are energized by it and numbed to their disobedience. Eventually, the risk seekers can't be excited by the normal anymore.

Still others seek to escape into a fantasy world that pretends to meet unmet, unrealistic expectations[5] or to resolve confusion about one's sexuality, or to rebel, or to relieve stress or insomnia.

Although the power and intensity of sexual arousal, activity, and release may temporarily relieve the emotions that drive many to the counterfeit, the behavior creates guilt and shame, emotions which send them right back into the elixir of sexual activity.

Think of a time of emotional pain in your life. How did you manage it?

Can you see the connection between personal pain and choosing the counterfeit? Does this change your thinking about a loved one who is struggling with a sexual counterfeit—or perhaps yourself? If so, in what way? If not, what do you think is the cause of their (or your) struggle?

_____

_____

_____

_____

Read Proverbs 27:19. What connection does this verse make between the heart and our actions?

_____

_____

_____

The heart is the pool from which every thought, emotion, attitude, and eventual action flow. As counterfeit messages embed themselves, our thought processes and belief systems shift as well. At this point, we give ourselves permission to give in to our sexual urges. It is only a matter of time before we act on them.

It is easy to condemn someone who is trapped in a struggle with sexual immorality. However, not everyone who is struggling with the counterfeit is a twisted pervert. Most are normal people who hate where they are. Nonetheless, left unchecked, they risk progressing to the more deadly forms of this struggle.

Let's look at the stages that lead to bondage:

Stage One: The Distracted Heart. Remember that back in the garden of Eden, Satan used distraction as his first tactic. When we are vulnerable—lonely, stressed, sad, rejected, bored, tired—we are more easily distracted, perhaps curious. We can forget God and focus on ourselves, our circumstances, our needs, our deprivations, and our emotions. We become ungrateful and nurture entitlement—"I deserve . . ." When this happens, lust has stuck its foot in the door and we set ourselves up for the next stage.

According to Mark 7:20–23, what is the spiritual condition of the heart at this stage?

_____

_____

_____

What does Ephesians 5:3–5 say is our protection and responsibility against the distracted heart at this stage?

_____

_____

_____

Stage Two: The Tempted Mind. We all come face-to-face with temptations created by counterfeit sexual messages. When we do, we have choices. If we let these messages become habitual in our heads, they will become habitual in our behavior. If we yield to the temptation to get our needs or wants met in all of the wrong ways, we chart a course toward bondage.

According to Matthew 26:41, what is our spiritual condition at this stage?

_____

_____

What do Matthew 26:41, 1 Corinthians 10:13, and 2 Corinthians 10:5 say is our protection and responsibility against the tempted mind at this stage?

_____

_____

_____

 EXTRA MILE

Sometimes believing God takes some serious energy, especially when we feel like the odds are against us. Read 2 Corinthians 5:21; Galatians 2:16 and 3:2–5; Ephesians 2:4–7; and Hebrews 10:10. What is it about these truths that assure us that we don't have to be or remain in bondage to any sin, let alone sexual sin?

Stage Three: The Compromised Body. When we give way to temptation, we move into the world of things, people, and circumstances that will set the stage for greater indulgence. We shift from being tempted to acting out our lusts and fantasies. We look for ways to create thrills through our chosen counterfeit.

According to Galatians 6:7–8, what is our spiritual condition at this stage? What's the warning?

_____

_____

What does Galatians 5:16–17 say is our protection and responsibility against the compromised body at this stage?

_____

_____

Stage Four: The Profane Practiced. The brain is wired to reinforce whatever we pursue. We are drawn to those places of temporary pleasure as if something at our very core is awakened. We won't permit feelings of sexual arousal to be tempered or governed by Holy-Spirit restraint. We permit our psyches to rationalize and justify why it's okay to do it rather than exercise the spiritual and mental discipline to walk away from the counterfeit. The majority of our passions are no longer directed toward God and the things of God. Instead, we have begun to live secret lives in pursuit of this idol.

According to Proverbs 27:20 and Ephesians 4:17–22, what is our spiritual condition at this stage?

_____

_____

_____

What do Ephesians 4:23–24 and 5:8–18 say is our protection and responsibility against practicing the profane at this stage?

_____

_____

_____

When we refuse to accept that we're in darkness, the shackles are secure. We no longer have "this thing"; this thing has us. It requires increasingly more to get the same sexual high. Now the counterfeit beckons us with persistence to pursue the temporary "feel good" more frequently and more intensely, with the desperate hope that it will eventually fill the holes in our souls. But it will never satisfy.

Stage Five: Bondage! Filled with and driven by darkness, we now pursue the object of our idolatry at every available opportunity and at any cost. We've turned from the Lover of our souls and are consumed with and by our new master. Enslaved, we either no longer want a way out, or we no longer believe there is a way out.

According to Romans 6:16, what is our spiritual condition at this stage?

_____

_____

What does Romans 6:5–13 say is our protection? Our responsibility?

_____

_____

_____

Based on Romans 6:14-23, what is our promise and provision (our hope)?

_____

_____

If applicable, describe how lust and temptation play out in your own sexual struggle or how you perceive it playing out in a loved one's struggle. Which stage most mirrors that struggle right now?

_____

_____

_____

One is in bondage if he or she . . .

- Copes with life in a compulsive way, whether physical or psychological
- Exhibits repetitive behaviors that are difficult to control or are out of control
- Engages in lies and deceptions
- Refuses to accept personal responsibility for choices made
- Needs a "fix" more often and more intensely
- Is unable or unwilling to relate intimately, is disconnected, isolated
- May also be in bondage to drugs, alcohol, gambling, eating disorders, etc.
- Experiences consequences due to sexual behavior (arrests, incarcerations, STI's; job, family, social, and legal difficulties)
- Is unable to stop sexual behavior despite risks or adverse consequences
- Attempts to limit sexual behavior and to control urges
- Exhibits severe mood changes around sexual activity: depression, irritability, anger, rage
- Spends inordinate amounts of time (and money) on obtaining sex, being sexual, or recovering from sexual experiences
- Neglects important social, occupational, or recreational activities because of sexual activity
- Is withdrawn or distant
- Neglects personal habits
- Leaves obvious evidence (missing money; outrageous phone/credit card bills; "900" number charges; computer or Internet site charges; pornographic magazines and movie expenses)
- Has an internal sense that something is wrong
- Abuses others as he or she was abused
- Explains away red flags[6]

As long as we choose to meet our needs in our own ways and on our own terms, we will continue our descent into bondage. That descent goes from small, seemingly insignificant choices to full-out enslavement—and we don't even see it coming. The outcome of almost every kind of bondage is destruction. And the march to that finish began with the turn from truth. But note this: Our God is gracious. He gives us the opportunity to turn back to truth. We . . . have . . . a . . . choice.

> Prayer: Lord, may Your truth wash over me and permeate my soul that I might depend on it rather than the counterfeit. *"For You are my lamp, O LORD; And the LORD illumines my darkness"* (2 Samuel 22:29).

DAY 3

COUNTERFEIT INTIMACY: THE RELATIONAL COUNTERFEITS

 IN HER SHOES

"I gave my life to Christ at age twelve, but the world was calling loudly, and my faith quickly faded into the background. In my early teens, I became aware that my primary form of power and control was my feminine sexuality. I used it aggressively to pursue and control the males in my life. In the deepest place of my soul, I knew that God wanted more than this for me—more than chasing the winds of control, more than believing my body was my only value, more than the emptiness that followed meaningless sex."

Charles M. Sell said, "Most of us do not want just sex; we long for what it means."[7] And the world, our flesh, or the enemy—or a combination of all three—will gladly promote lust as sexual intimacy if we are ignorant of or choose not to live according to God's design. But what they won't tell us is that counterfeit sex will eventually become shameful, joyless, and empty, while its bondage prevails.

In today's lesson, we'll address relationships that exist outside of God's divine design. They include premarital, marital (with false intimacy or no intimacy), adulterous, and same-sex relationships. We may know or encounter people in these relationships, so let's remember that Jesus was compelled by His Father's love to redeem the human race one heart at a time. He draws us to Himself or back to Himself by His grace and His truth (John 1:14). The two always operate together, and for good reason: Truth without grace is cruel and grace without truth is license. Therefore, if God calls us to engage anyone about his or her relational circumstance, we do so with grace and in truth.

 DID YOU KNOW?
What Are Values Neutral?

Because neurochemicals are "values neutral," they respond involuntarily to any stimuli, right or wrong, healthy or unhealthy. Whatever we make the object of our sexual interest will trigger those reinforcing chemicals in the brain. And the more stimulating the behavior, the more the brain adapts and molds to that behavior, reinforcing its repetition. We will become what we practice. How does Romans 6:16 address the "values neutral" impact on your life?

PREMARITAL SEXUAL RELATIONSHIPS

When God's purpose and plan for sexual intimacy are counterfeited by any sexual acts outside of a monogamous, heterosexual marriage covenant, the bonding chemicals still work, but they don't work toward God's goal—marital oneness. That's because these neurochemicals are values neutral. Therefore, as God's bonding process becomes adulterated by any of the enemy's substitutes (including sexual abuse or incest), the ability to bond with one's marriage mate (present or future) breaks down. In his article "Bonded in the Brain," Executive Vice President of American Family Association, Ed Vitagliano, quotes Joe S. McIlhaney Jr. and Freda M. Bush: "When young people—or those of any age—engage in casual sex or a series of sexual relationships, they are putting themselves through a continuous cycle of bonding and breaking up. This has the potential to damage the God-given ability to bond later. Their inability to bond after multiple liaisons is almost like tape that loses its stickiness after being applied and removed multiple times,"[8]

Do you remember the old teen stereotype of boy pursues girl? Move ahead a few decades. We discover a major shift in the tempo: Girls and young women are becoming more aggressive on e-mails, in social media, with texting, sexting, or chat rooms, many with open invitations for sex. They verbally pursue, visually entice, and physically invade guys' space with abandon. But the girls or women who pursue their sexual freedom are getting much more than they bargain for. They get men who view women's sexual freedom from a perspective of entitlement. A man like this is willing to commit to nothing— not to a long-term relationship, not to marriage, not to her security, not to her provision, and certainly not to her protection. And yet, sexual freedom is the modern woman's mantra. Christian theologian and pastor, John Piper, gives this great analogy about modern woman's desire for sexual freedom:

> There are sensations of unbounded independence that are not true freedom because they deny truth and are destined for calamity. For example, two women may jump from an airplane and experience the thrilling freedom of free-falling. But there is a difference: one is encumbered by a parachute on her back, and the other is free from this burden. Which person is most free? The one without the parachute feels free— even freer, since she does not feel the constraints of the parachute straps. But she is not truly free. She is in bondage to the force of gravity and to the deception that all is well because she feels unencumbered. This false sense of freedom is in fact bondage to calamity which is sure to happen after a fleeting moment of pleasure.[9]

Therein lies the difference between being bound to another in meaningful sexual intimacy—naked and unashamed—and being in bondage to meaningless counterfeit sex, which always begins with a lie. What follows are counterfeit messages that encourage premarital sexual activity. How would you address each one with grace and truth?

I can't control my lust. Besides, nobody's a virgin today.

I need somebody to love me, and sex makes that happen.

If I have sex with him, he won't leave me. It's just what girls have to do.

We're going to get married eventually. We have to know if we're compatible.

As long as I don't go all the way I'm not doing anything wrong. I'm still a virgin.

It's a biological need. What's the big deal?

Other?

How does 1 Thessalonians 4:2–4 address these messages? How does this apply to today's Christians?

According to a 2009 study, "Eighty percent of unmarried evangelical young adults (18 to 29) said that they have had sex"[10] And a number that are left are technical virgins, engaging in all but sexual intercourse while still considering themselves virgins. There is a huge disconnect today between what we do and "Whose" we say we are. Those who believe this counterfeit message must ask themselves: *Why do we say we know the truth and yet live apart from it?*

Another burgeoning phenomenon among young adults is cohabitation—the premarital experiment that many believe will determine their lifelong compatibility. Unfortunately, "cohabitation has increased nearly 1,000 percent since 1980, and the marriage rate has dropped more than 40 percent since 1960."[11] The divorce rate is twice that of those who didn't live together before marriage. "The unconventionality of those who live together does not explain their subsequent struggle when married. There is something about living together first that creates marital problems later."[12]

Cohabitation sets a habit of not being "all in." Marriage is an all or nothing proposition, the stuff of commitment. Cohabiting seems to instill an independent attitude of "business as usual" when the marriage finally takes place. Couples may have practical reasons why they choose to live together; however, they do not invalidate God's wisdom and order for marriage relationships and the value and protection of committed oneness. Dreaming of the eventual marriage while living apart physically and sexually keeps the mystery and beauty alive. It also honors God's call to make marriage holy and set apart. We want the assurance and security that someone is willing to risk everything for the sake of forever. Anything other than that is counterfeit.

 IN HER SHOES

"I had no idea what impact living with my boyfriend would have on my relationship with my future husband. I felt like a whore since I didn't end up marrying the man I lived with. For years I dragged my guilt and shame into my marriage bed, and they hovered over me like a dark cloud every time my husband and I had sex. And at the time, that's all it was—just sex."

Satan tailors his counterfeit for each one of us. What counterfeit messages have you listened to that may have encouraged premarital sexual activity (with or without cohabitation) in your life? Write it in your journal.

_____

_____

_____

Many today marry with sexual histories, and unless the truth replaces the lie, God's divine design for marital sexual intimacy remains distorted.

MARRIAGE RELATIONSHIP: FALSE INTIMACY AND NO INTIMACY

You've heard it said that as much effort should go into planning the marriage as went into planning the wedding. Each partner brings baggage into the relationship that they hope being married will fix, such as: "Now I'll never be lonely again" or "Marrying will take away my desire for pornography" or "She'll never find out about the prostitutes I've seen" or "He'll never need to know about my same-sex partners."

These hidden thoughts of the heart find their way into the marriage bed. If they aren't exposed, they launch a marriage into the netherworld of dishonesty, disappointment, disillusionment, and distrust. Fear, shame, childhood experiences, a gamut of abuses, cultural messages, gender confusion, bondage to sexual passions, or just plain selfishness can determine how vulnerable (naked and unashamed) couples are willing to be with each other. When emotional intimacy threatens to expose what we want to remain hidden and private, it impacts sexual intimacy. It can become fearful, stilted, cold, meaningless, or empty. We can avoid, neglect, and gradually withdraw from our spouses emotionally and sexually. All that will be left is false intimacy or no intimacy at all.

What follows are counterfeit messages that sabotage marital intimacy. How would you address each one with grace and truth?

I can ignore my spouse's sexual needs. Besides I'm just a sex object.

_____

_____

Sex is dirty, even in the marriage bed.

_____

_____

My body is too shameful for sex.

_____

_____

Pornography will spice up our sex life.

_____

_____

We're done having kids, so I'm done having sex.

_____

_____

I'm used goods; I don't deserve a good sex life with my husband.

_____

_____

Because of sexual abuse, I won't give myself permission to enjoy sex with my husband.

_____

_____

Other?

_____

_____

Revisit and seriously consider how 1 Corinthians 7:3–5 addresses messages that sabotage marital intimacy. What do you discover?

_____

_____

Author Nicholas Sparks wrote a wonderful book entitled *The Wedding*. He describes a long-married couple that had fallen into the pit of boredom, neglect, and complacency. Particularly memorable was the husband's description of his wife of twenty-nine years:

> *My wife is still beautiful. Of course, it's a softer beauty now, one that has deepened with age . . . We've made love infrequently these last few years, and when we did, it lacked the spontaneity and excitement we'd enjoyed in the past. But it wasn't the lovemaking itself I missed most. What I craved was the long-absent look of desire in Jane's eyes or a simple touch or gesture that let me know she wanted me as much as I longed for her. Something, anything that would signal I was still special to her.*[13]

Can't you just hear his heart? His longing clearly expressed his deep love for her. He missed her response to him sexually—her affirmation that he was still necessary to her life. The story tells us this deprivation wasn't one-sided. Life got busy, and mutual neglect fostered their aloneness and threatened their oneness. Often couples become so engrossed in "it's about me" that we miss God's intent for marriage. It's about "us".

Satan tailors his counterfeit for each one of us. What counterfeit messages have you listened to that encouraged false intimacy or no intimacy in your marriage? And if you're not married, how will you guard against false or no intimacy in your future marriage?

Remember: In a marriage, Satan waits for our unguarded hearts, our indifferent hearts, or our complacent hearts—and then he goes after our spouses.

ADULTEROUS RELATIONSHIP ~ INFIDELITY

Adultery is the epitome of betrayal—a breach of trust in a covenantal relationship that was to be shared with no other. Both men and women are equally at risk. Renowned divorce mediator and author Sam Margulies wrote: "Although most people assume that it is men who are most likely to have affairs, I have found in my practice that women are today as likely to engage in affairs as men . . ."[14] And although lies and deception attempt to cover up infidelity, there is no such thing as a secret sin.

 IN HER SHOES

"In the early days of the affair, as I laid there in the arms of another man, I could sense the Spirit saying, 'No! Get yourself out of this.' But I would stay and perform, just like I had learned from my childhood. As the affair continued, I no longer heard the Spirit telling me to stop. I slipped right back into who I used to be. I became infatuated with the rush of a new relationship and the attention he lavished on me. I was drugged again with the attention of another man."

Infidelity outside of marriage includes:

- A sexual relationship with or without an emotional commitment
- An emotional commitment but with sexual restraint
- Looking at, thinking of, fantasizing with sexual thoughts about another other than one's spouse
- Flirting, saying or doing anything designed to create sexual chemistry with someone other than one's spouse
- Using any media that adds another or others to one's sexual mix—whether visually and/or verbally—usually in the form of pornographic Web sites, books, magazines, catalogs, movies, chat rooms, cybersex, or phone sex.

What follows are counterfeit messages that encourage infidelity. How would you address each one with grace and truth?

My needs aren't being met.

I just can't help myself.

_____

_____

I can't endure this loneliness.

_____

_____

Being with this man feels right.

_____

_____

It feels so right it must be God's will.

_____

_____

I don't love him anymore.

_____

_____

What he doesn't know won't hurt him.

_____

_____

Other?

_____

_____

How do Exodus 20:14, Hebrews 13:4, and Luke 12:2 address counterfeit messages that encourage adultery?

_____

_____

_____

_____

> *"But there is nothing covered up that will not be revealed,*
> *and hidden that will not be known."*
>
> Luke 12:2 (NASB)

Adulterous actions matter on several fronts: They matter to current or future spouses; they matter to any children who are or will be; they matter to those over whom there is influence; they matter to the ones with whom these acts occur. And they matter to God from whom there is no secret. Christian sex therapist Douglas Rosenau maintains that if an affair is "emotional adultery and never culminates in physical sex, if it is lived out in the mind and never acted upon, or even if it is never discovered, the people involved and their marriages are damaged."[15]

Christian or not, we all want someone to commit to us deeply, passionately, and for a lifetime—never to be shared with another. This is a desire supernaturally programmed into human hearts by the Divine Designer, and He patterned it after His desire for relationships with us—committed, passionate, eternal. Is it any wonder that adultery is to a spouse what idolatry is to God?

Have you defended counterfeit messages that encouraged infidelity? Which ones? What justifications do you use or have you used to argue this counterfeit point? If you or a loved one is engaged in an affair, whose lives are at stake and in what ways? Does it matter? Write your answers in your journal.

HOMOSEXUAL, LESBIAN, BISEXUAL RELATIONSHIPS

Many struggle with both grace and truth when it comes to homosexuality, lesbianism, and bisexuality. That said, Christians are to exercise the combination of grace and truth no matter what the alternative lifestyle.

In 1 Corinthians 6:9–11, Paul listed those who practiced doing wrong. Does he differentiate between greater and lesser sins? Why do you think that is? What's the truth for those in any of these lifestyles? What's the grace for those in any of these lifestyles?

Paul was not being condemning; he was being truthful about those who were in jeopardy— who were actively practicing behaviors displeasing to God (truth). He knew they were also within the realm of redemption (grace). If the truth is that alternative lifestyles are not in concert with God's design, then the grace is that God in His love and mercy can provide help and hope for those who struggle to live according to His abundant design. Christian author Wesley Hill writes, "The Christian's struggle with homosexuality is unique in many ways but not completely so. The dynamics of human sinfulness and divine mercy and grace are the same for all of us, regardless of the particular temptations or weaknesses we face."[16]

What follows are counterfeit messages that women are tempted to believe about alternate lifestyles. How would you address each one with grace and truth?

God made me this way, or I was born this way.

_____

_____

I can't help the way I feel; marrying my partner will make it right.

_____

_____

She understands me.

_____

_____

We should be tolerant and accept this lifestyle.

_____

_____

Where there's love, gender shouldn't matter.

_____

_____

Other?

_____

_____

_____

Andrew Comiskey, himself having left the gay lifestyle, writes these poignant words: "Jesus embodies the transforming power of God's presence in human history. He is in our midst now, wanting to enter and alter our personal histories with his healing power. Consequently God invites us to live expectantly; we await and discover his kingdom breaking into our lives afresh. Through his Spirit, he transforms us more fully into his image and likeness. Homosexuality may have limited us in the past, but God breaks in and grants us kingdom power with which to live differently."[17]

 IN HER SHOES

"I was no longer under the weight of the abuse or of the gay lifestyle, but I did not know whether my fiancé would realize that or not. I prayed in preparation, cried in desperation, and got sick in anticipation, but finally one day I got back to my apartment and called him. I could not face him in person when I spilled my past. He just listened, not saying a word, then when I was finished, he simply asked, "Have you dealt with God about it?" I said, "Yes," to which he replied, "That's good enough for me." I had received God's forgiveness, but that was the first time I honestly felt that God would bring people into my life that would not judge me on my past but on God's potential for my future."

If you or others you know are in alternate lifestyles, how did you (or they, if you have this knowledge) come to be there? What have you told yourself (or have they told themselves) to validate this choice?

_____

_____

_____

_____

Many believe deceptive messages about sexual freedom and end up in any one of the relationships we have looked at today. Let's return to John Piper:

> *"Freedom does include doing what we want to do. But the mature and wise woman does not seek this freedom by bending reality to fit her desires. She seeks it by being transformed in the renewal of her desires to fit in with God's perfect will (Romans 12:2)."*[18]

EXTRA MILE
Resources for Help and Hope

For those who need additional help and hope on any sexual issues, visit Judy's Web page, www.eymministries.org, and click on the "Resources" tab.

> Prayer: Lord, I really don't want relational counterfeits for myself or for others I love. Help me receive Your grace and truth. Help me to impart Your grace and truth to those who need hope, help, and redemption.

DAY 4

COUNTERFEIT INTIMACY: SEXUAL COUNTERFEITS

When we believe counterfeit messages about sex, our conduct (or giving a nod to others' conduct) isn't far behind. What follows is an informational lesson on four sexual counterfeits that masquerade as intimacy. Be aware of what you believe about each.

DID YOU KNOW
What Are Sexual Counterfeits?

Sexual counterfeits are those that circumvent God's divine design for sex by engaging in a variety of isolating sexual activities. These include: sexual fantasy, masturbation, pornography, virtual/cyber sex, fantasy chatting, sexting, visiting chat rooms that lead to sexual encounters, offline hookups, swing clubs, voyeurism, exhibitionism, obscene phone messages, inappropriate touching, strip bars, prostitution, frequenting prostitutes, incest, childhood sexual abuse, child exploitation, child pornography, and more.

COUNTERFEIT INTIMACY: SEXUAL FANTASY OF THE MIND

Sexual fantasy (or fantasy sex) is sexual "pictures," scenarios, and obsessions of the mind that some use to break away from the humdrum or the pain of their personal realities.

Fantasy sex is its own great escape.

Harry W. Shaumburg writes, "All sexual involvement begins in the mind . . . At its core, sexual fantasy is a worship of self, a devotion to the ability of people to fabricate in their minds the solution to what they know is a need and believe they deserve."[19]

Tim Challies relates some truths about sexual fantasy:

- Sexual fantasy inclines us toward emotional isolation.
- Reality is rarely as wonderful as sexual fantasy.
- Sexual fantasy sets up unhealthy and unrealistic expectations of sex.
- Sexual fantasy rarely revolves around legitimate sex partners.
- Sexual fantasy can encourage faithful spouses to fill their minds with thoughts of others.

Challies maintains that a "single Christian man [or woman] . . .simply has no legitimate reason for pursuing sexual fantasy at all"[20] (brackets ours). Neither does a married Christian man or woman for that matter. However, *legitimate* imaginings can build intimacy with our spouse. Recall in the Song of Solomon that she daydreamed romantically about her beloved but would not let it lead her into sin. When we step outside of this legitimate exception, our fantasy breeds discontent and dissatisfaction. We can focus our mental energy on our spouses and experience healthier results.

COUNTERFEIT INTIMACY: MASTURBATION

Although Scripture says nothing directly about masturbation, it does speak to the lust of the mind that encourages and often accompanies the act. As women, we don't need much stimuli to meet us in our sexual longings: the good-looking new guy in the office, a new boyfriend, a fiancé, the coworker, neighbor, or man who seems to value us. But when the daydream morphs into lust, the mind opens to unhealthy compulsions.

How do Psalm 101:3-4, Matthew 5:27-28, and 1 Thessalonians 4:1-4 speak to sexual fantasy with masturbation?

Much has been said on this subject and whether or not the act of masturbation in and of itself is sin. Many agree that the major taboo about masturbation is where the mind goes during the act. In keeping with Scripture, no one other than our spouses is to take up intimate space in our minds. Masturbation can counter the goal of oneness that sexual intimacy should foster. There are valid reasons why we shouldn't turn to masturbation for sexual gratification, whether married or single:

- It violates God's holiness by compromising His divine design for sex (Genesis 2:25).
- It desensitizes the body's natural response to marital oneness (Song of Songs).

- It stimulates lust since it may involve a mental image of someone other than our spouses (Matthew 5:28).

- It appeals to the lazy, selfish side of our natures that won't exercise Holy Spirit self-control (Proverbs 25:28).

- It promotes a life of deception (James 1:16–17).

- It promotes isolation and division (Genesis 2:24).

- It deprives our spouses of sexual intimacy with us (1 Corinthians 7:5).

- It sidesteps honest communication and vulnerability with our spouses (Genesis 2:25; 1 Corinthians 7:3), robbing them of the opportunity to meet our needs.

- It can weaken marriages (Ephesians 4:15–16).

That said, there might be extenuating circumstances in some marriages that preclude sexual activity. Many yearn for the intimacy of the divine design but live with the pain of a spouse who is either disinterested or incapable due to health reasons. Others are forced to endure long-term separations. Christian authors Dr. Tim and Beverly LaHaye weigh in on this tough topic of masturbation: "All forms of masturbation have to be evaluated, not in the light of the physical experience, but in the mental attitude at the time. Usually, male [and female] masturbation is associated with pornography or fantasies that are pornographic, and that's when it's detrimental. Masturbation can also become self-addicting. . . . At the end of the day," LaHaye says, "masturbation is a matter between the individual and God. If you can do it without feeling the need to confess it as sin, the physical function of bringing oneself to orgasm is not in itself a sinful act—it's the mental thought process that makes it right or wrong" [21] (brackets ours).

Consider: Can a spouse contribute to the other spouse's problem with masturbation? Quite possibly, if either spouse repeatedly *neglects* and *rejects* the other, causing him or her to compensate for what the spouse should be providing. If spouses are remiss in fulfilling their sexual responsibilities (as outlined in 1 Corinthians 7:3-5, lesson 5) their neglect may encourage their mates to masturbate out of sheer sexual frustration. God will call neglectful spouses to account.

Consider also: And what about our children and masturbation? Children are naturally curious and actively learning about their bodies. As parents, we have both the age-appropriate opportunities as well as the obligation to shape their understanding of God's design for them sexually *without conveying shame*. Seek out the multiple Christian resources that are available on this topic. (See lesson 10, endnote 28.)

COUNTERFEIT INTIMACY: THE NEW EROTICA

In 2012, E. L. James wrote a book that took our culture by storm. In its first year, *Fifty Shades of Grey* sold over seventy million copies. Now a trilogy, this series "has done for women and erotica what the advent of the Internet did for men and porn...And among all American adults who read *Fifty Shades of Grey*, one in five were Christians. Today, erotica is the fastest-selling genre of books selling to women."[22]

Erotica is written fantasy that intentionally alters God's sexual and moral design, twisting and distorting it into a new—and well-received—sexual reality for women: "No man needed, no risks of heartbreak involved, you don't even need to put on makeup . . . Just start reading and you can have your body and mind awakened any time you want."[23] Erotica taps into the secret longings of a woman and is considered benign by most since it's not an actual physical encounter. But eventually erotica can take us to places we never thought we'd go: general dissatisfaction with our own lives and spouses, masturbation, pornography, off-line encounters, adultery—because even erotica will never be enough.

COUNTERFEIT SEX: PORNOGRAPHY

Pornography, in the form of sexually explicit imagery, is our culture's most explosive sexual counterfeit. It lures everyday people in every walk of life. Today forty million Americans are regular visitors—including 70 percent of 18-to-34-year-olds, who look at porn at least once a month. It has become "a whole generation's sex education and could be the same for the next." [24]

Pornography warps intimacy in relationships. When combined with masturbation, it renders intimacy pointless. In his book *Sex Is Not the Problem (Lust Is)*, Joshua Harris quotes Jeffrey Black:

> The goal of pornography and masturbation is to create a substitute for intimacy. Masturbation is sex with yourself. If I'm having sex with myself, I don't have to invest myself with another person. People who are "addicted" to pornography aren't so much addicted to lurid material as they're addicted to self-centeredness. They're committed to serving themselves, to doing whatever they can to find a convenient way not to die to self, which is the nature of companionship in a relationship.[25]

And when "it's about me", there's no compulsion we will refuse. That said, nothing can excuse, rationalize, or defend one's use of porn. It's a Pandora's Box that once opened, requires ever-increasing titillation to drive its user to deeper levels of excesses and self-indulgences. It becomes a secret life, an isolated life enshrouded by an obsessive pursuit that knows no boundaries.

Exposure to sexual imagery has a neurochemical impact in our brains. We are "releasing the tidal power of these brain-based chemicals. Early exposure to pornography—or simply sex on TV—may be opening pathways in the brain way before other faculties (like self control) can be engaged."[26] This is particularly true for children whose mental strength and discipline haven't been honed. Josh McDowell reports that "first exposure to pornography is now common for six- and seven-year-olds."[27] They're introduced to it at a friend's house, or when they push a wrong button on the computer, or as they're hit square-eyed with a book, magazine, or DVD that Mom or Dad or a sibling forgot to hide. Because kids aren't cognitively and developmentally mature, they are easily traumatized, captivated, and conflicted by what they view and how it makes them feel. And we kiss their sweet innocence good-bye.

Listen as Crystal Renaud, author of *Dirty Girls Come Clean,* tells her story: "I picked up the magazine. I opened the front cover. And it happened. In that one moment, in less than a second's time, I not only exposed my eyes to a concept I had never seen before, but I exposed my heart, my mind, and my body to a world that no ten-year-old should ever have entered."[28] Her counselors likened her experience to that of a rape victim, one both traumatized by her experience and yet one in which she placed the blame and shame squarely on her young self. Over time, Renaud confesses, "Pornography use took me places I never thought I would go. It kept me there longer than I intended to stay. And it cost me more than I wanted to pay."[29]

It is not uncommon for marriages that are struggling with pornography to discover that the spouses were exposed at an early age. Because they weren't emotionally mature enough to discern the impact that the images would have on their behavior, they continued to feed the dopamine-driven compulsion. Now years later, they are still glued to this same struggle. This can also be problematic for mature men or women who turned to sexual imagery as adults for stimuli and became hooked. It is then no longer an issue of maturity, mental strength, or discipline but a matter of bondage.

Were you exposed to sexual images as a child? How has your exposure played out? If you are married, do you know if your husband was exposed? And what about your children?

_____

_____

_____

_____

Over time, the feel-good fascination with pornography will impact the users' self-concept, wife or husband-concept, marriage-concept, God-concept—even if the user is single and especially if the user is a child. Tim Challies describes the imprint pornography can make on anybody's mind:

> Pornography reshapes our very understanding of sex, of manhood, and of womanhood. It is inherently violent, inherently unloving. It is not about mutual love and caring and commitment, but about conquests and vanquishing, about "having your way" (a revealing phrase) with someone else. It tears love from sex, leaving sex as the immediate gratification of base desires. It lives beyond rules and ethics and morality. It exists far beyond love. In this way, it is a perversion of sexuality, not a true form of it, and one that teaches depravity and degradation at the expense of mutual pleasure and intimacy.[30]

In most cases, pornography users have a love/hate relationship with the habit. Like any other habit, the harder they try to control, alter, diminish, or defeat it in their own strength, the stronger it grows. Even if pornography starts out as a casual pastime, it can quickly escalate from the merely visual. Users will inevitably become hooked. They will no longer control pornography; it will control them—their thoughts, their time, their relationships, their jobs, their money. It breaks down the inner restraint of moral boundaries, and the only thing greeting users on the other side is profound loss.

"When I met my husband, I knew that this man of purity was God's man for me. He wasn't interested in only my body. He was following God's plan for his life. Ten years later, this same man broke my heart. He confessed that he had been viewing pornography as early as one year into our marriage and was now addicted to it. A few days later, he confessed that he had had an affair eight years into our marriage."

If you are involved with pornography, what continues to allure you? If you're married, how is it affecting your view of sex with your mate? If you're not married, how is its use impacting your future marriage even now?

_____

_____

_____

What follows are some truths about this behavioral counterfeit:

Pornography isn't about sexual intimacy. Pornography use is often driven by non-sexual needs, longings, and desires. Most who are in bondage to pornography have sexual partners available to them.

Pornography won't create true marital intimacy. Some women may be pressured by their husbands to view pornography. Complying not only introduces someone else into the relationship, but it acclimates the couple to the counterfeit.

Pornography is not about you. In most cases, if our spouses are into pornography, we weren't there when the bondage began. We didn't cause it, and we don't have the power to change it.

Pornography is about power and control. The control that users have over sexual experiences makes them feel powerful while other aspects of their lives threaten impotency. But soon the tables turn, sometimes imperceptibly, and pornography has the power.

Pornography resets the neural pathways, "creating the need for a type and level of stimulation not satiable in real life."[31]

Pornography is infidelity of the mind. If left unchecked, it will lead to physical infidelity.

Pornography is a continuum of perversion. Users have a high probability of progressing to increasingly perverse hungers and desires, which potentially includes abuse and violence.

Pornography is a gateway to sexual bondage where freedom will require more than willpower.

If you're involved with pornography, how has it influenced your thoughts about sex? Your expectations of sex? Do you have a desire to get out of it? Do you believe you can let it go? If so, how do you know? If not, what is your greatest impediment to letting it go?

_____

_____

_____

_____

_____

_____

Christian author Thomas Schmidt, writes, "Moral questions have to do with the rightness or wrongness of my actions, regardless of the source or strength of my desires. Whatever I may attribute to my genes or to my parents or to my culture, none of them can force me, at the crucial moment, to turn a glance into a fantasy, or a fantasy into a flirtation, or a flirtation into a sexual act. At that moment, my _will_ is involved, and precisely such moments define my obedience and growth as a Christian."[32]

> Prayer: If you or someone you love is involved in any of these sexual counterfeits, pray and don't give up! There is hope and healing by the grace of God through Jesus Christ our Lord.

DAY 5

CONSEQUENCES OF COMPROMISE

 IN HER SHOES

"This sin [of child pornography] has affected our entire immediate and extended family, in addition to those who were and are friends of our children. Trying to find jobs for our sons and places for them to live is all the more difficult because both of them are now registered sex offenders. I think that the most difficult aspect of this whole situation has been that my dreams for our sons and their futures were shattered. There is still a great sense of loss as we think of all that was given up and taken away from us. The enemy is certainly the thief who comes to 'steal and kill and destroy' our children (John 10:10)."

The chief problem with counterfeit choices is that they lead to painful consequences that can impact generations to come. They include:

- Physical—sexually transmitted infections (STI's), unplanned and unwanted pregnancies, abortions, potential sterility

- Emotional—grief, guilt, shame, regret, anger, depression, anxiety, suicidal thoughts

- Spiritual—sense of separation from God, seeing oneself as unforgivable, unredeemable; hard heart

- Relational—stress, insecurity, abuse, violence, separation or divorce, single parenting

- Social—legal labels, rejection, isolation, promiscuity

- Financial—job loss, financial strain, potential poverty

Are you or a loved one living with consequences right now as a result of poor choices? Are you suffering consequences as a result of another's poor choices? Identify the choice and the consequences. Who was impacted and how? Be as specific as you can.

_____

_____

_____

_____

Even the consequences have consequences that can impact generations to come, all because of a divine design compromised. Let's look at a biblical example of how compromise impacted legacy.

The story of Lot is an example of consequences that came from being exposed to, choosing, and then getting comfortable with the counterfeit rather than being wholly bound to God. When God called Abram and his family to leave the city of Ur to go to God's Promised Land, Abram took his nephew, Lot, with him. Upon arrival Abram and Lot's herdsmen were competing for pasture, so Abram thought it wise to separate in order to keep the peace. Little did Abram realize how that separation would play out.

Based on Genesis 13:8–17, where did each choose to live, and what was the significance of their choices?

_____

_____

_____

Lot thought he got the best of the best when he chose the lush Jordan Valley, but in actuality he, his wife, and two daughters settled where *"the men of Sodom were wicked and were sinning greatly against the LORD"* (verse 13 NIV). Could he have realized his poor choice and changed his mind? Perhaps, but it appears that the perks of the land were more compelling than the perversion in the land.

Fast forward to Genesis 19:1–29. For our purposes, this story isn't so much about all of Sodom's evil men; it's about this one man, Lot. Read it carefully, and record all of the far-reaching consequences of Lot's poor choices.

_____

_____

_____

The Sodomite men were forceful; they were violent; they meant business! And Lot knew them all, calling them "my brothers," since he had moved from his tents outside the city into the city itself. He even shared the city gate with other officials and prominent men. He was a part of the community.

Lot's comfort level among sinners compromised his character to the point that his decisions were no longer in the best interest of his loved ones:

"Behold, I have two daughters" (v. 8). Really? Was this dad so desperate for his own life, his love so shallow for his betrothed, virgin daughters, his reputation so self-meaningful that he was willing to throw his daughters to these dogs?

"But he appeared to his sons-in-law to be jesting" (19:14). They didn't take his warning seriously. Sad. His daughters' futures perished with their father's lack of credibility.

"Up, take your wife and your two daughters who are here, or you will be swept away in the punishment of the city. But he hesitated" (vv. 15–16). Urgency from God! And yet, Lot lingered—hesitated! God's mercy was saving him and his loved ones, and he still held on to the very things that could kill him—and them!

"Now behold, this town is near enough to flee to. . . Please, let me escape there . . . that my life may be saved" (v. 20). Lot wasn't satisfied with the angels' plan, and yet God's mercy granted his request for "relocation" to a city among those destined for destruction but now was spared.

"But his wife, from behind him, looked back" (v. 26). It's possible that Lot's "waffling" cost him his wife. Perhaps Mrs. Lot thought that if the angels spared her husband when he'd made so many poor decisions that they weren't serious about their warning not to look back.

Now read Genesis 19:29 closely. Why did God spare Lot?

_____

_____

_____

Although the apostle Peter referred to Lot as a righteous and just man (2 Peter 2:7–8), Lot still made questionable choices. However, God saved Lot because righteous Abraham interceded on Lot's behalf. Let that sink in. What does that tell us about loved ones who face the consequences of their compromises? And what about us? If we're compromising God's standard, who's petitioning God on our behalf? We shouldn't get comfortable in compromise just because we know God spared Lot.

Lot left a legacy, and we must never dismiss the legacy we're leaving. God would have our legacy honor and glorify Him. And in His mercy, He may give us many opportunities to be saved from the consequences of our choices, but even as with Lot, opportunities run out.

Read Hebrews 3:7-15. How does this passage counsel the hardening heart? What is our responsibility to each other and why?

_____

_____

_____

When we peel away all the counterfeit messages, choices, and consequences, the bottom line remains: We give ourselves (and others) permission to do what we want without counting the cost in both the natural as well as the spiritual realm. We do so at our own peril. How does it speak to where you are right now? How does it speak to your response to a loved one in sexual sin?

Because of God's love for us, His grace and mercy are imbedded in consequences. He will use consequences to get our attention, imploring us, "Come back!"

> Prayer: Lord, choices have consequences, but the most terrifying is to fall away from You. My only hope is clinging to Jesus. While I hold fast to my hope in You help me to encourage others so that we don't have hard and unbelieving hearts.

LESSON 7

One of consequences of compromise (ours or another's) is its legacy of pain. Pain can even cause us to compromise in effort to escape it. We often don't realize that pain can be a driving force when critical decisions must be made in the midst of difficult circumstances. The negative thoughts and emotions associated with our pain compete with the precious time and energy that could otherwise go into our personal healing and restoration and/or into that with others.

We will all experience emotional pain throughout our lives in various frequencies and intensities. Pain cannot destroy us; however our responses to pain can.

DAY 1

A PAINFUL PATH

Pain is a peculiar word. Not only do we often react viscerally to the word, but we understand it differently based on our own experiences and how we view or tolerate pain. Pain can be physical, emotional, or even mental. But how many of us consider pain in its essence to be spiritual? Although Scripture uses the word *pain* infrequently, it gives many examples of how sin can become a source of pain. Think about it. Adam and Eve's sin brought about the fall and with it the knowledge of good and evil, the sentence of death, the separation from God, and the exit from the garden. Sin is often at the heart of our pain.

THE PAINFUL PATH TO GUILT

In order to understand this sin/guilt/shame/pain combination, let's return to Romans 1:18–20. In verse 18, what does Paul say is God's response to sin? What do you think it means to *"suppress the truth by their wickedness"* (NIV)?

According to verses 19–20, how did God make His truth known? What did this reveal about God?

_____

_____

_____

Look at the final line in verse 20. What does it say about suppressing the truth?

_____

_____

We are *"without excuse."* God provides us with revealed knowledge of Himself. He makes Himself evident. So when we choose to turn from Him to the world, to the flesh, or to listen to the lies of the enemy, we are without excuse. Guilty as charged. And unresolved guilt will lead to pain and shame.

Guilty is what we are when we do wrong. Guilt is what we experience when we become aware of our own wrongdoing. We've crossed God's line, and we know it. We don't like to feel guilty. Whether we acknowledge it or not, when we are charged as guilty, we need resolution because the guilt of our sin cuts us off from the Lover of our souls.

When it comes to guilt, there's good news and bad news. We'll give you the bad news first: The enemy uses guilt to condemn us—whatever will stunt us, keep us stuck, or stop us completely in our walk of faith. When he is able to do this in our lives, he knows we are useless to ourselves and to others because we become excessively self-focused. The good news is that God uses guilt to convict us for the purposes of repentance, forgiveness, and freedom. When it comes to our lives, God is always a forward-moving God. As with any sin, the guilt stands until we repent and ask God to forgive the guilt of our sin (Psalm 32:5).

 IN HER SHOES
What Is False Guilt?

One of the ways the enemy uses guilt to condemn us is to blur the lines of responsibility and choice. We can possess "false guilt" when we choose to own others' wrongdoings or falsely accuse ourselves of being complicit in their sin. This may be evident in others' sexual sins, as in the case of spouses' adultery or their bondage to pornography or worse. We can charge ourselves "guilty!" as we labor over what *we* could have done to keep them from committing such grievous sins against us. When we condemn ourselves or accept personal responsibility for their choices, we enable our spouses to reject personal responsibility for sin only they should own.

"I felt stupid and foolish and totally deceived, ashamed, and embarrassed—and heartbroken...and had all the thoughts that go along with the knowledge of infidelity: What did I do to deserve this? What is wrong with me? What could I have done better? Why wasn't I good enough? If I just had been prettier, nicer, sexier . . . "

Which guilt do you typically experience—condemning or convicting? If it's condemning guilt, how has it stilted your walk of faith? If it's convicting guilt, how has it freed you to walk forward in your faith?

Are you dealing with guilt right now? What do you think the source of your guilt is? Be specific.

Read Psalm 32:3–4. Where does guilt lead?

According to Psalm 32:1–2, 5, Lamentations 3:40, and Romans 8:1, where does Scripture lead us in our guilt? What's freeing for the believer about these truths?

THE PAINFUL PATH FROM GUILT TO SHAME AND DENIAL

Just before His arrest, Jesus warned Peter that something was coming that would affect him personally and profoundly. Read Luke 22:31–34. What did Jesus tell Peter was in store for him (v. 31)?

Rather than tell Peter that He would stop Satan, what was Jesus going to do for Peter and why (v. 32)?

What did Peter emphatically declare in verse 33?

_____

_____

And what was Jesus' response (v. 34)?

_____

_____

Poor Peter. Straight from the Savior's lips, Peter was told that Satan was out to get him. But Jesus also told Peter He would pray for him. What an opportunity for Peter to prove his faith genuine! And Peter was confident—perhaps overconfident—that he wouldn't disappoint his Friend. He declared that he would stand by his Lord under every circumstance. Perhaps it was this confidence that caused Jesus to respond with a painful but truthful comeback.

By now the Roman guards had seized Jesus in the garden of Gethsemane, and all of His disciples fled (Matthew 26:56). Let's get to the rest of the story. Read Luke 22:54–55. What did Peter do?

_____

_____

_____

Let's finish the account in Matthew 26:69–74. How many times was Peter confronted?

_____

_____

_____

How did Peter react to the first confrontation? The second? The third?

_____

_____

_____

Just exactly why did Peter deny Christ? Perhaps he thought he could help his Lord if he was able to remain incognito. Perhaps he was afraid for his life in the midst of the large contingent of soldiers. Perhaps he was afraid he too would be tortured and arrested. We cannot know what was in Peter's heart and mind, but we do know that his actions were to do the very thing that he declared he would not do—deny Christ. He spoke out of unbelief, and unbelief is sin. To compound Peter's sin, he lied. He experienced the gap that opens between humanity and God when we fail Him. This gap creates wrenching pain because we were not designed to be separated from God and His good for us. And with the pain comes the shame that can lead to denial—an unwillingness to acknowledge our sins.

When did you last experience shame as a result of feeling guilty? If it lead to denial, how did that resolve your guilt and shame?

THE PAINFUL PATH OF DENIAL

We've all been in a place where we felt that denial was our only option. When pressed, we swore that what we said was truth. And when pressed further, our denial escalated as did our defensiveness. Just like Peter. He *"denied"* (v. 70), then he *"denied it with an oath"* (v. 72), and finally he *"began to curse and swear"* (v. 74). "Curse and swear" doesn't mean he used every expletive he knew. It means that he began to "call down a curse upon himself if he were lying...to invoke heaven as a witness to his words."[1]

Did you note the progression of Peter's denial? Let's take it one step further by looking at the rest of the account in Luke 22:60–62. What did Peter remember when the rooster crowed (v. 61)? Why do you think Simon Peter *"wept bitterly"* (v. 62)?

"Though dependence upon the flesh had caused his memory of Christ's warnings to fail, the simple crowing of a rooster awakened Peter to the enormity of his sin as a [scorning] of Jesus' gracious attempts to forestall it"[2] (brackets ours).

The crowing rooster along with Christ's penetrating gaze brought Peter to the truth of his denial. Have you been there too? What has God used to remind you of the gap that may exist between you and God because of sin and denial?

THE PAINFUL PATH TO MORE PAIN AND SHAME

At the moment Peter's third denial left his mouth, the rooster crowed, Jesus looked at Peter, and Peter remembered. One can only imagine the penetrating sadness—and yet the compelling love—that Jesus' look conveyed to Peter. What a powerful, silent exchange between them at that moment. It must have devastated Peter—crushed him—knowing that he had betrayed his Lord and added to His sorrow. Oh, the guilt. And then shame set in.

Turn again to Luke 22. In verse 32, why do you think that Jesus prayed for Peter that his faith would not fail?

Jesus knew that guilt resulting in pain and shame crushes our hearts, which can shake our faith. When we find ourselves in a place of shame (whether earned, assumed, or unjustly thrust upon us), we often have great difficulty working through the painful emotions. The pain of shame can be devastating.

 IN HER SHOES

"Shame and guilt were my constant partners. I was an emotional wreck, and my mind was a mine field. I would be fine one minute and then begin crying for no reason. The weight of my sin was too much to bear. I had come to a point of total brokenness."

Shame can manifest itself as the "raincoat of the soul, repelling the living water that would otherwise establish us as the beloved of God. It prevents us from receiving grace and truth where we need them the most. Many factors contribute to shame, but ultimately the problem is that we resist the reality of the Father's love."[3]

> *"Lay aside every encumbrance and the sin which so easily entangles us, and let us run with endurance the race that is set before us, fixing our eyes on Jesus."*
>
> Hebrews 12:1-2 (NASB)

Are you still shackled by the shame of a sin you committed? How do you know? Why do you think you are still shackled? According to Hebrews 12:1-2, how will you be set free from it?

Some harbor shame as a result of sexual sin committed against them and own that shame. According to Hebrews 12:2–3, how did Jesus deal with the shame others thrust on Him? What do you think this means?

If you have undeserved shame, do you own it? If so, how do you justify owning that shame? What would it mean for you to *"despise and ignore"* (AMP) this shame. How will doing this set you free?

What a tangled mess—guilt, shame, pain, denial, more guilt, more shame, more pain, more denial. We are in deep need of the untangling power of God once we begin the path of pain. Pain and all of the emotions that make up our pain should lead us to the cross. It is God's way of telling us, *You need Me right now.*

God in His incredible grace met Peter right where he was. Look at John 21:14–17. By this time, Jesus had been crucified and resurrected, and appeared to the disciples for the third time. In this appearance, Jesus made a point of addressing Simon Peter. What was the first question Jesus asked Peter? What did Jesus ask of Peter after the initial question (v. 15)?

What was the second question Jesus asked Peter (v. 16)? And what did Jesus ask of Peter after the second question (v. 16)?

What was the third question Jesus asked Peter (v. 17)? And what did Jesus ask of Peter after the third question (v. 17)?

When Jesus confronts us with our guilt and shame, we can hang on to it and let it lead us down more painful paths, or we can let Him speak into us right where we need to be met.

Where are you on the continuum of sin, guilt, pain, shame, and denial? Has it created more sin, guilt, pain, shame, and yet again more denial? At any one of these places on this path, you have the option to return to the Lover of your soul. If this is you, how will you respond to this option *right now*?

Sin and its resulting shame don't need to have the last word in a believer's life. We have that choice.

> Prayer: Lord, I'm grateful that You remove the shackles of my shame. When I'm tempted to put them back on, may Your Spirit remind me that I am free.

DAY 2

EXPERIENCING THE PAIN

We all know what emotional pain feels like. Some of us might be in the midst of it even now.

When trust is breached, how quickly we close our hearts. We experience shock, and our foundations are no longer secure. Our reality shifts. Trust crumbles, threatening everything built on "what was." The relationship is no longer predictable, and neither is life. We no longer trust who we thought was trustworthy. And we no longer trust ourselves. We ask ourselves, *Why didn't I see this coming? What have I done to bring this on? What could I have done to prevent this? What should I do/can I do to make it go away?* Our thoughts are commandeered, consumed by worst-case scenarios. Our attitudes instantly morph, and in many cases, we sin in response to the sins against us. Grief, anger, fear, doubt, anxiety, guilt, shame, resentment, hostility, depression, despair, hopelessness consume us, determine our words, shape our conduct, make our decisions, and chart our courses. And if we've breached trust, we can experience these same emotions.

 IN HER SHOES

"Our lives were upside down and would never be the same again. My husband would have to be registered as a pedophile for the rest of his life (and of our lives together), and the public would assume he had been molesting children. The whole situation was a nightmare."

Whatever the source of our pain, we can all doubt God with questions. *Where is He in all of this? Why would He allow this struggle, pain, and heartache? Why didn't God stop _____?* How can you fill in this blank? What painful emotions have accompanied your thoughts?

_____

_____

_____

If you or a loved one is struggling with sexual sin, how has your emotional response affected you? Others in your life?

_____

_____

_____

Let's look at some of the most painful emotions from a biblical perspective:

Anger: is an emotion that tells us we need God now. It springs from unresolved pain, frustration, or fear. It also rises up when we don't get what we want or think we deserve: personal satisfaction, gratification, placation, contentment. From the root word meaning "to grieve," anger causes one "to burn, be kindled, glow with anger, be incensed, grow indignant. . . It has the sense of fretting" (*Webster*). Consider the analogy of anger to a kindled spark. When is it easiest to put out the fire? When is it most difficult? Someone once said that anger is one letter short of danger.

Read Proverbs 15:1; 22:24–25; 29:22; Ephesians 4:26–27; James 1:19–20. Where does anger lead? Where does Scripture lead us in our anger?

Anger itself is not a sin. It's what we do with it that may qualify it as sin. Do we withdraw, stuffing our anger, running from reality? Or do we go the dishonest route and become passive-aggressive, veiling our hostility with sarcasm or with words and actions that bait the object of our anger? Or do we become aggressive and enraged, rejecting healthy, Holy Spirit self-control? Even righteous anger can become self-righteous. If we don't deal righteously with our anger—that is, work it out before God and, if called to, express it in a way that honors God—it will often lead to both depression and aggression. Women ages "25 to 44 are most often affected by depression with a major cause being the inability to express anger."[4] That said, when and how we express anger will either improve or destroy opportunities to resolve problems.

We're all going to get angry. However, we can choose whether we remain angry. If we make this choice, it is sin. Sullen attitudes, abusive speech, disrespectful tones of voice, closed body language, cold conduct, and offensive behaviors are examples of unresolved anger—all intended to punish. Hanging on to anger deceives us into thinking we're powerful, but in truth, it squanders God's power in us.

Unresolved anger also gives Satan opportunities to tempt us to retaliate or get even. If we won't (not can't) control our anger, it will control us, and will eventually morph into depression and/or aggression. And the enemy has the upper hand.

How do you typically express your anger (or do you)? Where does your anger lead? How can you handle your anger differently?

Think carefully about your answer to this next question: Has an inability to express anger appropriately, if at all, led to depression or aggression? When and how did this begin? Where did it take you? Where are you now?

Resentment, hostility, and bitterness: If anger is left unresolved, resentment intensifies into hostility, the seed that fosters the growth of bitterness. And bitter people are in a constant place of biting, seething discontent.

Read Psalm 73:21–22 and Hebrews 12:15. Where do resentment, hostility, and bitterness lead? Where does Scripture lead us in our resentment, hostility, and bitterness?

_____

_____

_____

Can you relate? Have you ever been on the receiving end of the bitterness that sprang out of another's mouth and tarnished, corrupted, and degraded many? Have you been that person? In either case, what was the outcome? Who was affected by it? How did it affect relationships?

_____

_____

_____

Depression and hopelessness: Depression often comes from feeling powerless, even hopeless, as a result of unresolved pain. A Gallup-Healthways Well-Being Index survey conducted in 2009 revealed that approximately forty million American adults had recently been diagnosed with depression. As well, one in thirty-three children and one in eight teens also suffer from depression.[5]

Read Psalm 40:1–3; 42:1–11. Where does depression lead? Where does Scripture lead us in our depression?

_____

_____

_____

It's not our circumstances that will destroy us but our responses to them. For this reason, it is important to remind ourselves that our negative emotions are God's way of saying, *Seek Me! You need Me!*

 IN HER SHOES

"After my husband's confession, I couldn't stop picturing him with the other woman. With any other woman, except me. I couldn't picture him with me. All of the usual thoughts that a woman has when embracing her husband were replaced with horrifying images and sounds in my mind. It played out like a movie in my head, and there was no way that I could let him touch me after that. I slept in our guest bedroom. I couldn't get into bed beside him without bursting into tears. He was gracious and understanding and convicted and ashamed of himself, but there was nothing that he could do to help me in those moments."

If you have ever struggled with depression, have you been able to associate your emotions with a painful circumstance, a wounding, or intense stress? What did you tell yourself about these?

Note: if you have felt deeply sad, depressed, hopeless, or suicidal for a prolonged period of time and have not seen a doctor, please do so immediately. Modern medicine (to stabilize) along with biblical counsel (to apply God's mind-renewing truth to where you are in life) are gifts in the larger battle with depression.

Doubt: Doubt is the opposite of believing God. It saps our energy and causes confusion. We can spend hours or days looking for God to show up in our dilemmas but not believing He will. Or we can wait on God to prove Himself to us again, rather than drawing from those times when He already did. We may think that this supernatural God is too big to be bothered with our puny circumstances, though they are overwhelming to us. Or if we don't see Him, feel Him, hear Him—when He seems silent in our circumstances and our sufferings, we may think He doesn't care or want to work on our behalf.

Sharon A. Hersch, author of *Begin Again, Believe Again*, writes,

> When we experience the silence of God, we can cave in to desolation—anger and despair—or we can seek consolation. It is part of the human experience to question God's presence, especially during painful times. Questioning God is actually an act of faith because it assumes his existence . . . Moving out of our inevitable questions about God and toward consolation requires that we open our hearts and our hands and wait . . . Only a person who ardently believes in God will have the courage to endure desolation and wait for consolation.[6]

Read Psalm 13, John 20:24–29, and James 1:5–7. Where does doubting God lead? Where does Scripture lead us when we doubt God?

How can remembering God's faithfulness to you speak to any current doubt?

Worry and Anxiety: Worry and anxiety create a fog in the battleground of our minds. They work together to obscure reality. When life is not just out of control but out of *our* control, we worry and then become anxious about what will happen, how it will affect us, what we'll lose.

Read Psalm 37:1–8, Matthew 6:25–34; 10:29–32; Philippians 4:4–7. Where does worry and lead? Where does Scripture lead us in our anxieties and worries?

_____

_____

_____

Apply: Author Sarah Young says, "Do not hide from your fear or pretend it isn't there. Anxiety that you hide in the recesses of your heart will give birth to fear of fear: a monstrous stepchild."[7] What occupies you with worry, causing anxiety in your life? Is it hidden or does someone else know? How do you react to your anxiety (sexual compulsion, hyperventilating, panic attacks, eating too much, drinking too much alcohol, mood swings, hyper-control mode, shopping, praying, other _____)? What has that reaction produced?

_____

_____

_____

_____

Fear: Whatever we fear will master us. Whoever we fear will have power over us. We fear confessing our sexual failure because we're afraid of their disappointment, disapproval, and withdrawal. We fear confronting loved ones with their sexual sin because we're afraid of their wrath and rejection. We fear trusting God because we won't give up control; trusting others because we're afraid of betrayal; hoping because we're afraid of disappointment; forgiving because we're afraid to let another off our hook; feeling because we're afraid of being vulnerable; loving because we're afraid of what it will cost us; suffering because we're afraid of the pain. In any circumstance, the One we need never fear is God Himself. He will respond to whatever we bring to Him out of His perfect love and presence.

Read Psalm 23:4; 34:4, Proverbs 29:25, and 1 Peter 5:6–7. Where does fear lead? Where does Scripture lead us in our fear?

_____

_____

_____

Apply: What or who do you fear and why? Where has your fear led you?

_____

_____

_____

_____

Grief: Grief can be defined as "intense emotional suffering or acute sorrow associated with loss" to include loss of a relationship, loss of a loved one through death or divorce, loss of trust, loss of a job, loss of a reputation, loss of a dream, or loss of a battle with temptation. After Tamar was sexually violated, her loss is described in 2 Samuel 13:19 (ESV): *"And Tamar put ashes on her head and tore the long robe that she wore. And she laid her hand on her head and went away, crying aloud as she went."* When sexual sin breaches trust, the sense of loss is profound. Until the offense and the loss associated with it are acknowledged, grief may not be recognized as grief, let alone processed in a healthy manner. "[God] comes to us in the brokenness of our health, in the shipwreck of our family lives, in the loss of all possible peace of mind, even in the very thick of our sins. He saves us in our disasters, not from them. . . . He meets us all in our endless and inescapable losing."[8]

 IN HER SHOES

"Fearful, anxious, and depressing thoughts began to invade my mind, and I began the tedious practice of trying to take 'every thought captive to the obedience of Christ' (2 Corinthians 10:5). At times I felt like the breath had been knocked out of me. I felt flat, deflated, and my heart was heavy with waves of grief for what had been lost, especially the innocence of my son. I was so disappointed. My dreams had been dashed to the ground, and I felt overwhelmed, weak, and, at times, hopeless. I had been betrayed, hurt, and was broken and sad."

Read Job 2:9–10; Psalm 34:18; 51:17; Isaiah 53:3–5; Revelation 7:17. Where does grief lead? Where does Scripture lead us in our grief?

> *"For the Lamb in the center of the throne will be their shepherd,*
> *and shall guide them to springs of the water of life; and God will*
> *wipe every tear from their eyes."*
>
> Revelation 7:17 (NASB)

What loss did you grieve or are you grieving? How have you grieved, or how are you grieving the loss? Have you permitted God access to your grieving process? If not, why not? If so, how has God met you in your grieving?

Healing comes only as we submit our painful places to God. We can't change what has happened to us or to loved ones. We can't alter the unalterable. But God can redeem whatever caused the pain when we relinquish control and permit Him to work on our behalf and on behalf of those we love.

> Prayer: Lord, no one understands my emotions better than You do. Help me to remember how much I need to turn to You and depend on Your presence when emotions try to commandeer me. Help me to draw from Your Holy Spirit in me what I need for each day and sometimes each moment of each day. Grip me tightly, Lord, and take me to the other side of my pain in Your way and in Your good and perfect timing.

DAY 3

ESCAPING THE PAIN

Pain is designed to get our attention. Whether spiritual, physical, emotional, or relational, pain tells us something is wrong, something needs to be addressed, something needs to be confronted.

David understood the desire to escape a painful experience. In Psalm 55, David laments being betrayed by a close companion. Painful. According to verses 4–8, what was his response?

_____

_____

_____

 IN HER SHOES

"In the aftermath of my husband's confession, I learned how to cry out to the Lord. I read Psalm 55 silently to myself and then I stood up on my bed, and I screamed it at the ceiling, declaring that my heart was in anguish, that horror was overwhelming me, and that I just wanted to fly away like a dove and be free of it! And God was with me the whole time."

We too want to escape painful circumstances. And if we can't fly or wander far away, we'll default to an escape, the foundation of which is denial. For example, when something painful happens to us and we don't want to face it, we run, and that's denial. When we do something wrong that we don't want to face, we run, and that's denial.

Here's the bottom line: Pain ignored is pain denied. And pain denied is damaging. If we don't deal with our pain, it remains a lifelong influence that alters both how we view things and how we do things.

Although pain threatens our well-being, denial helps us run from the ever-increasing load. But the pain only continues to chase us.

Pain ignored is pain denied.

Two components of *denial* that we use to avoid pain are rationalization and justification. *Rationalization* is the "poor reasoning people use *as if* it were good reasoning"[9] in order to ignore the truth about a choice. We exercise this self-deception every day. While grappling with the emotional stress associated with this choice, we conjure up reasons and make excuses. We tend to blur our true motives in the process as we play out the scenario in our thoughts, emotions, and behaviors. Rationalization is the counterfeit means to deny and escape *conviction*. It is sin's friend since it typically distorts God's truth about ourselves, about others, or about our circumstances.

We may or may not act on our rationalizations, but when we do act we create the requirement to explain or defend our actions to ourselves or others. This is called *justification*. If rationalization is the process of false reasoning that leads to sinful actions, then justification is the argument to defend those actions as right, even if they're not. We do so to absolve ourselves of wrongdoing. Justification is the counterfeit means to escape *condemnation*. It is sin's friend, since it typically denies our accountability to God's truth.

Rationalization and justification rely heavily on each other, almost always traveling the road together as partners in denial.

Think of an adversity in your life that caused you pain. Did you try to escape the pain? Did you use rationalization to escape? What did you tell yourself? How did you alter the truth in your mind (rationalize)? How did you explain away the truth to others (justify)?

_____

_____

_____

_____

What's the *truth* surrounding the pain you were or are experiencing?

_____

_____

_____

 IN HER SHOES

"My husband woke up frequently with feelings of panic, but fervent prayer brought peace. He also read the Bible for hours a day and found God speaking to him through it, and not just words of comfort. God was showing him the lewdness of his own sin. Sometimes it was hard for him to face. He had rationalized so much during the years of sin."

RATIONALIZING AND JUSTIFYING OUR OWN SINS

Making excuses when we sin comes easily. They start in our thoughts as we ponder the ways we can get around our wrongdoings. We rehearse with our lips, crafting the perfect justification. Let's see how that worked for two sisters.

Sodom and Gomorrah had just been destroyed by God. Only Lot and his two daughters survived. At Lot's request, he and his daughters escaped to the town of Zoar but then were afraid to live in it. Pain, denial, rationalization, and justification drove this family to moral failures that would create pain for generations to come. Read Genesis 19:30–38. Where did Lot take his daughters after Sodom's destruction and why (v. 30)?

_____

_____

In verses 31–35, what plan did the daughters devise and why?

_____

_____

What excuses did they make (rationalize and justify) for their gross iniquities?

_____

_____

First, Lot allowed his daughters to manipulate him into getting so drunk that he didn't remember having sex with either of them. Second, His daughters rationalized and justified having sex with their father to escape being husbandless—lonely. Their rationalization and justification created painful outcomes.

And what sad outcomes! They unfolded an unpleasant, dangerous future. Reread Genesis 19:36–38. What did their sins produce?

_____

_____

We can only speculate about what these women were thinking, but their sexual choices were disastrous and long-lasting. On the face of it, they got to be moms; but in reality, their "two sons born of incest became the progenitors of Moab and Ammon, Israel's longstanding enemies."[10]

Have you ever rationalized and justified sexual sin? Have you used pornography, saying you were "just curious?" Have you engaged in premarital sex (whether a young single, divorced, or widowed), saying you were "in love?" Have you lived with your boyfriend, saying, "We plan to get married anyway?" Have you engaged in adultery, saying you were "lonely and rejected" by your husband? Have you embraced a lesbian relationship, saying it is "culturally acceptable?" If any of these apply, what rationalizations (self-satisfying talk) or justifications (arguments that absolve you or another) are you using?

_____

_____

RATIONALIZING AND JUSTIFYING OUR REACTIONS TO OTHERS' SINS

Perhaps we are not the ones who sinned, but were deeply wounded by another's sin. And perhaps we reacted negatively, intensifying our pain and leading us into sin ourselves which we may rationalize and justify. We want to comfort ourselves by what we tell ourselves, often with exaggerated or minimized truth. Then we seek to absolve ourselves when we say or do something against our offenders.

If sexual sin has been committed against you, what was your reaction? If your reaction has remained visceral and damaging to yourself and others around you, what are you telling yourself that rationalizes and justifies this continued reaction?

 IN HER SHOES

"I was incensed, enraged. I never thought this would happen to me. I was going to expose him, ruin his career, leave him, and take every single dime, turn every family member against him. I was going to leave him as empty and devastated as he had made me and then some."

Let's take a look at how one man rationalized his anger at a sinful people to justify his disobedience to God. Read Jonah 1:1–3. What did God ask Jonah to do, and what was Jonah's response?

Read Jonah 2:1–9. How does Jonah describe his distress? Where does he turn?

Doesn't it seem ironic that Jonah turned to the very One who put him in distress? Why do you think God did that to Jonah?

What happened in Jonah 2:10?

Before we go further, think about Jonah sitting in that whale belly for three whole days. He had to be covered with the gross contents of juicy tummy stuff. Isn't that just like God to let us face the yuck of bad decisions? And yet, He's still willing to work with us.

Read Jonah 3:1–3. What did God ask Jonah to do, and what was different about Jonah's response this time?

_____

_____

_____

You'd think that Jonah would be ecstatic at the result of his obedience, right? Let's see. Read Jonah 4. What is Jonah's attitude, and how does he justify himself to God (vv. 1–9)? How does God respond to Jonah's drama (vv. 10–11)?

_____

_____

_____

We see Jonah's self-focused heart in action here: *People don't treat me right; God doesn't treat me right; even plants don't treat me right. I just wanna' die!* Can you feel it? Been there? Jonah mourned the plant over the people because the plant brought him comfort while the people were a pain. Jonah would rather be separated from God than show compassion for the sinners. Sad.

Here's the bottom line: We can never justify a sinful response in the eyes of God, no matter how great the sinner or the sin.

Has your anger at someone ever been greater than your love for God? Is this not our hearts when we've been betrayed or violated by others? We know God's mercy, His goodness, His love, His forgiveness. And we want it. But we don't want it for our offenders. Is this true of you? Who is the Ninevite in your life?

_____

_____

_____

How have you rationalized and justified your reaction to your Ninevite?

_____

_____

_____

According to this story, how would God view your Ninevite? How do you reconcile your reaction with God's view?

_____

_____

Denial, rationalization, and justification are not only tools we use to escape pain or painful reality but also to get our own way. The enemy is desperate to keep us in the darkness by substituting denial for truth. But the truth is that rationalizing and justifying sins and pain will neither heal our pain nor exonerate our sins. There is only one justification for our sins, and it is at the foot of the cross. Romans 5:1 is clear. We are *"justified by faith, we have peace with God through our Lord Jesus Christ."* We can go no place else or to no one else except Christ. That is where the truth is. That is where He makes sense of (makes rational) our pain. That is where the healing takes place.

> Prayer: Lord, show me when I rationalize or justify my sin or my sinful reactions to another's sin. Open my eyes to those places where I'm comfortable with denial, rationalize away the truth, and justify my actions. Help me to see my sins and others' through Your eyes and with Your heart. In Jesus' name.

Day 4

The Purpose of Pain

A popular U.S. Marine motto reads, "Pain is weakness leaving the body." But for a Christian, pain is more than just replacing weakness with strength. Our pain has a higher purpose, a divine purpose. If we're not sure we believe this, we need only examine the One who dealt perfectly with His pain. This in no way minimized His experience or the intensity with which He agonized. His pain was real. And so was His purpose. His Father loved Him, His own dear Son in whom He was well pleased. And yet God required His life.

EXTRA MILE
Philippians 2:6–11

Do you question that Jesus suffered true pain while on His journey from Gethsemane to the cross? What does this passage illuminate about His suffering?

What was the purpose in Jesus' pain? We're it—every believer returned to the Father! And as God's children, there is purpose in our pain as well. Although we can't know what He has already written in His book for us (Psalm 139:16), we can know that God loves us so much that He won't waste one tear, not one agonizing moan, or one gut-wrenching, heartrending sob. Our suffering is His suffering.

Let's examine seven purposes for our pain from a biblical perspective:

TO TURN US TOWARD GOD

Famous pastor and author Max Lucado once said, "God is at His best when our life is at its worst." Pain shouldn't cause us to turn away from God but to turn toward Him, to humbly seek His presence, to press into His heart for comfort, guidance, and wisdom.

Read Hebrews 4:14–16. Why should we turn to Jesus when we face trials and tests? What can we receive when we draw near to Christ?

_____

_____

_____

Does your pain cause you to turn away from God or toward Him? If from God, what stops you from going to Him first? If toward God, what do you receive? Based on the truth you just read, what would await you if you went to the Lord first?

_____

_____

_____

If our pain is not drawing us into the heart of God, we are likely missing the purpose of our pain.

TO CHALLENGE OUR BELIEF SYSTEM—WHOM DO WE BELIEVE?

If God is not your first stop, where is the first place you turn to when faced with a compelling temptation, a severe challenge, a deep heartache, an agonizing tragedy, a wrenching betrayal? Pain shakes us from our comfort zones. This is good. Pain can also keep us in constant, emotional discomfort. This is not good. Either place compels us to seek a remedy.

Read Mark 9:14–24. Peter, James, and John were traveling with Jesus and had just come to the disciples. What problem had the rest of the disciples faced (vv. 14–18)? What was the dad's heartache (vv. 17–18)? What was Jesus' response (v. 19)?

_____

_____

_____

How did the boy suffer (vv. 20–21)?

_____

_____

Sometimes things get worse before they get better! What was the dad's appeal (v. 22)? How did Jesus answer the appeal (v. 23)? How did the father respond to Jesus' challenge (vv. 21–24)?

_____

_____

_____

Recall that the word _belief_ in the Greek is _pisteuo_ meaning "to cleave to, rely on, and have faith in." It's an active verb and indicates how we are to respond to Christ in everything! It's the stuff of trust.

"I do believe; help my unbelief."

If adversity has shaken you from your comfort zone and kept you in constant, emotional discomfort, what remedy have you sought? How has unbelief contributed to your pain? How would belief—cleaving to, trusting in, relying on, and having faith in Jesus—address your pain differently?

_____

_____

_____

Romans 1:17 (ESV) says that *"the righteous shall live by faith"*—by believing. If our pain is not strengthening our belief in Jesus Christ, we are likely missing the purpose of our pain.

TO TEACH US TO HOPE IN GOD

Hope is the sense of anticipation that God is on the move in our lives and in our circumstances. It is a by-product of belief, *pisteuo*, the foundation of all hope.

Romans 15:4 tells us, *"whatever was written in earlier times was written for our instruction, so that through perseverance and the encouragement of the Scriptures we might have hope."* One of the best accounts of an Old Testament believer is found in Genesis. Joseph suffered at the hands of his brothers when sold into slavery and at the hands of a seductress when accused of rape, landing him in jail for years—an innocent man throughout. Read Genesis 50:15–21. How did Joseph process his trials? Why do you think Joseph processed his trials this way?

_____

_____

_____

Joseph remained faithful because he knew the faithful hand of God was in each trial and on him. As he looked back, he saw both the necessity and the value of his adversities—the "God-picture." His trials not only prepared him for a higher realm of responsibility but also positioned him to impact others' lives—the nation of Israel, specifically.

Joseph's dependence on God throughout his trials is reflected in Genesis 41:50–52 when his sons were born. What was the significance of their names?

_____

_____

_____

We know it's impossible to wipe out egregious offenses from our minds. But Joseph not only said, *"God has made me forget all my trouble"*—the pain of his past, but *"God has made me fruitful in the land of my affliction"*—in spite of his past. *To forget* in Hebrew, *nasah*, means "to neglect or to not call to mind or to not let something dominate one's thinking."[11] Although he acknowledged the injustices, he didn't dwell on them. He was able to move forward in hope and bear fruitful outcomes.

Based on Romans 15:13 when it comes to hope, what is our part? What is the Holy Spirit's part? What is God the Father's part?

_____

_____

_____

Being in the Word is supposed to encourage us and give us hope. However, that isn't possible if we won't believe what we read. Joy and peace come by believing, and the Spirit's power makes hope come alive!

Can you identify with Joseph? Can you look back and see God's hand on a trial that yielded God's good—a benefit to you as well as to others? Describe it.

_____

_____

_____

What about now? Can you see the hand of God on this trial? If yes, how has He prepared and positioned you, and for what?

_____

_____

_____

Neither God the Father, Jesus, nor His Holy Spirit would ever impede or discourage your hope in them. What do you believe that impedes or discourages your hope? What truth about God can encourage your heart to hope?

_____

_____

_____

If our pain is not teaching us to hope in God, we may be missing the purpose of our pain.

TO BE CONFORMED INTO THE IMAGE OF CHRIST

The goal of redemption is to restore the image of God in humanity, and that only happens through our relationship with Jesus Christ. However, we tend to have a distorted view of His image. We don't translate His beauty into our lives—the beauty of His love, His grace, His truth, His mercy, His justice, His compassion, His suffering for our sakes. Instead, we see laws, works, judgment, and condemnation—much like the Pharisees.

What does Philippians 2:5–11 tell us about Christ's character? How should we respond and why?

_____

_____

_____

"What is Christianity supposed to do to a person? 'Long before he laid down earth's founda-tions, God had us in mind, had settled on us as the focus of his love to be made whole and holy with his love'" (Ephesians 1:4 TM). God is restoring the creation he made. What you see in Jesus is what he is after in you."[12]

Now read Romans 8:28–29. If we believe nothing happens to us that doesn't pass before God first, how does the promise in verse 28 speak to the painful events in our lives? What are the qualifiers of this promise?

_____

_____

_____

What does this mean for a Christian (v. 29)?

_____

_____

Remember, it's not our circumstances that destroy us; it's our response to them. And God will create or allow many opportunities to practice Christlike responses. He is eager to use the painful places in our lives to bring us to maturity in Christ—to make us more like Jesus. If we are given no other reason, this one alone is sufficient.

Has your pain transformed you? Explain.

_____

_____

_____

_____

If we are not being conformed to the image of Christ, if we are not sharing in His suffer-ing, if we are not letting God cause our pain to work for good, perhaps we have missed the purpose of our pain.

TO TRAIN US IN RIGHTEOUSNESS

We may view pain as punishment from a harsh or even a vengeful God as retribution for wrongdoing. We don't see the goodness or the love that pours out of God into our pain, especially when we do wrong. Hardship is no fun. But when was the last time you considered hardship as His glorious discipline, His loving correction, or even His spiritual muscle builder?

Hebrews 12 tells us how God designs our exercise program in order to build our spiritual six-pack. Every Christian has a program specifically tailored to her divinely designed "growth pattern." And God will apply whatever spiritual tension is required in order for her to reach that next rung of righteousness in her life. It will require His discipline—His correction or chastisement "for the purpose of educating someone to conform to divine truth."[13]

Read Hebrews 12:5–11. How should we regard discipline from God (v. 5)?

_____

_____

What methods does God use to discipline us (vv. 6–7)?

_____

_____

Look carefully at verses 6–10, and list reasons why God disciplines us.

_____

_____

_____

How does verse 11 qualify discipline?

_____

_____

What should God's loving, purposeful discipline yield in a believer's life (v. 11)?

_____

_____

Finally, what is our responsibility, according to verses 12–13 and why?

_____

_____

_____

God's loving correction—even though it is sometimes in the form of a divine spanking or scourging for a wrong that needs to be made right (v. 6)—is always for our good, always out of love, and always with the restorative intent to bring us back to the "very good" of His original design. Therefore, His discipline includes the "entire range of trials and tribulations which He providentially ordains and which work to [defeat] sin and nurture faith"[14] (brackets ours).

Think about a hardship or painful circumstance you're experiencing. In what ways can you discern God's hand of discipline in it? Do you perceive it as a loving hand or as a vengeful hand? Explain.

_____

_____

_____

_____

What righteous behavior do you think He's training you toward? Why do you think He chose this trial to mature you?

_____

_____

_____

What has your response been to His discipline so far?

_____

_____

What will you have to do to *"strengthen the hands that are weak and the knees that are feeble"* (v. 12)?

_____

_____

What path are you currently on that will have to be straightened (v. 13)?

_____

_____

_____

Something happens inside our heads and our hearts when we yield our circumstances to God as divine training exercises. If our pain is not training us in righteousness, we are likely missing the purpose of our pain.

TO PROVE OUR FAITH GENUINE

Perhaps we've never really given our spiritual authenticity much thought, much less felt the need to prove our faith genuine. When life is smooth, what's to prove? But when life is tough, the authenticity of our faith walk will be exposed, whether we set out to prove it or not.

Let's look at 1 Peter 1:3–7. Peter exhorts us to bless God for many reasons. What are they?

_____

_____

_____

The Greek word *poikilos* is translated "all kinds" or "various" and means "variegated, diverse, manifold" from which the English derivation *polka-dot* comes. Imagine a white board with various sized polka-dots from tiny specks to a huge, dark orb. What trial would the tiny speck represent in your life? What trial would the huge, dark orb represent? How could God use each of them to prove your faith genuine?

_____

_____

If our pain is not proving our faith genuine, we are likely missing the purpose of our pain.

TO GLORIFY GOD ~ TO KNOW HIM AND TO MAKE HIM KNOWN

Here's a tough truth: God didn't save us to make us happy, although belonging to Christ brings us joy. He saved us to make us holy in order to show a fallen world that He is enough, sufficient, satisfying.

Based on 1 Corinthians 10:31 and 33, what is Paul's instruction, and why?

When we *"do all to the glory of God . . . not seeking my own advantage, but that of many, that they may be saved"* (ESV), we reveal God's character in us, one that can draw others to Him, especially as they see Him in our tough circumstances. Circumstances don't alter God's character, and as we mature in Christ, circumstances become less likely to negatively alter our characters. Trials, temptations, hardships, affliction, or tragedies provide powerful opportunities to glorify God—to resemble Him and reflect His character. First Peter 4:19 (NKJV) says, *"Let those who suffer according to the will of God commit their souls to Him in doing good,"* to which Oswald Chamber lends perspective:

> Choosing to suffer means that there must be something wrong with you, but choosing God's will—even if it means you will suffer—is something very different. No normal, healthy saint ever chooses suffering; he simply chooses God's will, just as Jesus did, whether it means suffering or not. And no saint should ever dare to interfere with the lesson of suffering being taught in another saint's life. The saint who satisfies the heart of Jesus will make other saints strong and mature for God.[15]

Apart from the cross, our pain has no redeeming purpose. It would only be construed as a hostile onslaught from the enemy or deserved retribution for a self-inflicted wound.

If through our pain God is not made known more deeply to us and to others, we are likely missing the purpose of our pain.

> Prayer: Be merciful to me, O God, be merciful to me, for in You my soul takes refuge; in the shadow of Your wings I will take refuge, till the storms of destruction pass by. I cry out to God Most High, to God who *fulfills his purpose for me* . . . Your steadfast love, O LORD, endures forever. And I know that You will not forsake the work of Your hands. Therefore, I choose to exalt You, O God, above the heavens that Your glory be evident in my life (from Psalm 57:1–2, 5 and Psalm 138:8, ESV).

"MASTER"-ING THE PAINFUL PLACE

We dream about a pain-free life. One Christian describes her pain-free existence this way: "One night I sat out in the car after prayer meeting, waiting for my husband as he was stepping down from his position. A friend sensed that I was not myself and started asking questions. I remember her face as she realized that my husband had an affair with another man. She started to cry uncontrollably and reached into the car to hold me. I remember thinking that I so wanted to cry like she was and wondered why I couldn't. What was wrong with me?" The inability to feel doesn't mean we are pain free.

Author Kevin Goodrich writes that "our Western society provides just enough bait that millions of people believe such a life is possible. With the right medication, the right mate, and the right stuff, one might live a carefree existence without the pains and discomforts of ordinary life...Suffering is still a constant of life, but the new hope related to suffering for the average person is freedom from it instead of redemption in the midst of it as the Gospel offers."[16]

Teacher and author Beth Moore suggests that we confuse emotional wreckage and dysfunction with biblical brokenness. When we believe this lie, we remain in the bondage of oppression.[17] True biblical brokenness is when God uses the weight of His word against the lies we believe to bring us to a place of submission to Him. He graciously plans a healing path that will stabilize and free us.

Pain should take us to the place where all we want is the Healer Himself. And when we actively cooperate with the Holy Spirit to transform what we think, say, and do, healing begins. What follows are some helpful steps towards "mater"-ing our pain:

YIELD TO THE LORD

Read 1 Peter 5:6–11. In verse 6, what does it mean to you to humble yourself under God's mighty hand? Why is this necessary? Why is this safe? How does humility help us remain submitted to God?

_____

_____

_____

_____

Note the progression of this passage. We must first humble ourselves—yield to God before we can successfully move on to the next action. As we do, He will work on our behalf. What anxieties (worries) will you cast on God right now (v. 7)?

_____

_____

_____

The enemy is always waiting for opportunities in our circumstances. What is his goal in a believer's life (v. 8)? How would humbling ourselves first to God help us resist Satan? How do verses 8 and 9 instruct us and why?

Finally, in 1 Peter 5:10–11, what is guaranteed and why? What does this mean for the believer who is currently suffering or struggling with a recurent sin?

When we humble ourselves to God alone—no matter what and whatever it takes—we have a resting place as well as a place of protection in the midst of our pain. He *will* restore and secure us. With practice, submitting becomes a welcome and necessary habit of the heart.

SEEK GOD'S COMFORT

Who or what comforts you in your pain? If it isn't God, then your pursuit is imperfect and won't reach the deepest level of your pain. Only God can do this. Read Psalm 86. What do you find comforting about the psalmist's words?

Revisit 2 Corinthians 1:3–5. How does and will God comfort us?

 IN HER SHOES

"Dealing with friends at this time was not easy; family members even harder. All claimed to be Christians. My family wanted me to take the children and leave him. Friends wanted me to get even. One friend wanted me to take a baseball bat to his car. In some ways, it felt good for them to feel this way as I still felt nothing. Through all this clouded, numb, out-of-body-experience time, one thing became clear to me—God! I turned to my Bible and prayer. Though the Bible didn't always seem to make sense as I read it, it still comforted me. And though I didn't know how to feel or what I was to do or say, I could pour out my heart to God."

Confusion and fear reign in our painful places. Friends and family who want to comfort us may add to our confusion with their counsel, opinions, and advice. We need God desperately when we're confused because *"God is not the author of confusion but of peace"*

(1 Corinthians 14:33 NKJV). His comfort will meet us in our confusion and lead us toward His place of peace.

Consider what or who is the source of your painful place. Do you think the Lord understands all that you have experienced? If not, why do you believe this? If so, how or in what way has He shown you He understands?

_____

_____

_____

Have you asked God to show you His comfort in your painful place? He knows your temptations and failures. He knows if your heart has been broken; He also knows if you have broken another's heart. Seek God's comfort and be willing to receive it. Have no expectations about how He will comfort you, only anticipate that He will.

LET GOD MASTER YOUR THOUGHT LIFE

Dealing with our emotions begins in the mind, where the Holy Spirit does business in, with, and through believers. We're commanded to love God with all our minds (Luke 10:27). Letting Him master and renew our thought lives is critical to dealing with *any* of life's circumstances and it's a learned behavior. Let's start today:

Refuse to entertain unsettling or destabilizing thoughts and attitudes of the mind that are contrary to the truth. We cooperate with the Holy Spirit who searches our minds and knows our thoughts perfectly. Based on Psalm 139:23–24, Romans 12:2, and Philippians 4:8, how can we renew our minds?

_____

_____

_____

In Philippians 4:8, we're not called to think about what's true *or* honorable *or* right *or* pure, *or* lovely *or* commendable *or* excellent *or* worthy of praise. It's all or nothing. Something might be true, but if it doesn't share the other attributes, then we shouldn't camp out there. For example, we might think, *My husband left me for another woman. My life is over!* or *My choices are ruining my life! I'm such a loser!* or *I'm used goods. No decent man would want me.* If our thinking doesn't honor all parts of Philippians 4:8, then we're running a mental marathon of negative thoughts and lies that will result in emotional instability over time. Why? Because no emotion just happens; it's always preceded by a thought. What are you currently thinking about your painful place?

Consider instead: *Yes my husband left me for another woman, but God will never leave me nor forsake me.* Or, *As a child of God, I am not a loser. With His help, I can overcome my sin.* Or, *I know God can make me new. He can bring me Mr. Righteous, if that's His will for me.* These thoughts honor all parts of the Philippians 4:8 construct. It's up to us to protect our minds with God's truth, which is why we want God to search us and test us. Only then are our minds renewed. Right thinking is 90 per cent of the battle. It produces right doing.

Regarding your specific trial, identify a thought(s) about you, your situation, or a relationship that consumes you most. How has it unsettled or destabilized you emotionally? Apply the Philippians 4:8 construct: What's *true* about this thought(s)? Is it also *noble? Right? Pure? Lovely? Commendable? Excellent? Worthy of praise* to think on?

How does "Philippians 4:8-ing" this thought alter your emotions, your pain level, your decision-making, and how you treat a person involved in your circumstances?

We must guard our hearts vigilantly and with diligence above all else! What does "all else" mean? *Everything* we think matters. Further, we open ourselves to wrong thinking and wrongdoing when we lean on assumptions, guessing, or speculation about our circumstances, others, or their circumstances. Good or evil will flow out of our thought lives and determine everything that follows.

Second Corinthians 10:3–5 provides instruction for guarding our minds. What do we learn from this passage that can stabilize our thinking?

We have weapons with ammo that can demolish strongholds (whatever is entrenched in our minds and has a strong hold on us)! At any given time, we can "nuke" arguments in our heads (calculations, denials, rationalizations, and justifications) that determine our negative behaviors. We can jettison our pretentious notions (those lofty, prideful thoughts and attitudes that have become godless areas) so that we no longer exalt them higher than God in our lives. We have the Holy Spirit who works in tandem with God's Word to replace the thoughts we must *take* captive and *make* obedient to Christ. Can you sense exertion on our part to get our minds back on God's wavelength? It is a battle. And it's one we can win. The practice of guarding our minds results in stable minds. Who doesn't want that?

What emotions have a strong hold on you? What self talk keeps them well fed? What arguments (denials, calculations, rationalizations, and justifications) are going on in your head that keep these emotions alive? What lofty, prideful thoughts are you entertaining against another, God, or about your circumstances?

Replace consuming thoughts with God's truth. Lies or negative thoughts that consume us are like jingles in our heads that surface daily without prompting. They sink in and stick. Soon we are what we think. The only way to dislodge lies is to consistently bathe our minds with God's truths about our circumstances and about God in them until truth takes over. Scripture is our mental plumb line. We measure everything against God's Word. Read Jeremiah 15:16. How does the prophet Jeremiah, who was in a painful place, encourage you in your painful place?

_____

_____

_____

No more triggers! We inadvertently use words and phrases that trigger negative emotions. We must reject those words and phrases and replace them with the truth. Here are some familiar triggers:

Trigger #1: What if. . .? catapults us into the future over which we have no control. *What if this doesn't turn out the way I want it to?* or *What if he never changes? What if I can't change?* This is the stuff of fear and anxiety and reveals that we don't trust God with our future. How does 2 Timothy 1:7 address our "what if's?"

_____

_____

_____

Complete this question as it applies to your circumstance: What if _____

_____?

Now worst-case this *What if:* What if it does happen? What's the worst that could come of it? Play this out in your mind, and place God right in its epicenter. Is God trustworthy in this scenario—all the way to the end?

Trigger #2: If only... or I should (shouldn't) have... sends us careening back into the past over which we now have no control and which we can't change. *If only I had chosen someone else* or, *I should have seen this coming! I should never have let myself* _____. Guilt, regret, and shame consume us over and over again. This is the stuff of depression and reveals that we don't trust God to cover our past. The truth is that we will never know what could or should have been. We only know what is. The challenge is whether or not we'll choose to trust God where we are right now. He saved us for a purpose. How does Colossians 1:21–22 address our *if only's* or *I should have's?*

_____

_____

Complete this sentence as it applies to your circumstance: *If only/I should have* _____

_____.

Is God trustworthy in this scenario—all the way to the end? What biblical truth can you apply to your statement to get you out of this pit?

_____

_____

_____

Trigger #3: Why questions are valid and often heart-wrenching. Even David asked the question. But remaining focused on the why of our adversities will keep us stuck. *Why did that have to happen to me?* or *Why didn't I listen?* or *Why did he betray me? Why?* is a legitimate question until it commandeers our entire thought process, thwarting our ability to move forward. Based on Psalm 42, how did David counter his *why?*

_____

_____

_____

Complete this sentence as it applies to your circumstance: Why_____

_____?

What biblical truth can you apply to your "why?" to keep you from remaining stuck?

_____

_____

_____

Trigger #4: When questions focus on timing and expose our unwillingness to wait on God. *When will this be over, Lord?* or *When will he/she come home?* or *When will you work on my behalf, Lord?* Again, this is a legitimate, heartfelt question from one who is suffering. Psalm 13 is a wonderful example of when doubt meets faith. What encouragement do you derive from verses 1–2? Verses 3–4? How did David get to his place of peace (look closely at vv. 5–6)?

_____

_____

_____

How can Psalm 27:13–14 encourage us in our *when's?*

_____

_____

Complete this sentence as it applies to your circumstance: When _____

_____?

What biblical truth can you apply to your *"when?"* to keep you from remaining stuck?

Two safety mechanisms keep us from pulling the triggers of negative self-talk:

Safety #1: Stay in today. Yesterday is under the blood of Jesus—covered, secure. Tomorrow is in His firm grip for our good and for His use. We now focus on *what is*. Remember, Jesus Christ is the I AM (John 8:58), not the I WAS or I MAY BE. Read Matthew 6:34. What wise instruction does He give in this verse that you can apply to your yesterdays as well as your tomorrows?

What new truth will you tell yourself that will keep you in today, no matter what happens?

Safety #2: Instead of *Why, Lord?* and *When, Lord?*, ask <u>What</u> would You have me do, Lord? and <u>How</u> would You have me do it? The *what* seeks God's will. The *how* seeks His glory. According to Psalm 43, what should we do, and how should we do it when we know we've come to the end of our why's and our when's?

> *Instead of "Why, Lord?" and "When, Lord?", ask "What would You have me do, Lord?" and "How would You have me do it?"*

Remember these two questions, *What would You have me do, Lord?* and <u>How</u> would You have me do it? Keep them in concert with each other, so that when you're tempted to return to your why's and when's, these questions can recalibrate your thinking toward God's purpose.

Christian author Sharon A. Hersh writes that "daily and difficult human relationships contain the most intimate spiritual truths of all . . .The pain of brokenness leads us to the Healer and the gifts that come in surrendering to his healing touch...When we allow human relationships, in all of their agony and glory, to transform us into women of faith, hope, and love, then we are living a deeper story."[18]

The Legacy of Your Thought Life

Guard your thoughts; they become your emotions;

Guard your emotions; they become your behaviors;

Guard your behaviors; they become your habits;

Guard your habits; they become your character;

Guard your character; it becomes your destiny;

Guard your destiny; it becomes your legacy.

Prayer: **You have already written my story, Lord. Complete it to Your glory!**

LESSON 8

THE HEART OF THE MATTER

In this lesson, we're going to focus on the heart because the heart reflects and determines the depth of our allegiance to God. Do we have whole hearts, divided hearts, or cold hearts? Do we have judging hearts or discerning hearts? Do we have repentant, responsive, accountable hearts? Our allegiance to anything or anybody is unquestionably the heart of any matter we face.

DAY 1

THREE HEARTS

None of us is ever fully pure in our actions or our hearts' motives. If we are going to have healthy, effective relationships with people, we need to sort out the war going on in our own hearts. It's the war between our humility and our pride.

As we discovered earlier in this study, King David was a man after God's own heart (Acts 13:22–23). No matter what his failings, he always returned to God and served Him with a whole heart. Now it was time to crown a son as the next king. Would the son reflect his father's heart for God? Read 1 Kings 2:1–4. What did David command Solomon and why (vv. 2–3)? Another more important purpose is in verse 4. What is it?

In 1 Kings 3:1–14, what did Solomon ask of God?

Even in his dying, David's focus was on God and His purpose for His people, Israel. Solomon understood it as well because God spoke His purpose twice to him. What did God affirm in 1 Kings 6:12–13?

What did God say to Solomon in 1 Kings 9:3–9? Why do you think God added what He did in His second appearance?

_____

_____

_____

While dedicating the temple, Solomon ended his prayer with a benediction that reminded the people of God's purpose for them. According to 1 Kings 8:59–61, what was that purpose (v. 60)? What was Solomon's solemn exhortation to the people (v. 61)?

_____

_____

God not only granted Solomon wisdom but also wealth, prestige, and a long life. What gifts! Solomon was whole-hearted before God and started his reign with humility. He exhorted the Israelites to be wholly true to the Lord, as well. Read 1 Kings 11:1–8. What happened and why?

_____

_____

_____

Over time, God's promises became Solomon's pride. His heart was divided. The humility with which he began his reign became hubris—excessive arrogance and ambition—to the point that he not only married many foreign women, but he worshipped their gods. What a tragic irony: The same man who built a glorious temple to the Lord of glory also built high places for the detestable idols of the Moabites and the Ammonites. Do these two nations sound familiar? Remember the sons born to the daughters of Lot—Moab and Ben-ammi (*see* Genesis 19:30–38)? Worshiping these gods was directly and specifically forbidden by God. It eventually contributed to the downfall of the nation (*see* 1 Kings 9:1–9).

Let's fast forward to 1 Kings 12. After Solomon's death, his son Rehoboam reigned over all of Israel. The Israelites made a plea to their new king. What was it (vv. 1–4)?

_____

_____

How did King Rehoboam arrive at his answer (vv. 5–11)? What answer did his "buddies" tell him to give (v. 10)? What do you make of this answer (v. 11)?

_____

_____

_____

The "foolish advice of the younger men to Rehoboam is literally in Hebrew 'my little one is thicker than my father's thighs,' most likely a reference to his sexual organ rather than a literal finger. Power and sexual potency were very much connected in the ancient Near East."[1] Rehoboam was going to come at the people with "greater force than Solomon had exhibited."[2] "His "weakest measures will be far stronger than his father's strongest measures."[3] It was a supremely arrogant answer. Let's see where it took him.

Continue in 1 Kings 12:11–14 and 2 Chronicles 12:13–14. How would you characterize Rehoboam's heart, especially as it compared to his father's or grandfather's heart?

Read 1 Kings 12:15–20. What was the final outcome of Rehoboam's pride and arrogance?

IN HER SHOES

"God wanted all of me, not just the parts of my life that I wanted to give Him. One night as I was praying, I heard Jesus say to me, 'You can run, but don't you want to be healed?' I don't think this was an audible voice, but clearly I heard it plain as day. I had a choice to make. I could pick up my mat and walk, or I could stay stuck in the mud and mire. I chose to take a leap of faith and allow Jesus to minister to me and set me free. I finally surrendered all of my life to God."

Consequences. Whenever we choose to walk apart from the Lord, our personal price is high, but it doesn't stop there. Our decisions can impact others and in some cases, many others, and we may not even be aware of the damage being done. Are you on the receiving end of the consequences of another's pride? Explain. Has your own pride caused casualties among family and friends, yourself included? If so, how? How might your pride be thwarting a godly outcome of your current circumstances?

It was clear that the Lord sat on the throne of David's heart. Solomon began with a heart for the Lord but *"his heart was not wholly devoted to the LORD his God, as the heart of David his father had been"* (1 Kings 11:4). Rehoboam, on the other hand had a hard heart. All three are superb examples of the frail human heart.

If you were to qualify your own heart, who's would it look like? David's (whole heart), Solomon's (divided heart), or Rehoboam's (hard heart)? How did it get that way?

Micah 6:6–8 and 1 Peter 5:5–6 give us the remedies for Solomon's halfhearted faith walk and Rehoboam's hard heart. What are they? How do you think their outcomes might have changed had they followed these principles instead of their pride?

A whole heart is a humble heart—a heart yielded and responsive to God. There is no better example of humility than Christ's. How did He exhibit this in John 4:34 and John 6:38?

Read John 14:21. How should a believer's heart line up with Christ's?

The humble, yielded heart responds to God in obedience, just like Jesus. And in every act of our obedience, Jesus reveals Himself to us. This deepens our knowledge of, faith in, and allegiance to the one true God and Jesus, whom He sent (John 17:3). A humble, yielded heart develops an ever-growing, lifelong intimacy with the triune God.

EXTRA MILE
A Humble Heart

According the Scriptures that follow, what should a humble heart look like? Read Matthew 18:1–4; 20:1–16; 23:12; Luke 10:27; John 3:25–30; Romans 12:3, 9–21; Philippians 2:2–11.

Note that it is our responsibility to put our pride down and to humble ourselves. And sometimes—most of the time—that's a struggle. Christian author Chris Tiegreen said, "We have all, at some point or another, said, 'I will be my own Lord and follow my own authority.' It is pride, the foundation of all sin; and it is cosmic treason, punishable by death."[4]

Here's a tough truth: If we choose not to humble ourselves, God will do it for us. He will oppose our pride. The Greek word for *opposes* is *antitasso* and means "to set an army in array against, to arrange in battle order."[5] This definition should create a vivid word picture in our brains whenever our pride kicks in. And may we not be fooled: God doesn't want to wound our pride; He wants to kill it! So He will resist any effort of ours that is born of pride. He will not excuse it. If our pride is left unchecked, we will progress to the final condition of the hard heart. We may start out like David, even be comfortable and feel religious like Solomon and not think anything is wrong with our faith walk. But God made Himself very clear when He declared, *"I am the LORD, that is My name; I will not give My glory to another"* (Isaiah 42:8).

> Prayer: What business do you need to do with God in order to shift your pride to humility? Take this opportunity to meet Him there now.

DAY 2

THE JUDGMENTAL HEART

 IN HER SHOES

"'Guilty!—on three counts of sexual exploitation of children!' It grieved me, even though the courts had justly condemned him to three life sentences in a federal penitentiary. But unless he came to Christ, God would justly condemn him to an eternal death sentence in an insatiable inferno. That grieved me so much more."

We just learned that the humble heart pleases God. However, in our humanity, we don't respond well to sin, especially sin against us. We tend to become judgmental, critical, and condemning.

Judging comes naturally to the human heart. When we hear words or see behaviors we disapprove of, we can make assessments and draw conclusions. In a simple sense, we judge behaviors and actions to assess the dangers of sin, and that judgment informs our actions in obedience to Christ. But we can also default to the practice of being *judgmental*, passing judgment on both the sin and the sinner in a rash and unreasonable manner. Read Matthew 7:1–2 and Luke 6:37, what is Jesus' warning against this and why?

 WORD STUDY
Judges

As both verb and noun, the word judge means a number of things. As a verb it means to render a decision, to give or form an opinion after considering facts, or to discern or discriminate between right and wrong, good and evil. Greek-American Bible scholar, Spiros Zodhiates, defines the verb as "to form and express a judgment or opinion as to any person or thing, more commonly unfavorable."[6] As a noun, Vine's definition includes "one who passes, or arrogates to himself, judgement on anything."[7]

Jesus holds a strong opinion in Matthew 7:3. What comparison does He make? What is He saying about those who judge compared to those who sin?

In Matthew 7:4, what point is Jesus driving home? Why does He make this point?

Now read Matthew 7:5 very carefully. There is an important instruction that this verse gives before a believer addresses another's sin. What is it?

_____

_____

Have others judged you hypocritically (your speck/their log)? If so, how did that impact their credibility in your eyes? How did it impact your response to them? To the sin they addressed?

_____

_____

_____

Have you judged others hypocritically (your log/their speck)? How did it impact their response to you? To the sin you addressed? What do you think would have happened if you had first examined yourself through Scripture and the leading of the Holy Spirit?

_____

_____

_____

If someone scrutinized and judged you in the same way that you judge another, how would you respond?

_____

_____

_____

A careful read of the Matthew 7 passage tells us we are not to judge, which here means to try, condemn, and punish. First, we don't have the moral authority to do so. Second, judging others with disregard for our own deceitful hearts and sins (logs) damages the credibility of our faith walk with others—and potentially many others. Matthew does not say to avoid addressing the specks in others' eyes but to examine our own eyes first so we are not hypocritical, because hypocrisy brings judgment on ourselves. Beth Moore asserts "blameless people are rarely those who cast blame."[8] We may be part of the problem.

How do Acts 10:42 and James 4:12 qualify the only judge, Jesus?

_____

_____

Although Jesus qualifies as the only judge, let's be clear about why He came to earth. He had a specific mission. Read John 3:17 and 12:47. What perspective do these verses give you about Jesus' heart for humanity?

_____

_____

_____

Turn to John 8:15–16. Why don't we have the prerogative to judge the human heart?

_____

_____

Jesus didn't come to earth to judge sinners, but to bear their judgment on the cross. And when He returns, He will exercise His right to judge every human being. Until then, it is not a right we exercise in His absence. He said that we humans pass judgment *"according to the flesh"*—imperfectly. No good ever comes from our flesh. And although believers possess His Spirit, we don't possess Christ's judiciary qualities. We're not able to read hearts or gather information down to its "iota" in order to render a perfect and righteous judgment about others (John 7:24). We're also not perfect in loving others with the love and grace of Christ. Jesus said, *"As I hear, I judge; and My judgment is just"* (John 5:30). His knowledge and assessment of our sins and motives are perfect; His motives are pure; His agenda is God's will; His grace and truth are always in operation. Jesus judges with His Father's heart. Therefore, before falling into the trap of passing judgment inappropriately, we should be aware of God's perfect prerogative to judge and our own position before the Perfect Judge.

But we still want to exempt ourselves while in the throes of judging others. How do Romans 1:29–2:3 and James 2:10 address this notion?

_____

_____

Here's the bottom line about judging others: it requires that we ourselves are above judgment. Otherwise, judging others becomes sin. The power that we want to wield against others is not ours to wield. One of the reasons God, in His mercy, maintains this exclusive right is to keep us from condemning ourselves. He's protecting us and others because He knows the heart of man, and man's heart will judge unjustly.

Although Paul is addressing principles of conscience in Romans 14:10–13, he equates judging others with despising them. What is Paul's caution? How can judging others create stumbling blocks?

_____

_____

_____

Our condemning hearts can keep others stuck in sin (or us stuck in sin). We will not draw others to God if those of us who belong to Him convey by attitudes, words, or behavior that they deserve to be condemned. The condemned will run from the condemnation toward the very thing that makes them feel better—their place of bondage.

Christians who rest in God's love and grace can reach the hearts of others by that same love and grace. However, that love "should be more than sentimental; it should be knowledgeable and discerning. Having genuine spiritual knowledge (*epignosis*) of God and depth of insight into His ways enables Christians to love God and others more."[10]

If we truly understand the death knell that accompanies condemnation, we will resist the temptation to judge others. The human heart will judge out of self-righteousness rather than God-righteousness, out of retribution rather than redemption, with our own wills and agendas in mind rather than God's. Is it any wonder that Jesus said, "Don't do it!"

 **IN HER SHOES**

"My husband was carrying such a load of shame and condemnation about his sin that when he saw the opportunity to confess and repent and be free, he took it without hesitation. However, I will say that I believe that my reaction to the confession was a critical component in his response. If I had reacted with anger, condemnation, and judgment toward him, I believe that he would have felt attacked and he might have gone into a place of self-defense and justification. By responding to him with grace and love, I allowed him the space to be fully honest and to acknowledge his sin."

Prayer: Lord, You who test the minds and hearts, You are the judge of all people. Judge me, O Lord, according to Your righteousness. May I not be quick to judge but to discern so I can respond with Your loving knowledge and wisdom and pray when I am tempted to condemn myself or others.

DAY 3

THE REPENTANT HEART

When God is calling us to repentance, we hear it much like in Isaiah 44:22, *"Return to me, for I have redeemed you."* At that call, we know that we have no more excuses, no more denials, no more deceptions, no more lies, no more rationalizations, no more justifications, no more enabling. We have been totally and utterly exposed to *ourselves* by God. When that happens we can only move from self-focus to self-examination. We can no longer blame others. Rather, we know in our hearts that it's time to take personal responsibility for our choices and our reactions. There is only one word that describes this journey back to God. It's not a palatable or often-spoken word, but it is the pivotal point between freedom and bondage. It is *repentance*, and it is essential to the healthy and authentic Christian walk.

Recall from a previous lesson that *repentance* means to "turn around, change one's mind, relent, and in the theological sense involves 'regret or sorrow, accompanied by a true change of heart toward God.'"[11] Apart from repentance—to turn from sin and toward God—believers will continue to saunter toward their own Gomorrah.

Many of us have heard the story of the prodigal son. Let's take a fresh look at Luke 15:11–24. What did the second son request, and what was the result (v. 12)?

_____

_____

_____

In that culture, it was unheard of for a child to receive an inheritance prior to his father's death. The request was an astonishing act of insolence. That the father granted the request was an astonishing act of grace.

In verses 13–15, what did the younger son choose to do with his wealth? What was the personal outcome of that choice?

A wealthy young Jewish boy given over to feeding swine! Since swine were unclean animals, to come into contact with them was to defile oneself in the very worst way. It was "the lowest possible humiliation for a Jew."[12] It is noteworthy here that it was not the famine that had created his need. His choices did.

According to Luke 15:16, how bad did his circumstances become?

The prodigal son takes a hard assessment of himself, a self-examination if you will. What does he conclude (vv. 17–18)?

IN HER SHOES

"I give God the credit for our recovery. His Spirit touched my husband and brought him to repentance. His Spirit opened my mouth with wisdom and allowed me to speak with grace instead of judgment. His Spirit cleansed my husband and gave him a new heart. His Spirit quieted my anxious heart and gave me a firm place to stand."

Before the prodigal strayed, his generous father gave him everything he needed. He possessed riches beyond inheritance. He possessed security, love, provisions, position, and purpose. Instead, his ingratitude, rebellion, and insatiable lust gained him humiliating servitude and poverty. This story paints a powerful picture of one who chooses the servitude of sin over the wealth and freedom given us by our generous heavenly Father.

Consider this: We will always sin against God before we sin against another. We choose sin against God when we ignore His Spirit's promptings or reject His warnings. The Prodigal affirmed this in verse 18. How did King David affirm this in Psalm 51:4?

According to 1 Corinthians 11:32, what happens when sin puts us on the receiving end of God's judgment?

Returning to Luke 15:19 and 21, what understanding does the Prodigal come to about his condition? How does he act on this understanding?

_____

_____

According to Romans 2:4, what prompts repentance?

_____

_____

The Prodigal could have returned home with a sense of entitlement but instead *"he came to his senses"* (Luke 15:17). He saw the depravity of his choice; he saw himself unworthy to be called his father's son. In deep regret and remorse, he didn't just change how he thought about himself and his circumstances, but he acted on them. He knew that restoration could only take place when he returned and faced his father with a humble heart. This is repentance!

In Luke 15:20–24, what was his father's response to his son's return?

_____

_____

Shame didn't bring the prodigal home; godly sorrow did—right into his father's open arms!

Read 2 Corinthians 7:9-10. What is the difference between godly sorrow and worldly sorrow (v. 10)? What do you think this means?

_____

_____

_____

Although worldly sorrow is just a feeling, it is also a by-product of worldly living. It erupts after personal failures, humiliations, or exposures, and keeps us stuck in a place of deep humiliation. Worldly sorrow is counterfeit repentance. Godly sorrow, on the other hand results when we are painfully aware that we offended the Lover of our souls. It drives us to the cross in repentance and into God's welcoming arms because we desire to please Him more than we desire to please ourselves. Sorrow that is *"according to the will of God"* will do the will of God. That's the power of repentance.

> *"For the sorrow that is according to the will of God produces a repentance without regret, leading to salvation, but the sorrow of the world produces death."*
>
> 2 Corinthians 7:10 (NASB)

Oswald Chambers maintains that "repentance always brings a person to the point of saying, 'I have sinned.' The surest sign that God is at work in [a believer's] life is when he says that and means it. Anything less is simply sorrow for having made foolish mistakes—a reflex action caused by self-disgust"[13] (brackets ours).

Think about the last time that you were sorrowful for sin. Was it godly sorrow or worldly sorrow? What did your sorrow produce?

_____

_____

_____

You have an opportunity right now to lay this burden down. Take a minute, and consider the following: Do you harbor sexual sin or a sinful response to another's sin? Have you confessed it to the Lord and asked for forgiveness? If not, will you do so now? The ultimate lie is that we really don't need to repent to be set free from sin. Will you repent and lay this burden down?

_____

_____

_____

IN HIS SHOES
What Happens When We Won't Repent?

From what did each of these Christian churches have to repent? What does Jesus say would happen if they didn't repent? How does each of their problems relate to today's believers? Read Revelation 2:1–5, 12–16, 18–22; 3:1–3, 14–19.

Repentance is God's way home. Peter called all to *"repent and return, so that your sins may be wiped away, in order that times of refreshing may come from the presence of the Lord"* (Acts 3:19). When we repent and return, He will be waiting with open arms.

Prayer: Lord, when I offend You, free me by the power of repentance.

DAY 4

THE RESPONSIVE HEART: INWARD RIGHTEOUSNESS, OUTWARD EVIDENCE

An upright, repentant heart responds to God in measurable ways. What's on the inside will be evident on the outside. However, even unrepentant hearts may "look" righteous on the outside.

John the Baptist and Jesus confronted religious leaders over this very issue of inward righteousness and outward reflection. Read Matthew 3:7–8 and 23:27–28. What were their indictments and why?

_____

_____

_____

These religious leaders looked good on the outside, but they had unrepentant hearts. We all can look pretty good on the outside but may have hearts unresponsive to the Holy

Spirit. As our hearts respond to His promptings, leading, and guidance, the outside and the inside begin to align. The evidence of this alignment is called *fruit*.

> *As our hearts respond to the Holy Spirit's promptings, leading, and guidance, the outside and the inside begin to align. The evidence of this alignment is called "fruit."*

To understand how inward righteousness becomes outward evidence or fruit, let's look at Romans 12:1–2. What did Paul urge and why (v. 1)?

What circumstance is testing whether or not you are conforming or being transformed?

The word for *urge* or *beseech*, *parakaleo*, means "one who comes alongside someone else, as close as he can get, and then begins to passionately call out, plead, beckon, beg, and beseech that other person to do something on his behalf."[14] *The Amplified Bible* writes Paul's plea this way: "*I appeal to you therefore, brethren, and beg of you in view of [all] the mercies of God.*" Paul's sense of urgency rose out of God's great mercies. This compassionate God deserves a passionate response from those He saved.

Verse 1 (AMP) continues, "*to make a decisive dedication of your bodies—presenting all your members and faculties—as a living sacrifice, holy (devoted, consecrated) and well pleasing to God, which is your reasonable (rational, intelligent) service and spiritual worship.*" For a Jew, to present anything to God—whether a bull in sacrifice or the dedication of his firstborn son—was a holy and righteous act. Paul specifically uses the word *present* or *offer* or *dedicate* with the intent that we deliberately choose to yield not only our physical selves but "the totality of one's life and activities, of which his body is the vehicle of expression."[15] This, too, is an act of holiness and righteousness. What we do reflects the whole of who we are.

Fruit is the outward evidence of inner character. What do the following Scripture verses tell us about the fruit our lives can produce? What are the benefits of good fruit and/or the consequences of bad fruit?

Matthew 12:33–36

John 15:1–8

Galatians 5:22–23

Ephesians 5:8–10

Hebrews 12:11

James 3:17

"Therefore I urge you, brethren, by the mercies of God, to present
your bodies a living and holy sacrifice, acceptable to God, which is
your spiritual service of worship."

Romans 12:1 (NASB)

When we offer ourselves as living sacrifices, we will always produce good fruit. This is the evidence that we are rejecting the world's ways and yielding to the Holy Spirit's transforming power, a lifelong process. His power in us renews our minds, changes our hearts, and reshapes our characters. By His power, we learn to live out righteousness in our variety of trials, circumstances, and practices. In so doing, we guard our thought lives and self talk, temper our emotions, change reactions to responses, and soften our words. This is the outward reflection of inward righteousness.

Do your inside and your outside agree? Romans 12:9–21 indicates measurable evidence of the fruit you're producing as you grow in Christ, ways that reflect whether you are conforming to *"the pattern of this world"* (NIV) or being transformed by *"the renewing of your mind."* In the list that follows, put a "**C**" on the line in which you are more *Conformed* to the world's practice or a "**T**" on the line if you are being *Transformed*. Then record "fruit" that is evidence of either being conformed or becoming transformed, especially as it relates to how you respond in your current circumstances. You may be stronger or weaker in some of these areas.

This exercise just gives you a picture of the degree to which you are reflecting the One within.

___ Let love be without hypocrisy. Fruit?

___ Abhor what is evil. Fruit?

___ Cling to what is good. Fruit?

___ Be devoted to one another in brotherly love. Fruit?

___ Give preference to one another in honor. Fruit?

___ Don't lag behind in diligence. Fruit?

___ Be fervent in spirit. Fruit?

___ Serve the Lord. Fruit?

___ Rejoice in hope. Fruit?

___ Persevere in tribulation. Fruit?

___ Devote yourselves to prayer. Fruit?

___ Contribute to the needs of believers. Fruit?

___ Practice hospitality. Fruit?

___ Bless and don't curse those who persecute you. Fruit?

___ Rejoice with those who rejoice. Fruit?

___ Weep with those who weep. Fruit?

___ Be of the same mind toward one another. Fruit?

___ Don't be haughty in mind. Fruit?

___ Associate with the lowly. Fruit?

___ Don't be wise in your own estimation. Fruit?

___ Never pay back evil for evil to anyone. Fruit?

___ Respect what is right in the sight of all. Fruit?

___ Be at peace with all men. Fruit?

___ Never take your own revenge. Fruit?

___ Leave room for the wrath of God. Fruit?

___ If your enemy is hungry, feed him/her. Fruit?

___ If your enemy is thirsty, give him/her a drink. Fruit?

___ Do not be overcome by evil. Fruit?

___ Overcome evil with good. Fruit?

Write the number of C's you have here:_____. Write the number of T's you have here:_____.

Why is it important for you to know where you stand on the continuum of your faith walk? Do you see a particular pattern of conformity to the world or transformation? How does your pattern of *conformity* influence your struggle with your sexual sin or your reaction to the sin against you or a loved one? Be specific.

How does your pattern of *transformation* influence your struggle with sexual sin or your reaction to the sin against you or a loved one? Be specific.

Finally, Philippians 1:6 has an uplifting encouragement for those who truly desire to conform no longer but be transformed by the renewing of their minds. What is it?

The heart responsive to truth is responsive to God's maturation or transformation process and power. Transformation develops true inward righteousness that will always be reflected outwardly to the glory of God the Father.

> Prayer: Lord, I present my entire self to You as a living sacrifice—daily—holy and acceptable to You. May Your fruit of righteousness become more evident in me as You transform me by renewing my mind. May others see You as real in my life, whether I've caused much pain or have experienced much pain. Continue to transform me so that Your fruit of righteousness is evident more and more each day. In Jesus' name, Amen.

The Accountable Heart: Inward Accountability, Outward Reliability

 IN HER SHOES

"While I was active in church and having a daily relationship with God, I was faithful to my husband. When I took my eyes off God, then I went back to my cheating ways. So I divorced again. But even in single relationships, I could not remain faithful."

Accountability. Personal accountability. Accountability groups. Accountability partners. Hold me accountable. Hold you accountable. What does the word *accountability* conjure up in your mind?

_____

_____

Accountability in life strikes against humanity's self-serving hearts. For a variety of reasons, many shudder at the statement, "You need to be accountable." We are all accountable or answerable for the many obligations and requirements of life. When we give account, we make a statement explaining our conduct to include reasons, causes, and motives rather than rationalizations and justifications. Being accountable for who we are and what we do matters to others. It's the measure of our reliability and integrity. And it matters to God since we ultimately give account to Him.

Today we are going to focus on sexual accountability. It's a good thing when it's a God thing. Read Philippians 2:12–13. For what is a Christian accountable? What is God's part? How can this apply to sexual morality?

_____

_____

What does Luke 16:10 tell us about accountability? Now consider this verse from the perspective of sexual accountability. What is it saying? How does this verse speak to degrees of sexual activity?

_____

_____

Can you see a pattern of accountability in your life? Are you more accountable in some areas than others? Which one(s)? Are there any areas that are hands off when it comes to accountability? Would you say that you are accountable sexually? What is your response to God holding you answerable for your conduct? Do you think that sexual accountability to God is important for the believer? If so, why? If not, why not?

_____

The believers of Philippi were told to "work out, to put into practice in their daily living, what God had worked in them by His Spirit. They were not told to work *for* their salvation but to work *out* the salvation God had already given them."[16] In other words, we are to make our inward accountability to God outwardly reliable to others.

DID YOU KNOW?
God Owns the "Rights"

When someone creates or authors "a work," he has the copyright or patent on it. A copyright lasts for seventy-five years, at which time the original work shifts to public domain. Anyone may use the material without citing its whereabouts. On the other hand, a patent expires in seventeen years, after which the creation is up for grabs. Not so with God's creation or authorship. What God has created never ceases to be His. Therefore, creation will always be accountable to the Creator.

Here are some points to consider about being sexually accountable to God:

Sexual accountability to God recognizes and affirms His authorship of the act and its purpose. Revisit how Genesis 1:26–27 and 2:24 affirm this point?

What does it mean for you to be accountable to God as the Creator of your sexuality and its use, whether married or unmarried? Why should this matter to you?

Think about this: If you're currently in a sexual relationship outside of the marriage covenant, not only are you accountable to God for your choices, but you are accountable for your part in how your partner faces God on this matter. If you are married, you are also accountable to God for your choices in your sexual relationship with your husband.

Sexual accountability to God affirms His lordship. How do 2 Corinthians 6:16 and Ephesians 4:30 affirm this point?

What would accountability to God as Lord look like in your sexual relationship? Why is His lordship important in this?

We were designed to be mastered by the One who designed the "very good" and wants it for us. If we are not mastered by God, we will be mastered by evil, however benign its appearance.

Sexual accountability to God requires self-examination. What do Psalm 19:12–13 and 2 Corinthians 13:5 say or imply about self-examination? How does this relate to sexual accountability?

Do you openly and honestly examine yourself and your choices, especially as they relate to your sexual activities? What criteria do you use?

Pastor and author Mark Buchanan maintains that the whole Bible is "God-breathed and useful. If this stuff gets in you, down in your guts, it is going to shape you in ways beyond your asking or imagining . . .We don't probe and hairsplit and dissect the Bible; *it does that to us.*"[17] Accountability is determined by how we process God's truth. It's the Holy Spirit's job to lead us into all truth. He will reveal it to us. We just may not want to hear it.

Sexual accountability to God establishes dependence on Him for righteous sexual behavior. Healthy dependence on God will enable healthy interdependence with our spouses or future spouses. According to Psalm 139:1–12, what should compel us to be dependent on God for righteous sexual conduct?

> "Where can I go from Your Spirit? Or where can I flee from Your presence?"
>
> Psalm 139:7 (NASB)

Are you dependent on God for your sexual choices? If so, what do you do that reflects that dependence? If not, what do you do that rejects that dependence?

How can dependence on God's design for sex foster healthy interdependence with your husband? How can independence from God's design for sex foster unhealthy interdependence with your husband?

If we are not dependent on God, then we're apt to make poor sexual choices, married or not. The truth is this: Independence from God's divine design for sex eventually leads to bondage. God knows us perfectly. He scrutinizes our public ways as well as our most intimate moments. We can't hide from Him. Only the all-knowing, everywhere-present God can pierce any darkness, secure us, and equip us for righteous sexual conduct.

Sexual accountability to God promotes reliability and fidelity in a relationship. What does Romans 13:8–14 reveal is behind reliability and fidelity in a relationship?

Okay. Let's get real here. Why is reliability in your singleness, or marriage, or future marriage important?

How is love, like that described in Romans, reflected in your sexual choices, whether married or single? What does this say to God about the reliability of your relationship with Him? What does this say to others about your relationship with God? About the reliability of your relationship with your spouse or future spouse?

If we're to *"put on the Lord Jesus Christ, and make no provision for the flesh, to gratify its desires"* (Romans 13:14 ESV), then we must starve the old nature and feed the new nature.

Sexual accountability to God chooses and practices Holy Spirit self-control. Doing so builds spiritual strength and maturity. Based on 1 Corinthians 10:13 and Hebrews 4:14–16, what promises help us with sexual accountability? How do these build our strength and maturity?

We will protect someone we truly love from anything harmful, anything that would jeopardize their standing with Christ. And we should expect this same protection from the ones who say they love us. To say we love, yet live at the expense of another, makes us neither reliable nor trustworthy.

> *To say we love, yet live at the expense of another, makes us neither reliable nor trustworthy.*

Sexual accountability to God sets healthy sexual boundaries inside and outside of marriage. According to Matthew 5:27–30, 1 Corinthians 7:1–2, and Hebrews 13:4, what are the sexual boundaries God has set for us?

Do you resist God's boundaries on your sexual choices? If yes, why? If no, why not? What has been the outcome of your unwillingness or willingness to be sexually accountable to God?

Scripture is clear. As believers, His Word is our boundary.

We can choose to practice healthy, Holy Spirit-dependent self-control over flesh-dependent self-gratification. No matter what our temptations, Jesus Christ experienced them and overcame them. We can count on the Spirit's help to do the same in us. Practice makes permanent!

Where do you most need self-control in your sexual life? If self-control has been missing, how has it affected your strength and maturity? What escapes has the Holy Spirit given to you that you have ignored? Why have you ignored them? Please be candid with your answers.

Only within God's boundaries will we know sexual freedom, peace, blessing, and bounty. When we are accountable to Him, we will be reliable in our relationships. And we will have no fear when we are called to give account.

> Prayer: Father, You are Creator and Lord. Where can I go from Your Spirit? Where can I flee from Your presence? Help me to take an honest accounting of my sexual choices before You and before those to whom I am accountable. I receive Your extended hand of help and thank You for Your faithful presence, protection, and power in my life.

LESSON 9

THE FREEDOM FACTOR

We just finished talking about keeping our hearts accountable before God. However, sometimes we need a change in perspective before we can yield our hearts fully. We discover God's perspective when we look again to the cross. It was there that Christ bought our freedom. We must return there in order to access that freedom.

DAY 1

THE UNFORGIVENESS FACTOR

Our unwillingness to forgive does far greater damage to us than the original wound ever could.

We all wrestle with the issue of forgiveness. And we tend to measure its importance by whether we're asking for it or if we're asked to give it. Often, forgiveness makes no sense, making the Bible's requirement to forgive others far easier "read than done."

Therefore it's important to grapple with the issue of forgiveness.

The questions that follow are penetrating, perhaps even exposing, but purposeful. Before you begin, understand that you are in the presence of God and free to answer "naked" (with vulnerability) and "unashamed" (with abandon). This page is for your eyes only and not to be shared with anyone but you and God. Ask Him to help you answer the questions clearly and correctly, with truth and discernment. Do it alone and undisturbed. Note: You may not be dealing with forgiveness issues related to sexual sin. Regardless, do not neglect this exercise. All of us have offended or been offended in other areas, and we trust the Holy Spirit will speak to you. If you're genuinely not struggling with *any* offenses (yours or another's), don't think you must come up with something. Praise God with thanksgiving for this blessing. Let's begin.

Describe the sin that has impacted/is impacting your life.

_____

_____

_____

To what degree do lies or deception play a part in this sin?

What does your thought life consistently tell you about this sin and the person involved?

Identify the negative emotions you're dealing with as a result of this sin?

What impact are these emotions having on you?

What impact are these emotions having on your loved ones (husband, children, friends, person involved)?

What impact are these emotions having on your ability to live out your daily life (home-making, parenting, routine jobs and responsibilities, career, other commitments outside the home)?

What relationships have been the most seriously impacted as a result of this sin?

Do denial, rationalization, and/or justification play a factor at any time in how you coped with the sin or its discovery? If so, in what way?

How does the sin impact trust in your relationships?

What has been the most difficult aspect of dealing with this sin?

What impact does the sin have on your relationship with God?

This might have been a difficult exercise for you. But we want to encourage you that it has a purpose and a direction just like the painful experience itself. No matter how many books you read, no matter how many counselors you see, no matter how many friends you canvas, there really is only one answer to the offense of sexual sin or *any* sin. It is forgiveness through Jesus Christ—the costly purpose of the cross.

> Prayer: *"I will lift up my eyes to the mountains; from where shall my help come? My help comes from the LORD, Who made heaven and earth." . . . "I am the LORD your God, who upholds your right hand, Who says to you, 'Do not fear, I will help you.'"* Lord, forgiveness makes no sense, especially when it is undeserved. I am ready to understand, Lord. Teach me. (from Psalm 121:1–2 and Isaiah 41:13)

DAY 2

THE FORGIVENESS FACTOR

IN HER SHOES

"My husband dropped to his knees and crawled toward me as I dropped down beside him. He put his head into my lap, and we cried together. I told him that I loved him and forgave him. I told him that God loved him too and that he didn't have to live with this shame and guilt for one more second. The Holy Spirit spoke through me that day. I was dying inside. I was hurt, angry, bitter, vengeful, and broken inside. But I held my tongue and begged God to help me, to keep me from doing more damage than had already been done. God was faithful."

When we forgive, we're truly free—free to understand all relationships from a healthy perspective, free to discern which ones need healing and which ones need boundaries with the hope of healing, and free to move forward appropriately.

Unforgiveness inflicts its own wounds. It not only shackles others, it shackles us. The truth is that our unwillingness to forgive does far greater damage than the original wounds ever could. It weighs us down with ugly mental and emotional reactions to an offense. We become self-focused, offender-focused, and offense-focused. The Greeks have a visual for this concept of unforgiveness: The one unforgiven is roped to the back of the one who is unforgiving. We bind ourselves to one who has offended us most. Who's really carrying the burden? Think about that! Unforgiveness is a counterfeit bonding agent. We will be ever bound to its burden.

Consider the definition of forgiveness: "to let go from oneself, . . . to let go from one's power, possession, to let go free, . . . to let go from obligation toward oneself."[1] When you read this definition—especially in light of Day 1's exercise what's your first response?

Forgiveness makes no sense from our human perspective, but it makes perfect sense from God's perspective. Forgiveness frees us to focus on God, looses us from our offenses or from the effect of our offenders, and restores us to God. Think about that! Forgiveness is a divine bonding agent. We will ever be bound to its blessing.

You might say, *But wait a minute! What about the consequences of what he, she, or I have done?* We're not saying that there are no consequences associated with offenses, especially sexual offenses. We are saying that forgiveness is the only way to bring God's good and glory out of any offense and its consequences.

Scripture makes forgiveness and unforgiveness perfectly clear. Matthew 6:14–15 (AMP) says: *"For if you forgive people their trespasses [their reckless and willful sins, leaving them, letting them go, and giving up resentment], your heavenly Father will also forgive you. But if you do not forgive others their trespasses [their reckless and willful sins, leaving them, letting*

them go, and giving up resentment], neither will your Father forgive you your trespasses."
What do you think reckless sins are? What do you think willful sins are? What does this
passage mean for you as it relates to sexual offenses against you or a loved one, or perhaps
your own against another?

_____

_____

_____

The parable that follows makes the previous passage come alive. Matthew 18:23–35 tells
the story of the unmerciful servant. As you read the account, picture the king or master
as God, who wants to settle accounts with His servants. Picture the servant, who owes
much, roping the fellow servant, who owes little, to his back. What was the debt the first
servant owed his master (vv. 23 and 24)?

_____

_____

Consider this astounding fact: The servant owed his master the equivalent of thousands of
years of labor! In contrast, this same servant was owed by the other servant the equivalent
of one hundred days of labor.

Continuing in Matthew 18:23–35, when the master confronted the first servant about
the great debt owed him, how did the servant appeal to him (vv. 25–26)?

_____

_____

What were the master's three responses to the appeal (v. 27)?

_____

_____

Once the servant left the master's presence, what did he do? How did he treat his debtor
(v. 28)?

_____

_____

Did you note that the first servant went looking for the servant who owed him? When
someone owes us, we too, may want to grab him by the throat and yell, You owe me! And
maybe he really does owe us. The offense is legitimate. Often our deliberate intent is to
inflict punishment, rather than forgive. What was the debtor's response (v. 29)? What did
the first servant do (v. 30)?

_____

_____

_____

In Matthew 18:27, how did the master's approach differ from the first servant's approach to his debtor?

_____

_____

_____

When the master heard of how the servant treated his debtor, what did he do (vv. 32–34)? What does this mean for all who refuse to forgive?

_____

_____

_____

What was Jesus' warning in verse 35? What do you think He meant? What do you think it means to forgive _"from your heart"?_ [2]

_____

_____

_____

What the servant really owed his forgiving master was gratitude, praise, and honor, because his debt had been so great and impossible to pay. Because the servant didn't consider the master's mercy and extend to his debtor that which he had received, he was imprisoned for his hard, merciless heart (v. 35). In the same way, unforgiveness in our hearts will imprison us. When we refuse to forgive, God will turn us over to our jailers and torturers—anger, bitterness, hostility, resentment, anxiety, depression, and more. Yes, we can make our debtor pay a high price but not nearly the price we'll pay spiritually, physically, mentally, emotionally, and relationally for the sin of unforgiveness. Remember, the person we won't forgive is tied to our back. We're carrying the load; we're carrying the burden. And it's heavy.

Here's the tough truth about unforgiveness: If we don't take seriously God's command to forgive, we cheapen Jesus' work of forgiveness on the cross. When we take for ourselves all that it cost Jesus to free us from our incalculable debt and refuse to free others from their sins against us, we are in sin. Founder of Desert Stream Ministries, Andrew Comiskey, put it powerfully:

> We need to exercise the power of resurrection by forgiving our wounders. This is crucial. In order for Jesus to bear our suffering, we must release our captors to him. Our sufferings are bound up into the wounds of Christ when we entrust our perpetrators to him. When we refuse to forgive, we continue to bear suffering without his release. This is a process, which often involves many choices to forgive. But forgive we must for Jesus' sake and on behalf of our own freedom. Sufferers who go the way of the cross in their wounds become healers. [3]

IN HER SHOES

"If we confess our sins, God will forgive us and cleanse us. How could I live with God forgiving me and God forgiving my husband but my not forgiving my husband? Thankfully, the Holy Spirit won, and I forgave my husband before he asked for it. I didn't excuse his actions, but I forgave him."

Would you agree that all believers receive compassion, release, and forgiveness from the Master for their incalculable debt? This is the basis by which you can choose to forgive another from your heart. With this in mind, if you (or a loved one) were sinned against, what does your debtor owe you? What have you done about that debt? If you have reacted like the first servant, what do you hope to gain by exacting payment from your debtor? If you refuse to forgive like the first servant, where does that leave you with the Master?

_____

_____

_____

If you owe another, what have you done to seek forgiveness? If he or she refuses to forgive you (as if you were the second servant), how would you respond to the one who won't forgive? Where does that leave you with the Master?

_____

_____

_____

How would you apply this parable to your personal circumstances?

_____

_____

_____

If you're thinking that what you've done or another has done is unforgivable—too costly—what has this parable taught you?

_____

_____

_____

IN HIS SHOES
Hosea 1—3:5

It's not easy to forgive. God knew this and gave us a picture of what His forgiveness of us looks like. Read this account in Hosea. List what Hosea forgave and why. What happened in the end? How does this illustrate God's love for us?

Many of us may be unable to forgive ourselves because of our struggles with sexual sin or its consequences. Consider this: Nowhere in Scripture are we commanded to forgive ourselves. If we have accepted God's forgiveness for our sins and yet we won't forgive ourselves, then we're saying that what our Savior did on the cross was not payment enough for what we've confessed. Receiving God's forgiveness says, "I agree that I am forgiven." It's that simple.

 IN HER SHOES

"I took my sin to the foot of the cross, the only place where one can receive true freedom. In time, I was eager and determined to fully be healed. I completed a post-abortion Bible study through my local crisis pregnancy center along with three other post-abortive women. Only by knowing Christ, realizing that He died for all my sins (even my abortion), and receiving His forgiveness, grace, and mercy could I be fully restored. God's offering of mercy and forgiveness was instantaneous, but it took time to heal psychologically, emotionally, and spiritually. When doubt sets in, I remember to check these thoughts against Scripture and renew my mind with God's truth."

What we really owe our Master for His forgiveness of all our debts—past, present, and future—is *gratitude*. Only then can we forgive others from our hearts.

Just prior to this parable, Peter asked Jesus a tough question, to which Jesus gave a tougher answer. Read Matthew 18:21–22. What was Peter's question?

_____

_____

What was Jesus' answer, and what do you think He meant?

_____

_____

Jesus' message of "seventy times seven" or "seventy-seven times" is that our requirement to forgive has no limit. This might be difficult to accept since forgiveness makes us vulnerable from a human perspective. But from a spiritual perspective, forgiveness is the power of God.

If there has been repeated sin resulting in repeated wounding in your life (by the same person), and you had just told Jesus about this sin cycle, how would you genuinely respond to His answer to Peter's question?

_____

_____

What follows are some thoughts you may have about forgiving: What if . . .

He's (she's) repentant, but I'm not ready to forgive yet? Like all of God's principles, forgiveness offers us the opportunity to obey God. When you forgive, you're not condoning another's activity; you're releasing that person to God for His work in his or her life. Revisit Matthew 6:14–15. Why does Jesus command you to forgive, ready or not?

_____

_____

_____

I still can't trust him (her)? Forgiving isn't the same as trusting. One is required; the other is earned. Distrust is a legitimate consequence for betrayal; therefore, your present inability to trust should be conveyed to your offender. The good news is that when you can't trust someone, you can trust God with that someone. Read Psalm 3:5–6. What would giving your distrust to God look like in your case?

_____

_____

_____

He's (she's) unrepentant and justifies the sin? Read Jeremiah 5:3, Psalm 7:11–12, and 1 Corinthians 5:1–5 in that order. We can't make others repent. Only the Holy Spirit can convict them of sin. And God knows what it will take. That's when we pray, "Whatever it takes, Lord." Repentance may be a long time coming or may never come. But when we follow God and decide to forgive, our emotions are no longer in charge. God is, and we'll be where God wants us— able to discern which relationships will need healing, which will need boundaries, and how to walk forward in both. Why do you think this person justifies the sin? What insight does your answer give you into this person?

_____

_____

_____

He (she) keeps on doing the same thing over and over again because he (she) thinks I am weak, a doormat, or am giving him (or her) permission? Forgiveness isn't about sanctioning sin but about doing the right thing in the strength of the Lord. Read Ephesians 6:10. On whose strength are you currently depending? How would God ask you to stand differently so that His way and not your own is accomplished?

_____

_____

_____

He (she) gets off without punishment? That's unfair! Really wrap your mind around God's job. Read Romans 12:19. If we refuse to forgive, we are exercising God's prerogative. What have you entertained in your mind that would avenge what your offender did to you or a loved one? How would that help? And if you're the offender, think about what would turn your heart around or what did. Christian counselor June Hunt says, "*Forgiveness is not based on what is fair. It was not fair for Jesus to hang on the cross, but He did so that we could be forgiven.*"[4]

He (she) doesn't understand how badly I've been hurt? This too is no excuse for unforgiveness. God knows how badly you were hurt. Run to Him for understanding, comfort, and direction. Then your heart will be prepared to forgive. Read Lamentations 3:55–59. Why is it important to cry out to God when you have been badly hurt?

_____

_____

He (she) won't reconcile with me? Forgiveness and reconciliation are not the same. A willing heart forgives; two willing hearts reconcile. And much like repentance, we can't make others reconcile. We can only take care of our part and leave the rest to God. Read Romans 12:18. What is your part?

_____

_____

Note the self-focus in all of the preceding "what if's." What are the "what if's" associated with forgiving your offender?

_____

_____

And if you're the one who requires forgiveness for sexual sin, do you have a "what if?" If so, what is it?

_____

_____

_____

Do we really want to have others punished? Some of us might respond with a resounding yes! But let's ask this another way. Do we ourselves really want to be punished? No, not really. Not even close! We want help; we want hope; we want a chance to course correct; we want grace and mercy. We want forgiveness. We *need* forgiveness and everything the cross offers. And when we receive it (which we did), how can we not pay it forward?

> Prayer: Lord, You forgave my trespasses, my reckless and willful sins. Prepare my heart to do the same—to forgive as You have forgiven me. In Jesus' name.

DAY 3

FORGIVENESS UNWRAPPED

Christ has given us assurance that we are forgiven; therefore, He gives us a compelling reason to forgive from our hearts. But how do we do that? Forgiveness is an ongoing choice to obey God out of gratitude for His forgiveness of our sins. Let's unwrap what forgiving should look like.

Forgive from the heart before entering into dialog toward resolution. Read Ephesians 4:29–32. When we enter into dialog determined to forgive based on another's response, we're not forgiving as Christ forgave. What does the Ephesians passage say in support of this point?

Trust that God won't minimize others' egregious offenses against you. Read Psalm 37:7–9. We can't pretend something didn't happen. Through forgiveness, we can release an offense to God, who won't minimize it but will properly deal with it and the offender in His timing, in His way, and with His wisdom. He can even bring great blessing from it. Do you trust God to properly deal with the offense? With the offender? If so, why? If not, why not?

As it relates to forgiveness, don't cooperate with the world, the flesh, or the enemy but walk in the Holy Spirit. Read Ephesians 4:26–27, and James 1:19–20. If we forgive as God forgave, we will bear spiritual fruit. If we forgive according to the world, the flesh, or the devil (conditional forgiveness, no forgiveness, or get even), we will bear worldly, fleshly, or evil fruit. If you've been unforgiving, what fruit has that produced? If you haven't been forgiven, what fruit has been produced?

Be willing to entrust yourself to God. Read 1 Peter 2:23 and Romans 12:17–21. When we do this, we will have no reason to "get even." Forgiveness doesn't mean that we must "allow those who have injured us back into our lives, and more importantly into our hearts, without *them* making an effort. If the *other* person doesn't make some sacrifice or invest-ment in the process of healing, the relationship cannot be restored to its former state. If a true process of reconciliation is to take place, it requires two people working together collaboratively to repair and reestablish the relationship."[5] If our offender is repentant, we owe him or her every opportunity toward restoration. How does this insight change the way you respond to your offender? If you are struggling with sexual sin, what do you think entrusting yourself to God could mean for you?

_____

_____

_____

Don't ignore recurrent sin. Read Galatians 6:1. Forgive and then address it in truth and in Christ's example of love. If the Lord leads us to address sin, and we won't, we enable the offender to continue on a destructive path. God's goal through Jesus Christ in us is about restoration not about condemnation. Would God have you address this recurrent sin? If so, in what way? If not, how is the Spirit leading you to respond to this sin? If you are struggling with recurrent sexual sin yourself, has anyone addressed you? If so, how did the person do so and how did you respond? Whether you addressed another or another addressed you, are you holding onto unforgiveness regarding those interactions?

_____

_____

_____

Be prepared to bear potential consequences of the sin you forgive. Read 1 Corinthians 13:7 and 2 Corinthians 1:3–4. When we choose forgiveness, God will faithfully see us through any and all consequences of the sin, strengthening us as we continue to trust and depend on Him. Author Meg Wilson writes, "When our injuries are great, we need to process through layers of forgiveness . . . I needed time to process through all the consequences I was agreeing to live with. The first layer was forgiving him for the pain of the overall betrayal, but additional layers were uncovered that had to be sifted through. Emotional, spiritual, financial, and family issues are just a few of those layers. It took time for me to realize how many layers there were and how each area had been affected.[6] What consequences were/are attached to a sexual sin you must forgive? How has that affected your willingness to forgive? When will you begin to process forgiveness? What consequences were/are attached to a sexual sin for which you must ask forgiveness of God and potentially of another or others?

_____

_____

_____

Don't assume that quick forgiveness is full forgiveness. Read Psalm 51:6. June Hunt makes this point: "Many well-intentioned people feel guilty if they don't extend immediate forgiveness, so they 'forgive' quickly. They have *neither* faced the full impact of the events nor grieved over what happened. Rarely is the full impact of sin felt at the moment it occurs."[7] The person involved in the sexual sin may not understand the impact it had on your lives and/or your family. As you encounter new knowledge about the sin and the offender, you may have to extend new forgiveness. If you are struggling with sexual sin, do you expect or encourage a quick forgiveness and then move on? What is your responsibility as it relates to a loved one's forgiveness of your sin?

_____

_____

_____

Pray for your offender, no matter how painful your ordeal. Read Matthew 5:43–45 and James 5:16. You don't have to *feel* forgiveness before you pray, because prayer is an obedient act of your will in response to the will of God. It's enabled by the Holy Spirit. How would God have you pray for your offender? If you are struggling with sexual sin, is anyone praying on your behalf?

_____

_____

_____

Let forgiveness guard you against bitterness. According to 1 Corinthians 13:5, how does bitterness begin? What does Ephesians 4:31-32 reveal as evidence that we're already bitter and the remedy? Where are you on a continuum of bitterness toward another?

_____

_____

_____

In what way has your struggle with sexual sin embittered loved ones? In what way has your struggle made you bitter? Toward whom? Whether offender or offended, how can forgiveness guard you against bitterness?

_____

_____

_____

Forgiving is not the same as trusting. Revisit Ephesians 4:31–32. For the one or ones who violated or betrayed you or one you love, forgiving is an act of faith and trust in Christ and not in the offender. God will provide the courage to forgive; He will also provide the discernment and wisdom when trust is breached. Forgiveness and trust "are closely tied and are simultaneous processes. Trust takes longer to rebuild."[8] But it is impossible to build trust at all when unforgiveness stands between two people. Are you withholding forgiveness because trust has been breached? What will you do about that?

_____

_____

_____

> *"Let all bitterness and wrath and anger and clamor and slander be*
> *put away from you, along with all malice.*
> *Be kind to one another, tender-hearted, forgiving each other,*
> *just as God in Christ also has forgiven you."*
>
> Ephesians 4:31–32 (NASB)

Forgive your offender "from your heart"—a heart of gratitude for how you've been forgiven. Read Psalm 103:12, Mark 11:25, and Hebrews 8:12. When we forgive, we no longer bring up our offender's sin to use against him or her. We may not be able to erase the memory, but we can choose to quit replaying it in our minds. God will meet us in this place of obedience. How do you rehash offenses against you? Over coffee with a friend (or lots of friends)? With your children about their father? With anyone who will listen? Remember to check your self-talk to see how it feeds and supports your forgiveness.

Let forgiveness change you. Read Romans 6:8–11. Forgiveness is the ultimate act of death to self and God's greatest agent of change—our change and potentially the change in others. What is your response to this?

_____

_____

God would never require anything of us that He didn't first require of Himself through the person of His Son, Jesus Christ: *"Father, forgive them"* (Luke 23:34). And by the power of His Holy Spirit, we have the capacity to do the same.

> Prayer: Father, forgive my debts as I forgive my debtors . . . from the heart!

DAY 4

FREE AT LAST! OUR PART AND GOD'S PART

How long have we carried around our offenders? Though Scripture encourages us to carry one another's burdens, God never intended that we carry the unforgiven around as burdens. In order to lay those burdens down at the foot of the cross, we need to understand the difference between the work that we do and that which God does.

GOD'S PART AND OUR PART: SEXUAL SIN AGAINST US OR ONES WE LOVE

Day 1 exposes the offender(s) that God requires us to forgive. We are able to forgive these people because God in Christ forgave us. And because He dwells in us, we now have the capacity to forgive as He forgave, or He wouldn't require it.

What do Mark 11:25; John 8:32, 36; 15:5, and Philippians 4:13 imply is our part in forgiving? What is God's part?

_____

_____

Return to Day 1. We've addressed every aspect of forgiveness. If your offenders are still roped to your back with the cords of unforgiveness, it's time to cut the cords, set them free, and unburden your heart before the Lord.

 IN HER SHOES

"I have sought the Lord not only for healing for myself and my children but in truly forgiving my spouse. Many times by the grace of God, I really believe that I have forgiven, but there are still times I must choose to let it go and not go back there. A very wise counselor told me once that 'you can't move forward looking in your rearview mirror.' I try to recall all that Christ gave up for me and the forgiveness only His death could accomplish. All the pain I have experienced does not come close to His sacrifice."

Out of obedience to the Father, choose to forgive your offender(s)—whoever hurt you or betrayed you, whoever disappointed you, whoever did not meet your expectations—as God in Christ forgave you. Your decision to forgive is not based on how you feel but on your willingness to obey God's command. When you do the right thing, the right feelings will follow with time. God will see to it.

As you sit before the Lord with your mind focused on Him, be assured that He is with you right now. He is loving you, encouraging you, guiding you, because He is for you. The prayer of forgiveness that follows can settle this once for all just as Jesus settled your sins once for all.

Prayer of Forgiveness: Father, by the great sacrifice of Jesus' death, You forgave my sins. Now, as an act of my will and out of obedience to You, I forgive (name the offender) _____ for (name the offenses) _____ I have permitted these offenses to create in me feelings of (name the feelings) _____ _____. My unforgiveness has mastered my thoughts, my emotions, and my actions toward this person. I desire now to let him/her off my hook for every offense and to be mastered by Your Holy Spirit. Help me to follow His leading. I entrust _____ to You, Lord. I also entrust myself to You. Glorify Yourself in this act of obedience. Work in me to will and to act according to Your good purpose, especially when I'm offended in the future. In the matchless name of the living Word, Jesus Christ, "It is finished."

"So if the Son makes you free, you will be free indeed."

John 8:36 (NASB)

According to Psalm 103:12, God separates us from our sins *"as far as the east is from the west,"* and He says, *"I will remember their sins no more"* (Hebrews 8:12). This does not mean that God has forgotten our sins, because He is omniscient. It does mean that He won't use our sins against us anymore. He requires us to forgive in the same way. There may be more sins to process in our circumstances and more forgiveness yet to grant, but with each opportunity to forgive, we are free to move forward.

A word of warning: Down the road, Satan will try to convince you that you've not forgiven your offender because of the way you sometimes feel. Remember, God was a witness to your decision to forgive, and He is rejoicing over you. Continue to put your thought life under His authority, submitting it to Him. Resist the enemy's attempts to return you to jail. Practice the habit of correct thinking (Philippians 4:8) and, over time, the correct feelings will follow. The prayer of continued release will help you practice this habit:

> Prayer of Continued Release: Dear Lord, I forgave _____ for _____, and I will not re-rope him/her to my back. I place these thoughts under Your authority, Jesus, and move forward to stand firm in the forgiveness I have already granted. I will think on *"whatever is true, whatever is honorable, whatever is right, whatever is pure, whatever is lovely, whatever is of good repute, if there is any excellence and if anything worthy of praise, [I will] dwell on these things"* (Philippians 4:8 brackets ours) so that You might be glorified in my obedience. In Jesus' name. Amen.

When any new offenses occur—and there will likely be some—keep a clean slate, and start fresh by working through the first prayer again.

GOD'S PART AND OUR PART: WHEN WE ARE STRUGGLING WITH OUR OWN SEXUAL SIN

How does forgiveness apply to someone who is struggling? Have you asked for forgiveness only to find yourself giving way to temptation and falling back into sexual sin? It's not how many times we ask for forgiveness, but what our heart's motives are when we ask. God will work with the truly repentant sinner until the bondage is broken, no matter what it takes.

According to Acts 19:18, James 5:16, and 1 John 1:9, what is our part? What is God's part? What do you think it means to confess your sins? What do you think it means that God is faithful and just to forgive you? To cleanse you from all unrighteousness?

The definition of confession is to "speak back." When we are honest about our sins with ourselves and with God, we speak back *to* Him what we just heard *from* Him.

Psalm 143 is a penitential psalm that makes us aware of our deep need for forgiveness, rescue, and restoration. Prayerfully read this psalm aloud to the Lord in order to prepare your heart for confession.

Take time now to confess your sexual sins before God. Be specific.

Next, from 1 John 1:9 and for each sin, express God's faithfulness and righteousness to forgive you for that sin: "Lord, You are faithful and righteous (just) to forgive my sin(s) of _____."

Last, from 1 John 1:9 and for each sin, express God's faithfulness and righteousness to cleanse you from that sin: "Lord, You are faithful and righteous (just) to cleanse me from my sin(s) of _____."

Remember, when God forgives you, it is finished! Settle your heart and mind before the Lord, confident that your confession has been heard. Then choose to believe that God has forgiven you, that you are guilt free. He will finish the good work in you that He has begun (Philippians 1:6).

DAY 5

FORGIVENESS IN ACTION

We're not only to forgive as God forgives but to love as God loves, and His love is *agape* (God's love in us). As with forgiveness, allowing God to manifest His love through us toward those who have wounded us is a decision we make, not an emotion we wait for. We do so in obedience to His command to love. Forgiveness opens the door to *agape*; *agape* keeps the door open to continued forgiveness. We cannot walk in God's *agape* if we are unwilling to forgive, and we cannot forgive without *agape* at work in and through us. *Agape* is the only love that can heal wounded hearts. And because God is its source, *agape* can never be exhausted. *Agape* is so pure and untainted by fickle emotions that it can withstand any relational wounding or threat and still mature its giver. God's way works, especially when circumstances seem impossible. First, we must trust God's way; then we must practice it! God will prove Himself on the other side of our faith and obedience.

> EXTRA MILE
> God's Love in Us
>
> Read 1 John 2:9–11, 12–18; 4:7–21. List all the ways in which God's love in us (*agape*) is evident.

We may ask, *So what is agape supposed to look like in real life and in painful situations?* The most practical biblical guidance is found in 1 Corinthians 13:1–8. If you have read or done a study on this passage before, we encourage you to do the exercises that follow as if for the first time. Verses 1–3 give three examples of an impotent, fruitless Christian walk. Whenever you read the word *love* in these three verses, substitute the word *agape*. As Christians, if we don't have *agape*, what will our walk look like in:

Verse 1

Verse 2

Verse 1 describes treasured gifts as purposeless and meaningless when used without *agape*. Verse 2 describes powerful gifts as futile and useless when used without *agape*. Verse 3 describes sacrificial gifts as empty and worthless when offered without *agape*.

Agape is the ultimate, critical, and essential component of relationships. Whatever we say or do that is without *agape* counts for nothing.

Agape abides in a Christian because God abides in the Christian. When the Bible tells us that God is love, it is literally saying that God is *Agape* (1 John 4:16). Romans 5:5 affirms that *"the love of God has been poured out within our hearts through the Holy Spirit who was given to us."* Now read 1 Corinthians 13:4–8 and substitute "God's love in me" every time the word *love* or its pronoun is used. What do you conclude from this exercise?

In the chart that follows, some of the attributes of 1 Corinthians 13:4–5 are *outward behaviors* of *agape*. Circle the traits that are most difficult for you. Then in the next column, write how you can practice each *agape* behavior (circled or not) toward the one who has wounded you in any way. (Note: Even if your offender is far removed, which characteristics can you apply even if only in your own heart?)

Outward Behaviors of *Agape* (Habit)	Situations in Which I Can Practice Each *Agape* Behavior
Endures long, is patient	
Kind	
Never is envious; doesn't boil over with jealousy	
Is not boastful; is not vainglorious, does not display itself haughtily	
Is not conceited, arrogant, or inflated with pride	
Is not rude (unmannerly); does not act unbecomingly	
Does not insist on its own rights or its own way; not self-seeking	

IN HER SHOES

"Like a festering wound, the sin had to be opened up and brought into the light so that all the filth could be thoroughly cleaned out. After all that exposure, a good number of friends and acquaintances expressed their continuing love and prayers for us. We were truly humbled by God's amazing provision of so many loving and forgiving friends. They did not condone the sin but were there to help us heal."

In the chart that follows, the attributes of verses 5–8 are positive *inner attitudes* of *agape*. In the right column, write how you can practice these attributes of *agape* in your personal circumstances, (Note: If your offender is far removed, which characteristics can you apply in your own heart?

Inner Attitudes of *Agape* (Heart)	How I Can Practice *Agape* in My Circumstances?
Is not touchy, fretful, resentful	
Keeps no record of wrong	
Agape rejoices when right and truth prevail and over whatever could lead another to repentance.	
Agape "bears up under anything and everything that comes" (AMP)	
Agape is "ever ready to believe the best of every person" (AMP). When we can't trust a loved one, we can trust God with him/her.	
Agape's "hopes are fadeless under all circumstances" (AMP). God is able to bring good out of any circumstance	
Agape "endures everything [without weakening]" (AMP). Persevering love strengthens us to love perseveringly and do the hard and righteous things. As we exercise *agape*, God applies His strength moment by moment. *Agape* doesn't give up, give over, or give in.	
Agape "never fails [never fades out or becomes obsolete or comes to an end]" (AMP)! Human love will fail us when we face egregious sin. God's *agape* in us will never fail us or another because it is both merciful and just. Will *agape* change our loved one? Perhaps, perhaps not. But it will change us.	

This 1 Corinthians 13 passage tells us what believers' outer behaviors and inner attitudes should look like regardless of our circumstances. How does this picture differ from your heart and conduct currently?

_____

_____

_____

"Love never fails."

1 Corinthians 13:8

Pastor and counselor Tim Alan Gardner illuminates *agape* by maintaining that loving unconditionally doesn't mean we "put up with harmful, destructive behavior. God does not want us to tolerate abuse, a sexual affair, a partner's addiction to pornography, alcohol, or drugs, or any other destructive behavior. Those situations must be dealt with head-on and without retreat or compromise."[9] True agape requires courage.

Agape is not afraid but resolute. What encouragement does 1 John 4:18 give about addressing one's own sin? What encouragement does it give as we relate to others who are in sin?

_____

_____

_____

The Common English Bible puts 1 John 4:18 this way: *"There is no fear in love, but perfect love drives out fear, because fear expects punishment. The person who is afraid has not been made perfect in love."* We might find ourselves cowering, enabling, or cooperating with sin in relationships out of fear of others' responses or the outcomes. We may also find ourselves punishing others so that they cower in fear. And if we're the offenders, we may be afraid to approach God or others. Although we may not trust who hurt us or who we hurt, we can trust God with both.

Oswald Chambers writes, "When a moral person is confronted with contempt, immorality, disloyalty, or dishonesty, he is so repulsed by the offense that he turns away and in despair closes his heart to the offender. But the miracle of the redemptive reality of God is that the worst and the vilest offender can never exhaust the depths of His [*agape*] love"[10] (brackets ours).

> Prayer: Lord, may Your *agape* enable me to forgive, to live above my circumstances and pain. I entrust my situation to You, because Your purposes for me are pure, Your plans for me are sovereign, Your power in me is sufficient, Your promises to me are precious, and Your love for me is perfect—a love that remains in me as I remain in You.

LESSON 10

A LOVED ONE'S STRUGGLE

Does anyone respond well to the discovery of a loved one's pornography use or infidelity, or worse? Our instinctive and visceral emotional reaction is normal. Often when our initial reaction subsides, many of us just want to get beyond the problem. However, God may call us to be part of the resolution, and, if so, He'll give us the means to do so. That begins with understanding the problem and our place in its solution.

There are signs when a loved one is struggling with sexual sin. In this lesson we offer suggestions on how to prayerfully *confront the problem* and *engage the person* with care and intent. These terms *confront* and *engage* are purposefully used throughout the rest of this lesson. We ask that you do the entire five-day lesson before you act on anything you know or think you know. Even if you don't know anyone who is struggling, please do this lesson for the insights you will gain.

> *Our prayer is that you will learn to prayerfully*
> *confront the problem and engage the person.*

Although there is no guarantee that relationships will be restored or that a loved one in sexual sin will give it up willingly to follow God's divine design (John 3:19–20), as you continue to follow God, your relationship with Him will grow and strengthen. May our loved ones come to the realization that God alone is the source of all that is real, true, and fulfilling. He alone "can overcome the sin in our hearts that damages our relationships."[1]

DAY 1

RECOGNIZING THE PROBLEM

 IN HER SHOES

"My husband lied to me for nine years. He lied to me about the pornography, about his relationship with God, and about his affair. I had a strong gut feeling that something wasn't right. I specifically asked him about it (in a joking way so as not to offend), and he responded with anger. He accused me of not trusting him and declared that I should get over my fear. He lied a lot and for a long time."

RECOGNIZING THE PROBLEM

Sometimes prospectors will mine for rare stones by looking at the outward rock and land formations. It does not always yield what they believe is there, but it is a place of beginning. This is true for any checklist of signs pointing to sexual sin or bondage. Lists are only places to begin. But before we begin, a caution: Many may rely on intuition when trying to arrive at answers to questions or suspicions. Intuition is a gift that tells us something might be wrong, but it usually doesn't tell us what is wrong. Until evidence is found and sexual sin is verified, we need to exercise caution in the assumptions we make. There may be more than one cause for what is observed. For example, a husband may not have a pornography habit just because he's withdrawing from lovemaking. It may be because he doesn't trust that his erections will meet the requirements, especially if age and stress have taken their toll on his body. And a loved one may not be in an adulterous affair if his hours away have increased. Work may be a genuine concern and preoccupation that could affect mood, time, and connectedness. Ask God to expose any sin, *"for there is nothing concealed that will not be revealed, or hidden that will not be known"* (Matthew 10:26). He will clarify the facts.

What follows are typical signs that suggest a problem.

Pornography: How do we know if a spouse is involved with pornography? The signs that follow can indicate struggles. If any of these apply, circle the bullets:

- Diminished intimacy
- Loss of interest in sexual relations (Note: Loss of interest due to pornography should not be confused with that associated with medical or emotional anomalies.)
- Insatiable, compulsive sexual appetite
- Introduction of unusual or bizarre sexual practices in the relationship
- Preference for masturbation over sexual relations with spouse
- Sexual relations that are rigid, rushed, without passion, detached
- Withdrawal from family
- Neglect of responsibilities in the home or on the job
- Increased isolation (such as late night hours on the computer)
- Intensified irritation, highly defensive reactions, irregular mood swings, or depressed moods
- Unexplained absences
- Unusual or unexplained financial transactions
- Evidence of hiding computer usage
- Discovery of notes, Internet sites, unexpected packages in the mail[2]

Based on what you have circled, what are you seeing or perceiving that sends up red flags? Be specific. Is there tangible proof that a problem may exist? Can you deduce a reason other than pornography use?

_____

_____

_____

How do we know if a child is involved in pornography? "Boys are not the only ones vulnerable to pornography. In the past, girls seldom got involved in viewing hard-core materials (although this is rapidly changing because of the Internet). Now, girls and women become hooked on pornography mostly through the 'gateway' of romance novels and Internet chat rooms or forums."[3] The following are warning signs of a child's possible involvement in pornography:

- Suspicious phone activity: pictures, texts, or charges (sexting or use of 900 numbers)

- Inordinate amount of time on the computer; visits to pornographic sites

- Loss of interest in usual activities

- Falling grades

- Embarrassment or quick to hide things when one unexpectedly enters the room

- Distractibility; inability to concentrate; fidgety

- Disrespectful, casual, frequent humor about sex

- Moodiness when deprived of TV, video, or Internet privileges

- Unaccounted-for periods of time or time spent secretively or reclusively in order to access pornographic material

- Deceit, lies that cover up activities or whereabouts, especially after school

- Stealing to support habit including from parents' wallets and shoplifting

- Possessing sexually stimulating materials in his or her room: wall posters, music, or magazines

- Wearing sexually stimulating clothing styles: tight, revealing clothing, t-shirts with sexual innuendos on them[4]

Based on what you have circled, what are you seeing or perceiving that sends up red flags? Be specific. Is there tangible proof that a problem may exist? Can you deduce a reason other than pornography use?

_____

_____

_____

_____

> *"You are a slave to whatever controls you."*
>
> 2 Peter 2:19 (NLT)

Second Peter 2:19 (ESV) tells us that *"whatever overcomes a person, to that he is enslaved."* A sin practiced becomes a lifestyle. And pornography is usually a progressive practice. Left unchecked by conviction and repentance, pornography will pull one ever further into darkness.

Adultery: How do we know if a spouse is unfaithful? If any of these apply, circle the bullet:

- Change in physical appearance: clothes, jewelry, cologne
- Change in behavior, mood
- Change in spending patterns, unexplained bills
- Change in schedule—working later or on weekends, more business trips
- Fewer personal conversations
- Less emotional intimacy, vulnerability (sharing from the heart)
- Fewer discussions of future plans
- Less spontaneity
- Less sexual intimacy
- More faultfinding
- More emotional distance
- More unexpected gifts (guilt gifts)
- More anger at being questioned[5]

Based on what you have circled, what are you seeing or perceiving that sends up red flags? Be specific. Is there tangible proof that a problem may exist? Can you deduce a reason other than adultery?

_____

_____

_____

_____

If we discover that a loved one is in sexual sin, we will experience a gamut of emotions. This reaction is normal and the associated feelings are valid, especially in light of potential physical problems (STI's) along with financial, legal, emotional, and relational consequences. And although expressing our feelings is essential to the healing process, how we express ourselves is critical to its outcome. We want to respond in a way that ultimately encourages our loved one's acceptance of personal responsibility for the damage and pain caused by the sin, as well as recognition of the need for help, preferably in the form of professional counseling or therapy.

Should we discover sexual sin, there is hope and help, because we don't serve a God of hopelessness. He provided the way out of bondage. His name is Jesus! How can Luke 4:16-21 apply to one's struggle with sexual sin?

It is important to remember that God loves us and our loved ones. Believing this builds faith and opens endless opportunities for God to work in us and through us—to His glory. We'll examine this further in Day 2.

> Prayer: Lord, there may be confusion and concern if we don't have all the answers, but You already know them. Reveal the truth, Lord. Build our hope in You so that Your very best outcome will unfold in Your timing.

DAY 2

BEFORE YOU ENGAGE THE PERSON

 IN HER SHOES

"I have not had the courage to ask my husband about his bondage. It is so uncomfortable to mention. And it just always feels like the same ride when I bring it up. He admits to backsliding. I get angry, cry, fret and then move on. I wait several months (or more) and then repeat. I often wonder if I make a bigger deal out of this than it is. So he looks at dirty images on the computer when I'm not around. So what? I'm sure a lot of guys do that. He's not taking it any further, right? No biggie. But when I'm smacked in the face with the reality of it, I can't help but get angry, feel hurt, and know it is wrong. Such inner turmoil."

PREPARING OUR HEARTS AND MINDS

Just as our stomachs often drop out from under us on a steep roller-coaster ride, so our hearts can drop out from under us when we realize that sexual sins have entered our world. By virtue of this discovery, our world and our future are threatened. So where do we go from here?

God would encourage us to turn to Him before we engage loved ones who are in a dangerous and destructive place. Why is this so important? It's not because they have hurt us (which they have). It's not because they deserve retribution (which they probably do). It's not because we are angry and want revenge (which they may "deserve"). It's not because we're afraid for loved ones (which is valid). Based on Mark 2:17, what is God's goal?

Because God knows perfectly our circumstances and those involved, He knows how to apply perfect pressure perfectly. No matter how He presses in, He does so out of love, not retribution, to redeem and restore, not to destroy and discard. When we desire His goal as *the* goal, the outcome is His.

> *No matter how God presses in, He does so out of love, not retribution, to save and restore, not to destroy and discard.*

How does this knowledge affect your approach to your loved one?

_____

_____

What follows are valuable considerations when confronting a loved one's sin. (*Note:* Some of these points may not apply when dealing with a severe psychological or potentially dangerous disorder. When this is the case, it is best not to engage the loved one. Professional counsel should be sought immediately, and shelter, if necessary.)

In order to prepare our hearts and minds for engagement...

We pray, lifting our circumstances and everyone involved before the Lord. How does Psalm 121 speak to this?

_____

_____

 WORD STUDY
Keeper

Hebrew, *shamar.* With God as our "keeper," He is our vigilant guard, security, stability, and hedge day and night, surrounding those who look to Him.

We seek wise, professional Christian counsel early in this journey but most definitely before engaging a loved one. Whenever possible "rely on a Christian counselor...who not only understands the Bible and what it says about the nature of life and people but also comprehends the complexities of sexually addictive behavior."[7] If a loved one is in this trouble, silence will guarantee even more destructive outcomes. Resources are in place for our benefit and that of our loved ones (see works cited at the end of this book).[8] (Note: Sexual issues, such as incest, child pornography, sexual exploitation or abuse, voyeurism, exhibitionism, and rape have legal ramifications or dangerous consequences to us and our families. Sexual behaviors such as these are complicated and are difficult to resolve without outside, professional treatment.)

What does Proverbs 19:20 say about wise counsel?

_____

_____

_____

 IN HER SHOES

"I realized I needed help as the shock set in. I seemed paralyzed, so I called a dear friend. She helped me cook dinner for the children and get them into bed and think through how I would engage my husband. She prayed for me, and though I continued to shake, I felt peace in my heart, a stirring that God was with me through this."

We find a safe, discreet, biblically grounded sister who can walk this journey with us, hear our wounded hearts, and not pass judgment when we freely express even dark or frightening emotions; one who will not let us persist in anger, helplessness, hopelessness, profound sadness, or victimhood, but will lovingly hold us accountable for our responses and conduct; one who will help us get help when needed. According to Proverbs 15:23, 27:5–6, and Galatians 6:1–2, what qualities should that friend have?

We remain courageous and willing to confront the problem. Read James 4:17. Harry Shaumburg tells us, "Refusing compassionate and restorative involvement with someone caught in sin is not an option."[9]

Are you willing to engage your loved one toward resolution? If not, why not? What are you telling yourself about doing so?

We check the spiritual condition of our hearts, trusting God and His truth with where we are right now. Where does Psalm 16:7–8 say our trust will lead?

We ask God for protected hearts—not hard hearts but strengthened hearts that submit to Him and resist the enemy. We need to realize that our loved one is not the enemy. Satan is the enemy who is influencing him or her. According to Ephesians 6:10-11, what part do we play in our protection?

We make sure our slates are clean by checking our own eyes for logs. According to Psalm 51:13, what is the outcome of a clean slate?

We make sure our motives are pure. How does Psalm 26:2 say we will stay on the right track?

_____

_____

We educate ourselves about whatever concerns us most. Read Proverbs 18:15. We gather reading material, research Christian Web sites, and seek support groups in order to confront the problem and engage the person in a way that can benefit him (her) and glorify God.

How can getting smart about your concern help you where you are right now?

_____

_____

We get our thoughts (and therefore our emotions) in God's order. Let's revisit 2 Corinthians 10:5. If our thoughts are not under God's authority (Lesson 7, Day 5), our emotions will not be in check, and they will take us and our circumstances to places we do not want to go. This is the time to *"take every thought captive,"* and let Scripture and the Holy Spirit address fears, anxieties, anger, hurts, and any other wounds or negative emotions.

What have you been telling yourself about your loved one's sexual sin that has been keeping you from thinking straight? Write your consuming thoughts here:

_____

_____

_____

If Jesus were sitting across the table from you right now listening to your consuming thoughts, what do you think He'd tell you, and why?

_____

_____

We choose to respond rather than react. Read Proverbs 15:28 and 1 Peter 3:9–12. The difference between responding and reacting is subtle, but powerful and direction-setting. A reaction is preceded by unchecked negative thought patterns resulting in sudden, sometimes uncontrolled emotions that potentially determine our behavior. These unchecked, negative thoughts exercise "self" and escalate already difficult situations. *Responses* are preceded by deliberate, purposeful thoughts that can temper our behaviors regardless of the emotions. They are fueled by the Holy Spirit and exercise self-control, which calms situations: *LORD, You knew. How would You have me respond?* We may be tempted to unload on those who have hurt us, to pay them back, to put them in their own hell. The sad truth is that they're already in their own hell or this wouldn't have happened.

In your current circumstance, are you reacting or responding? Explain what you do when you react. What impact has this had on your situation thus far? Explain what you do when you respond. What impact has this had on your situation thus far?

_____

_____

_____

We avoid inflaming the situation with a frontal attack. Read Proverbs 15:1. When we use "I" statements rather than "you" statements, we own our own feelings: *I feel/felt … when…* rather than *You make/made me feel…* Also, refraining from "you never" or "you always" statements eases the tension and the tendency to go on the defensive. We can be forthright without being verbally destructive.

How will addressing your situation in this way be different than you've addressed it in the past?

_____

_____

_____

We don't embellish the facts or our feelings, but state the truth plainly and simply, and leave the results to God. Second Thessalonians 3:15 (ESV) tells us not to "*regard him as an enemy, but warn him as a brother.*" How can this guidance help us when we engage?

_____

_____

We trust God to reveal what more, if anything, we need to know. Although we shouldn't take matters into our own hands by compulsively looking for further evidence, we can't ignore signs, indicators, or obvious evidence that God allows us to discover. How do Proverbs 10:9 and Hebrews 4:13 support this?

_____

_____

When dealing with a spouse, we prayerfully consider our options. Read 1 John 5:14-15. When sexual sin is discovered in a marriage, the hope is that our loved one would seek help in order to restore relationships with God and with others. Better that we listen to God through His Word and Holy-Spirit guidance, as well as through biblically grounded counsel than to the urgings that come from others' personal opinions. Marriages in the worst places have known the greatest victories when a believing spouse has yielded to God's grip on her life and not given up. And God is glorified.

From whom have you received wise counsel? Have you received counsel that is not trustworthy? If yes, how did you know it was erroneous counsel? What's your measure?

_____

_____

_____

We wait patiently for God to move us toward engagement. Impulsive, emotion-driven engagement is typically self-driven engagement that will likely backfire. What do Psalms 25:21, 27:14, and Isaiah 40:31 tell us to do and why?

"Do not regard him as an enemy, but warn him as a brother."

2 Thessalonians 3:15 (ESV)

We'll know when we feel more contempt than compassion. Contempt can be a protective defense mechanism that says, *If I keep my heart hard, he can't hurt me again; he can't disappoint me again if I already believe the worst about him.* Shaumburg says, "Contempt is like wearing a stiff brace; it hinders our movements but protects us from further injury."[10]

When we operate out of contempt, we might feel protected, but *nobody* is, and there will be no forward movement. Based on Romans 15:1 and Galatians 6:1, what can dispel contempt?

We can meet repentance with grace. That said, we must remain aware that this is just the beginning of the healing process. He or she may relapse, repent, and require continued grace. Bondage is like an onion. It may need to be peeled one layer at a time. According to Ephesians 4:32, how would grace respond to repentance?

We must understand that fear may exist in repentant loved ones who are struggling with sexual bondage. Revisit 1 John 4:18. They may fear that once we know who they really are and what they really do, our wrath and disgust would turn to the ultimate rejection—abandonment. It's a place many in sexual bondage have experienced long before we entered their lives.

Have you considered that your loved one may have fears about disclosing his/her sexual activity? Would this change your approach? If so, how? If not, why?

We can remain thankful while we wait. According to Psalm 50:14–15 and 23, why is thanksgiving to God in time of trouble a sacrifice? What will our thankfulness yield?

God promises His outcome for those who come to Him with their problems. When we trust Him, we can send tough messages without dishonoring the hearers even if their bad choices have dishonored us. We must be true to God in the worst of circumstances because He is true to us and eager to work on our behalf and on behalf of our loved ones.

> Prayer: Lord, if You are calling me to confront the problem, then You will prepare my heart and mind to engage my loved one. I wait on You, Lord, to teach me what I need to know, to discover, to assess. I depend on Your heart of compassion to quell any contempt in mine. May I see my loved one through Your eyes, Lord. In Jesus' name.

DAY 3

DEFINE AND CLARIFY

Being prepared to engage a loved one who is in sexual sin requires clear communication. We need to express our care and concern; to clearly define our understanding of the problem; to be clear about how his or her sins are impacting us and others; to clearly articulate what behavioral changes need to be made. These points need to be organized and well thought out. In today's lesson, we will go through practical exercises that can help to equip us to confront sin with clarity, engage our loved one with care, and express defined boundaries and desires with resolve.

THE BLESSING OF BOUNDARIES

Boundaries in a relationship that is dealing with sexual sin allow a separateness that "protects us from the outside while giving us an area in which we can feel safe."[11] They are lines that we draw in the relationship for the good of each involved. In their book *Boundaries*, Henry Cloud and John Townsend paint a clear picture of what boundaries are:

> In the physical world, boundaries are easy to see. Fences, signs, walls, moats with alligators, manicured lawns, or hedges are all physical boundaries. In their differing appearances, they give the same message: THIS IS WHERE MY PROPERTY BEGINS. The owner of the property is legally responsible for what happens on his or her property. Non-owners are not responsible for the property. . . . In the spiritual world, boundaries are just as real, but are often harder to see. . . . These boundaries define your soul, and they help you to guard it and maintain it. . . . We are responsible *to* others *for* ourselves.[12]

Boundaries are not what we put around others or put into their lives. That's control, and nowhere in Scripture are we instructed to control others.[13] Boundaries are what we put around ourselves for righteousness' sake as well as for our protection and welfare.

EXTRA MILE
Psalm 101

What boundaries did David lay out for himself in Psalm 101? How would these boundaries apply to believers today?

We are responsible to our loved ones for our responses to their behaviors. According to Micah 6:8, what response pleases God? How would these three qualities form a healthy boundary in a broken relationship?

_____

_____

The New Living Translation puts Micah 6:8 this way: *"O people, the Lord has told you what is good, and this is what he requires of you: to do what is right, to love mercy, and to walk humbly with your God."* It is not the boundary that is at issue but the motive of the heart when we set the boundary—to do what is *good* in our situation. When setting a boundary, we do what is right (what is just and necessary), do it with mercy (kindly administered), and carry it out humbly (hand in hand with God's will). Our motives can also be vindictive. And we know the difference. We must check our hearts' motives when establishing boundaries. For example, in the case of pornography use, an appropriate boundary (both right and necessary) that is kindly administered (mercy) as determined through prayer and wise counsel (in line with God's will) could include: filters to all computers and other "screens," an explicit commitment to stop all exposure to pornography, and a commitment to Christian counseling. In the case of infidelity, a wife's appropriate boundary (both right and necessary) that is kindly administered (mercy) as determined through prayer and wise counsel (in line with God's will) could include: an immediate end to all contact with the other party (or parties, from communication to sexual activity) both spouses being tested for STI's, and both committed to and pursuing restoration of the marriage through professional Christian counseling.

THE DISCLOSURE BOUNDARY

When we talk of disclosure boundaries, the question of how much we need to know about our loved one's sexual activities often comes up. The circumstance will determine the disclosure boundaries. For example, a spouse doesn't need the lurid details of unfaithfulness, but a parent would need specific details of sexual activity or abuse in order to help provide protection and healing for a child. Whether or not we receive vital information also depends upon the heart of the person who is in sexual sin. If he or she is unrepentant, resistant, or afraid to disclose, we are more likely to experience continued denial, lies, and deceit. However, a repentant loved one needs to openly disclose *all needful* information. And we must encourage this with the right questions, because anything concealed, with the exception of graphic details, will delay or prevent true healing for all involved.

 IN HER SHOES

"Satan had used secrecy to continue to keep my husband in bondage."

For this reason, and with wise counsel, we should prayerfully consider the level of details we think we need. Full disclosure may come all at once, slowly, in pieces, or over time. And it will be painful. But God knows, and as He leads us through this, He will protect our hearts.

We will want answers to...

Who: Every human being involved, whether consensually or as a victim, matters. Even though this information will be painful to hear, we need to understand if we or others have been exposed to health risks. This full disclosure will also begin our loved one's recovery process.

What: The full scope of activity is important to understand in order to see patterns. For example: Was he/she using only pornography, or did sexual sin extend to other areas? Accurate and informed pictures of his or her hidden life matter for our understanding and for the protection of all involved.

When: This helps us understand the beginning and practice (frequency) of the sexual activities and lends further perspective to the depth of bondage. As well, answers to this question fill in many of our blanks and dispel and/or confirm our wild imaginings. As it relates to our loved one, disclosure helps him or her to face the lies, deceptions, and excuses that go with hiding these activities.

Where: In the office? At home? On a business trip? At a brothel? At youth camp? *Full* disclosure. Understanding the where of activity alerts us to all patterns and places that must be avoided in the future.

Why: This is the pressing question that we want answers to but will likely require professional insights in order for even the one in bondage to understand. This is one reason professional counseling is so highly recommended. Answering the why is critical to breakthrough and healing.

How: Caution! Because salacious, intimate, and voyeuristic details are wrapped up in the how, this is where we draw boundaries (unless children were violated). The only answers we need here are those necessary to protect our health, such as what kind of protection was used. As for the exhaustive details of the sexual activities, we really won't want those answers. They are almost always counterproductive, haunting, and inhibiting to our healing and our loved ones' recovery.

The following exercise can be written in your journal. With each point, prayerfully consider how you would engage a loved one. Note: If you are seeing a counselor, therapist, mentor, or are in a support group designed for those whose loved ones are in bondage (highly recommended), you may want to share these exercise results with them.

 IN HER SHOES

"I joined a group of Christians who had loved ones struggling with the same sexual addictions, though all the others were parents of loved ones. I was the only spouse. We encouraged each other, prayed for each other, and were there to listen and help if needed. I was able to deal with the hard issues of my worth, who I could trust, my children, and our marriage. It gave me perspective and was like a shot of hope each time I went."

Define the problem. Think your statements through before you engage. Make a bullet-list of recent behaviors/activities that strongly suggest sexual sin. Read Ephesians 4:29. Keep this part brief and to the point without an overload of emotion. Write your statements in your journal as List #1. Add to or remove from them as necessary.

Convey the emotional impact that the behaviors/activities have had on you. Keep this brief as well. What feelings do you want to express? Doing so is not intended to manipulate your loved one but to genuinely and forthrightly convey the pain he or she has caused (*I feel betrayed...; I felt threatened when...; I'm afraid for our/your future...*). Hear the psalmist's heart in Psalm 62:1–8. Write the feelings you want to express in your journal as List #2. Add to or remove from them as necessary.

Be prepared to gently yet forthrightly tell your loved one how you would like to see his/her behavior change. Read Hosea 3:3. Hosea required his wife's compliance to specific boundaries in order for their relationship to heal (v. 3:3). With the Spirit's leading, seek a pastor, counselor, mentor, or support group that can give you wise counsel on your list of changes specific to your loved one's current behavior. Write them in your journal as List #3. Add to or remove from them as necessary.

Be clear about the personal boundaries you need to draw in this relationship. According to Job 27:6, how should we draw and hold our personal boundaries? Write your boundaries in your journal as List #4. Add to or remove from them as necessary.

Determine how you will respond should your loved one defend, rationalize, deny, justify, lie, or blame. Own none of them. They are manipulative and detract from the truth. Read Proverbs 27:4-6. Determine to be firmly resolute in your response—unwavering, steadfast. Answer the following questions in your journal: Have you been willing to support or tolerate deceptions and manipulations from your loved one? How will you respond to your loved one's defensiveness, denial, lies, blame now? Take the time to think these through. This is List #5. Add them or remove them as necessary.

Determine how much you think your loved one needs to disclose about his or her sexual activity. The reason is two-fold: Disclosure determines if you or others are at risk. (Has there been sexual involvement outside of marriage?) Exposure also opens the door to his/her healing process and yours. Read James 5:16. Lies, denial, blame, and defensiveness will continue until he/she owns the sin. You want full disclosure and total honesty. Remember that your loved one may be afraid to be forthcoming initially, so this step will likely be revisited. Avoid the intimate details. Write your questions in your journal as List #6. Add to or remove from them as necessary.

Be prepared to create consequences (outcomes resulting from poor choices) when they are needed or when your loved one is unrepentant or resistant or these behavioral changes are ignored or not taken seriously. Well-reasoned consequences (best when designed with an expert familiar with your circumstance) will give the offender every opportunity to turn around. Poorly designed consequences (threats, manipulations, warnings, and other forms of power and control) can make matters worse and create defensiveness. Read Proverbs 25:12. Write the consequences in your journal as List #7. Act on them if it becomes necessary.

Do your homework! Read Proverbs 24:5–6. Have your list of counselors, websites, treatment centers, twelve-step recovery programs, accountability groups, and churches that deal with sexual bondage with phone numbers ready. Add these to your journal as List #8. Add to or remove from them as necessary. (Note: if pornography is your loved one's struggle, visit www.covenanteyes.com. It will monitor usage and send weekly reports to an accountability partner. Best to download on every tool that gets Internet access.)

Be prepared should things get worse before they get better. Read Psalm 46:1. Remember Who your strength is. In your journal, write Scripture verses that assure and strengthen you. This is List #9. Revisit them often. Continue to add to them as this confrontation/engagement process unfolds.

IMMEDIATELY BEFORE ENGAGING YOUR LOVED ONE, REMEMBER...

Our hope is always for the salvation of an unbeliever and restoration to God of a believer.

This process may unfold over time, so don't expect an immediate resolution. Reengaging a loved one is not unusual, but expected. This is not license; it's reality.

Prayerfully choose the right time and place with no interruptions.

Remember, you are not confronting the problem alone. Nor will you be engaging your loved one alone, for the Lord your God is with you. Determine to be strong in the Lord and in the power of His might. In Day 4, we will explore the specifics of engaging your loved one.

> Prayer: Equip me, Lord, not only with knowledge but with resolve to do the hard but right thing so that my loved one will know how much I love him (her), and more important, how much You love him (her).

DAY 4

ENGAGING THE PERSON

If we have a loved one who's struggling with sexual sin, do we love (*agape*) him or her enough to address the issue? Ask yourself this: If my closest friend brought facts or suspicions to me similar to my own, would I encourage her to shove them under the rug and ignore the problem or face the problem to save a life (or lives, relationships, families) from potential destruction? Love is willing to take a good, hard look at the facts or even the valid suspicions and engage the loved one.

Let's look at Jesus' divine construct for confronting sin and engaging a sinner with grace and truth. Although Jesus is directing this construct to believers, He also offers insights when engaging an unbeliever. This process is designed to restore people to God, and where applicable, to each other. Read Matthew 18:15. What specific guidance is given? What is the hoped-for outcome?

Dr. Mark Laaser, founder of Faithful and True Ministries, tells us to "courageously [engage] the person in a one-to-one conversation. Address only the behaviors you know about. You might begin by saying, 'I care about you, but I am concerned about some of your behaviors. By those I mean...' "[14] (brackets ours). The initial engagement should be one-on-one to eliminate the extent of exposure to others and protect both you and the one you love. It's factual. And although our emotions may be high, our approach shouldn't be laden with fear, guilt, anger, or attempts to control. Rather, it's a prayerful, "waiting-on-God" opportunity to express truth. (Note: if possible, both parents should be available to engage a child.)

It's important to engage our loved one with compassion. Compassion is not the same as sympathy, which can draw us into another's emotional web. Sympathy is more about *feelings* regardless of truth. Compassion is *action* based on truth. It should never "*determine our beliefs* about [sexual sin]; it should only *determine our response* to those who struggle with [sexual] feelings and behaviors. . . . Compassion should make us gentle and humble in heart when dealing with another's sin, but truth, as found in the Word of God, must determine what we believe."[15] True compassion cares enough to engage a loved one with the hope of repentance, redemption, and restoration. We stand for truth while we engage with grace. That's compassion.

If you are preparing to engage your loved one, consider how you have engaged him/her on difficult matters in the past. What, if anything, would you do differently? What evidence is there that the person you engaged did or didn't listen? (*Reminder*: One should not engage alone or without professional counsel if physical violence has been experienced with this loved one.)

Assuming a one-on-one engagement failed, Jesus' guidance provides the next step which can be applied to both believer and unbeliever alike. In Matthew 18:16, how are we instructed to approach a loved one if he/she chooses not to listen?

It is important to note that these are to be witnesses for the second engagement and not necessarily witnesses of bad behavior. How do Proverbs 12:17 and 14:25 characterize a godly witness (which includes you)? What can a godly witness accomplish?

Who would you call as godly witnesses? Be sure to base your choices according to the Witness's Job Description that follows. Write their names in your journal. What are your motives for selecting these witnesses?

A Witness's Job Description

Witnesses (or third parties) are not to be used as hammers on the head or heart of your loved one. They should:

- Be trusted believers, who have had a previous positive impact in that person's life
- Be known, trusted, and respected by both parties
- Be discreet, able to keep confidences
- Be able to assist in keeping the discussion on task
- Be helpful in diffusing tough, emotional responses
- Be able to gently encourage your loved one to get help
- Be compassionate throughout the discussion
- Be objective and perceptive observers
- Be forthright about their knowledge of the sexual behavior without moralizing or sermonizing

If a loved one refuses to listen after the second engagement with witnesses and will not repent, Jesus lays out a tough boundary for a believer. Read Matthew 18:17. What happens?

The intent of this third step in Jesus' construct is not to do evil *to* our loved one but to undo evil *in* our loved one. We know the involvement of our church body may sound risky because we don't know what will happen on the other side of Jesus' instruction. It may be necessary to involve an appropriate body of believers to appeal to this loved one (caring believers within a home church or other Christians who are related to the loved one). In the case of an unbeliever, a Christian counselor trained in crisis intervention should be considered as a necessary recourse working in concert with those who have been directly affected. Family members, friends, a co-worker, an employer—those who can express their care and concern based on how they have been affected—can also be beneficial to the process.

But even with all this effort, a loved one may refuse to listen. The apostle Paul described releasing an unrepentant, defiant sexual sinner. Read 1 Corinthians 5:1–5. To "whom" was he released and why? What do you think the "destruction of the flesh" means? For what purpose?

_____

_____

_____

As the churches' spiritual leader, Paul took extreme measures with hopes that this man's fleshly appetite would be destroyed and his soul saved. This is not retribution, but compassion in action. It is spiritual "tough love." Whether our loved one is a believer or not, what this release looks like in practice today will be different in every case and can only be brought into sharp focus through prayer and Spirit-led Christian counsel.

The painful reality is that God will judge sin. What does Psalm 7:12–16 say will happen if a person won't repent?

_____

_____

_____

Concentrate on the first word of verse 12: "If a man does not repent..." God is waiting for, encouraging, urging a repentant heart. This also "helps the faithful to prefer and wish that their oppressors would turn to God rather than suffer punishment."[16] The point is, we should fear the potential outcome for our loved ones more than we fear the engagement.

We recognize that at any point in this process there is a risk that the loved one may throw down the gauntlet and threaten to leave. But there is a greater risk: Our physical, emotional, and spiritual health and that of others we love may be at stake. We must fight for our loved one in trouble, for our relationships, our families, and pursue the help we need. The help is out there. We are not alone.

Psalm 37:5–6 gives two commands with two promising outcomes. What are the two commands (v. 5), and what will our obedience to them yield (v. 6)?

_____

_____

_____

> *"Commit your way to the Lord; trust in him and he will do this:*
> *He will make your righteousness shine like the dawn, the justice of*
> *your cause like the noonday sun."*
>
> Psalm 37:5–6 (NIV)

These promises stand no matter how our loved ones respond to our efforts to bring them back. However, if we choose to make no effort, there may be no improvement, and the situation will continue to deteriorate. Before engaging, remember...

- Ask discreet biblically-grounded sisters to pray for you before and during.

- Engage one-on-one at first.

- Reassure your loved one that you love him (her) and care about his welfare.

- Don't deviate from your "bullet" list of facts (List #1) or feelings (List #2). Doing so will jeopardize the effectiveness of the engaging process.

- Be sure to have List #8 ready (resources).

- Avoid judgmental (condemning) language that will create defensiveness.

- Address *only* those activities or behaviors that you know about or have observed (List 1).

- If appropriate, express empathy for what it might be like to be in his/her struggle and in this confrontation. For example, *I know this may be difficult to hear...* or *I sense this struggle may be exhausting and perhaps even frightening...*

- Don't mistake a bumbling struggler with an unrepentant sinner in denial. Expect embarrassment, shame, even initial defensiveness. These are natural reactions to confrontation. Pray for discernment.

- Listen as much as you talk.

- Again, reassure your loved one of your love and support.

- Remember you are confronting the problem and engaging the person.

ENGAGING YOUR LOVED ONE

When engaging, succinctly state from your journal the lists you've compiled in the suggested order that follows. It is designed to best facilitate engaging your loved one. That said, the order may change as your conversation unfolds. Begin with...

- *These are the things that concern me.* (List #1)

- *This is how it's affecting me (and/or others) emotionally.* (List #2)

- Have your responses ready should he/she defend, deny, lie, or blame (List #5)

- *This is what I need to see changed.* (List #3)

- *I think you'll need help to make these changes.* (List #8)

- Be ready to communicate boundaries that protect you. (List #4) (Review "Blessings of Boundaries" in Day 3 if necessary.)

- Full disclosure may not be possible at the initial engagement. However, over time, it will be required. Refer to disclosure questions from List #6.

- **Do not** use the consequences in List #7 as an "or else." Doing so may create defensiveness in your loved one and potentially derail the process. Use them wisely should he or she refuse to respond to your requirements.

- If possible, end this engagement in prayer together.

What if he (she) promises easy fixes? When it comes to recurrent sexual sin and bondage, easy fixes aren't easy—or real. Steve Gallagher, author of *At the Altar of Sexual Idolatry*, writes, "The Lord almost always deals with those in sexual sin through a gradual, well-organized process of transforming the man into a new creation. . . . When a person has to fight and struggle to break the powerful grip of sin, he will appreciate the freedom he eventually experiences."[17] Look for genuine effort and progress rather than pledges of easy fixes. There will be slips (relapses). At a time like this grace and truth can go a long way to getting him or her back on track.

What if he (she) gets arrested or worse? If your loved one has committed a sexual crime, such as rape, child sexual abuse, production, distribution, and/or collection of child porn, indecent exposure, voyeurism, or any criminal sex act in which there are victims, God knew this was coming. That your loved one got caught is both just and merciful. You may be watching 1 Corinthians 5:1–5 in action. Do you trust God with both your loved one and the consequences of poor choices? Are you willing to let God take this where it must go in order to get your loved one's attention? Pray that this is a "rock bottom" experience, a "hell" that convinces him (her) that the only way "up" will be radical change, that his own efforts have failed him, that nothing else will work to bring him out of that pit but Jesus Christ Himself. Are you willing to be there for him? To make this sacrifice? To walk out these consequences with him? Even a jail term? And again, at a time like this grace and truth can go a long way to getting him back on track. Where there is repentance, there is amazing testimony waiting for those who walk through this together.

We can't see what's ahead for us or for our loved ones. But isn't that the stuff of hope? We must stand firm in our faith. Isaiah 7:9 (NIV) reminds, *"If you do not stand firm in your faith, you will not stand at all."* That may sound a little scary, or at the very least intimidating. But it's true. Jesus can work with however much faith we have—even if it's just a little.

Remember faith doesn't mean everything goes our way; it promises that everything will go God's way as we trust Him. In His sovereignty, He puts believers "where they will bring the most glory to Him, and we are totally incapable of judging where that may be."[18]

And now you wait and watch. Not in fear or depression but fully vested to your reality alongside our mighty God who is working on your behalf. How will you do this?

When your loved one is repentant and responsive, let God prepare your heart over time to trust again (Lesson 12). How does Psalm 28:6-7 encourage you?

Continually (daily and sometimes moment by moment) relinquish your heart and your hurt to God. He's always waiting. Then follow His lead. According to Luke 9:23, what is Jesus' specific instruction for a journey such as yours? How can this help you on a daily basis?

_____

_____

_____

Take it slowly. In our instant gratification culture, we want everything fixed and everyone perfected yesterday. But that is not how God works if the work is to be permanent. According to 2 Peter 3:8–9, what is God's timeline when it comes to perfecting us and why?

_____

_____

Accept where God has you right now rather than dwell on dashed hopes, expectations, or illusions. God has a new reality that will shape your future. How does Isaiah 43:18–19 support this notion?

_____

_____

_____

If you've done your part, be at peace, especially if your loved one is unrepentant. According to Isaiah 32:17, what is our part and what is the reward?

_____

_____

Engaging another isn't only about us; it's about proactively seeking God's good and glory as we follow Jesus in this process, for the sake of our loved one's soul.

> Prayer: Lord, You are my strength and my shield. My heart trusts in You, and I am helped; therefore, my heart exults, and with my song I shall thank You as You guide me through this process.

Day 5

Has My Child Been Violated?

 IN HER SHOES

"My 12-year-old son came home from camp and confided in me that a sexual experience was forced on him by an older boy. He also confided that, while the first encounter was forced, he returned to the individual for more later on in the week. The second encounter was far more traumatic, way beyond the bounds he had previously experienced. He expressed mostly trauma but also much fear, shame, and guilt. I was first confused and then angry! We put our son in camp because his father frequently traveled, and we wanted him to have other male mentors. I felt betrayed. I was deeply saddened and afraid for my son. I also put some of the blame on him for what happened. I didn't back him up enough."

Every child is curious. But few children are wise when it comes to sexuality. Tragically, childhood sexual abuse abounds. June Hunt, founder of Hope for the Heart, a worldwide biblical counseling ministry, asserts, "When it comes to abuse of any kind, too many people become like an ostrich, hiding their heads in the sands of denial. Although it is terribly hard to do, facing the truth that child abuse is taking place is the first step to healing."[19]

We are going to look at some tough truths today with the hope that we can offer prevention of childhood sexual abuse. To those for whom prevention comes too late, we pray this lesson will provide some guidance toward healing

From the information that follows, underline every aspect of childhood sexual abuse that you did not know before reading this:

Childhood sexual abuse is any physical, visual, or verbal interaction with a minor by an older child or adult whose purpose is sexual stimulation or sexual satisfaction. A victim of such abuse is any boy or girl under the age of 18 who has suffered one or many experiences of sexual abuse. . . Sexual abuse of a child is almost always committed by someone the child knows or with whom the child has frequent contact.[20] Childhood sexual abuse takes advantage of weaker, younger, more vulnerable children in order to take control. It is usually planned beforehand and in most cases, repeated. Many victims know their victimizers and often even love them.

VICTIMIZERS CAN INCLUDE:

Relatives: those biological, adoptive, step-relatives, or in-laws who perpetrate sexual abuse with children or adolescents. The most common perpetrators are males in the families.

Children molesting children: those who carry out sexual acts against or perform sexual acts in front of younger children. They include incestuous sexual activities with older siblings, stepsiblings, or cousins, or other children under eighteen who babysit, are in the neighborhood, or are in sports and other activities.

Trusted adults in neighborhoods, schools, childcare centers, or organizations: those who take physical liberties or perform sex acts on or in front of vulnerable youngsters.

Adults or older children who introduce pornography: those who expose pornography in the form of any medium to younger siblings, friends, or relatives.

Males or females who force sex: those who coerce or force sex on their dates or companions typically while in high school or college. The National College Women Sexual Victimization Study estimated that between 20 and 25 percent of college women experienced completed or attempted rape during their college years.[21]

Pornographers and sex traffickers: those who solicit and exploit children (as well as parents and guardians who are complicit). "The FBI estimates that well over 100,000 children and young women are trafficked in America today. They range in age from 9 to 19, with average age being 11."[22]

 IN HER SHOES

A woman who suffered childhood sexual abuse by a female daycare worker recalls: "I remember nights I would lie awake praying, "Please turn me into a boy"—over and over in hopes that God would take pity on me and change me, believing that all my problems would be solved, that I would feel better about myself—that I would actually like the person looking back at me in the mirror. My sexual identity crisis went with me throughout my life."

HOW DOES SEXUAL ABUSE HAPPEN?

How does Psalm 36:1–4 explain the evil of a sexual abuser?

_____

_____

_____

June Hunt lays out the typical, progressive, four-part path that the sexual abuser follows:

Seduction takes place as the victimizer gains the trust of the child. Through gifts, rewards, and/or preferential treatment, the abuser develops a friendship or closeness that lets the child know he or she is special.

Stimulation may be in the form of wrestling, light hugs, physical affirmation (pat on the fanny), back rubs, and the like. By the time the abuser encroaches on the sexual level, the child is sufficiently desensitized and vulnerable. He or she may not like the physical advances that the abuser is making but is often responsive to the sexual stimulation. This can be confusing and frightening for the child. Hunt writes, "A child victim of sexual abuse feels overwhelmed and powerless. A child has no choice about being abused, does not have the ability to stop the abuse, is defenseless against the emotional pain, and feels helpless and totally alone... By God's design, the body naturally responds to sexual stimulation. While children eventually feel conflicted over the mixture of pain and pleasure, no guilt should ever be attributed to the child—the guilt belongs to the abuser alone."[23]

Silence is forced on the child through tactics of intimidation and threats in order to prevent the child's disclosure of the abuse. The abuser uses guilt to make the child believe that he or she is to blame for the relationship, that disclosure will destroy their families, destroy the child's credibility, disappoint significant people in their lives, or even cause death. The abuser may even threaten to kill himself (herself) or another if the child tells. It's an evil tactic that causes the child to perceive devastating consequences for speaking out.

Suppression is the child's response to a hopeless situation. Without discovery or disclosure that leads to rescue, they believe that there is no hope. The betrayal will likely set up a lifetime of distrust toward everyone, even of God.[24]

HOW WILL WE KNOW? WHAT ARE THE INDICATORS?

Childhood sexual abuse can be difficult to discover. It's often discovered by physical or behavioral evidence or some kind of disclosure by a child: unusual questions, role play with dolls, pictures drawn, and the like. Behavioral indicators include guilt, shame, secret crying, gender confusion, substance abuse, emotional detachment, conflict about being alone with the abuser, sleep disturbances and flashbacks, anxieties/nervousness/phobias (such as obsessive compulsive disorders), alienation, depression, and suicidal behavior. As well, *separation* from the reality of sexual abuse may become a new normal. When children feel there is no escape, no help, and no hope, the only way they can cope is to somehow disconnect from what has happened. This can manifest with an inability to distinguish right from wrong and fantasy from reality. It can also manifest in hyper-sexuality. Everything is sexualized: conversation, clothes, body language, interactions. Sexual activity can begin earlier and is often more dangerous and more promiscuous, as if without consequences.

Ephesians 5:3–17 offers important teaching on improper sexual behaviors. Observing any of these behaviors in adults or children (others or our own) should be a warning to parents regardless of who exhibits them. What are these behaviors (vv. 3 –5)? What warnings does this passage give (vv. 6–10)? Specifically, what do verses 11–14 promise as help when we are dealing with the darkness of sexual abuse? According to verses 15–17, what part do we play in that help? What is the warning and instruction (v. 17)?

We must stay aware of the evil around us and when we recognize it, exercise wisdom in how we proceed.

ENGAGING THE CHILD WHO IS THE VICTIM

When we're unsure if our child has been abused, further information *carefully* gathered is helpful in determining when to engage a professional. How we gather information is important because of potential trauma to the child and other family members. There may also be the potential for legal action.

Observing notable change in a child's behavior would prompt a mom to ask her child about it: *You've been pretty sad (or angry, anxious, detached) lately. Is there something you'd like to talk about?* Should he (or she) be willing to talk, a mom should:

Reassure the child that he is loved and can share anything. Because children are tender, fragile, and highly suggestible, we must be careful not to ask leading questions that fill in truth for them, such as, *Did he touch you here?* Rather, ask *Will you tell me what happened?* or *Did you experience something uncomfortable or confusing?*[26]

Be careful to speak language at a level the child understands when engaging him or her. Children can be confused not only by our tone but by concepts and language that are beyond their level of understanding.

Should the child disclose sexual abuse, be careful not to accuse, blame, or suggest that the child is at fault with such statements as *Why did you let this happen (or let him do that)?* or *What were you thinking?* or *You know better.* These may seem like reasonable "parenting" words at the time, but they blame the victim, which is unjust. They also magnify a child's guilt and shake his trust in the one he should trust the most. This creates further trauma and helplessness. It's important to stay calm and keep anger or fear in check. If the child was threatened by the victimizer, our overt negative reaction may intensify that fear, and the child may delay or stop disclosure altogether.

Reassure the child that he/she is safe.

Reassure the child that he/she is believed. This is further securing for the child.

If our concern is further validated, our first response may be to avenge our child, but overreaction will traumatize him or her and can shut down the opportunity for the child to be forthright with the truth. We must become our child's defender no matter who the perpetrator is—family or otherwise. Emotions will be strong, so if there ever was a time to depend on God and be under Holy Spirit self-control, it would be now.

Under-reaction or to do nothing will cause a child to feel further betrayed and hopeless, rendering him at risk for future sexual abuse. German Lutheran pastor Dietrich Bonhoeffer said, "Silence in the face of evil is itself evil: God will not hold us guiltless. Not to speak is to speak. Not to act is to act."[25] The sad truth is that left unaddressed and untreated, the victimized child can be victimized again or grow up to become a victimizer. Therefore, everything we say and do must be Holy Spirit-led, prayerful, measured, and in keeping with what's best for the child.

According to Proverbs 20:18, what is the wise approach to a child's abuse?

_____

_____

_____

It's important that we not act on our own. To act before getting wise counsel would be irresponsible and potentially damaging. Therefore, if abuse is strongly suspected or discovered, we must be prepared to:

Immediately seek professional help. Professionals can ask deeper questions that get to the truth without further traumatizing the child. And how information is gathered will be critical if legal action needs to take place.

If the previous step warrants, take the child to a local emergency room or pediatrician (whether the violation is recent, ongoing, or in the past). Physical examination can often verify sexual activity or the past effects of sexual activity. If there is verification of abuse, medical personnel are required to follow the policies of the local jurisdiction. The system is in place to help and protect children.

Know and understand the legal options. Sexual violation of a child is a crime and must be reported. Don't engage the offender or the parents of an offender. Engage the legal system. To neglect to do so is not only unlawful, but puts a child and potentially other children at further risk. Child advocates are in place to prepare both the child and the parents for legal procedures. Local law enforcement and an attorney may be required.

The child will likely need counseling. Professionally trained Christian therapists are in place with the expertise to address a child's mental and emotional trauma and help heal the soul.

ENGAGING THE CHILD WHO IS THE VIOLATOR

Read Proverbs 20:11. What are we called to discern and how?

Sometimes a child becomes sexual with another child out of innocent curiosity. (Playing doctor comes to mind.) In most cases, this may just require calm and gentle education. However, if our own child violates another, as heartbreaking a reality as this might be, we must defy denial and act on behalf of all involved. It's crucial to aggressively seek counseling from a biblically trained professional in order to help our child, prevent future victims, and mitigate legal ramifications.

KEEPING CHILDREN SAFE

Parents must be observant, mindful of how and what their children play with other children. They must be especially aware if any of their children have been exposed to graphic images like those on today's prime-time television or on the Internet. In their book, *Protecting Your Child in an X-Rated World*, Frank York and Jan LaRue quote Mark Laaser as saying, "Satan works on the naturally curious mind, tempting it to find out what it knows nothing about."[27]

Know your children. Know their whereabouts. Know their friends. And finally, know what they know about sex, about pornography, about their bodies, and confirm that it's truth. (For excellent resources, visit works cited at the end of this book.)[28] Laaser suggests that "both Mom and Dad be involved, so that both a male and a female perspective are offered. Mom can express her feelings about how pornography treats women as less than human, as nothing more than sex objects meant for pleasing men, rather than as creations of God with feelings and a need to be valued as whole people. Dad can discuss the lasting effects porn has on boys and men"[29] and more so today than ever in the past, on girls and women. Teaching our children, in age-appropriate stages, truth about God's divine design for sex, can serve to protect them from the lies and deceptions of an abuser.

Read Proverbs 1:10. What warning must we help our children heed?

Tim Clinton and Ron Hawkins report, "sexual abuse violates personal boundaries. The abuser crosses a person's boundaries to take what he or she wants. A key to helping the abused person is to set up boundaries that cannot be crossed."[30] What follows are a few parental guidelines:

Help children develop a strong relationship with Jesus Christ. This is first and foremost. Even if a child is resistant to Him, live Him for this child. Don't preach; model. Model His love, His mercy, His justice, His discipline, His forgiveness.[31]

Teach children that they are *"fearfully and wonderfully made"* in the image of God, and so is every other human being (Psalm 139:14). Teach self-respect and "other"-respect.

Be their sex educator and help them establish healthy boundaries with their bodies, their thoughts, their friends, their acquaintances, teaching them when and how to say no. No fear tactics; just faith-based facts.

Educate them with age-appropriate information about God's divine design for sex so that they can mature toward accountable sexuality.

Children are a gift from God and require whatever physical, emotional, and spiritual resources we have to ensure safe and sacred sexuality.

> Prayer: God, I am so grateful that You are a God who redeems when humanity fails us, who restores what the locusts have eaten, who provides what we do not possess, especially when faced with the heartbreak of a sexually abused child. Cover my child, Lord. Equip me to encourage and strengthen continued growth—whole and healthy.

NOTES

LESSON 11

OUR OWN STRUGGLE: LET'S GET PERSONAL

This lesson is written for those who struggle personally with the impact of sexual sin. However, if you've never been sexually violated or you're not struggling with personal sexual sin, you likely know someone who has or is. Therefore, in order to understand what imprisons us and what frees us, please do not skip this lesson.

DAY 1

VIOLATED!

 IN HER SHOES

"I heard my bedroom door creak open, and I immediately felt sick to my stomach with dread. I knew exactly what this meant: I would hear the whisper in my ear that it was okay and just to stay quiet so I wouldn't wake up mom or dad. I would feel the hand slip between my legs. At age eight, I couldn't say no to my sixteen-year-old brother who I knew loved me."

"Sexual abuse and rape victims are sitting in our pews every Sunday. We have domestic violence in Christian homes. We have the sex trafficking of young girls in our towns and cities. We must face what we find no matter how ugly it is. These things are hidden because they disturb and overwhelm us. However, to turn from these evils, to pretend or deny them, is to be complicit in them."[1]

We see this complicity in the story of David's daughter, Tamar. Read 2 Samuel 13:1–2. It is a powerful depiction of how lust steals all that is good and ultimately destroys everyone touched by it, especially the innocent. What is Tamar's relationship to Amnon? How is Amnon's attraction to her described?

_____

_____

In the Hebrew, the *love* that Amnon had for Tamar is "illicit eroticism and pure lust."[2] Mosaic Law prohibited intercourse between brother and sister as well as half brother and sister (Leviticus 18:9), which made Tamar "forbidden fruit" in Amnon's eyes—and perhaps a bit more desirous.

Who is Jonadab in 2 Samuel 13:3–5? What was his counsel to "lust-sick" Amnon?

_____

_____

Read 2 Samuel 13:6. Who does Amnon deceive, and what were his three requests?

_____

_____

It's possible that Amnon wasn't able to have an audience with his dad, the king, unless he devised a compelling ruse. His "illness" brought the king's visit and perhaps along with it a little sympathy which may have softened David to his son's request. All three requests seemed somewhat intimate for a brother and sister since Amnon "had few opportunities to see the unmarried members of the royal harem, probably none to see Tamar alone."[3]

According to 2 Samuel 13:7–8, what happened next?

_____

_____

In 2 Samuel 13:9–11, in what way did Amnon continue his deception, and to what end?

_____

_____

How did Tamar respond, and why do you think she responded the way she did in 2 Samuel 13:12–13?

_____

_____

Tamar protested, giving the cultural argument in her defense from Levitical law which states, _"You shall not uncover the nakedness of your sister, your father's daughter or your mother's daughter, whether brought up in the family or in another home"_ (Leviticus 18:9 ESV). She also gave the moral argument as it related to both of their reputations. And finally, we believe she may have been trying to thwart the inevitable or even escape by reasoning with Amnon.

What happened to Tamar in 2 Samuel 13:14?

_____

_____

According to 2 Samuel 13:15–17, what powerful emotion overcame Amnon, and how did he treat Tamar after he had gotten what he wanted? What does Amnon's treatment of Tamar say about his "love" for her?

_____

_____

_____

Amnon exposed his true nature when he discarded Tamar. This was not about love but about power. He dismissed her with the same disdain as he would dismiss a prostitute. It appears that he showed no remorse. As a matter of fact, he had a great hatred for Tamar. This exposed his lust. This exposed the real Amnon.

Rape is a painful reality for anyone who, like Tamar, becomes the object of another's lust for power. The violator threatens, forces, or deceives in order to attain his (or her) goal, and all with no shame. Violation can fall within different categories: statutory rape (rape of a male or female under the legal age of consent); stranger rape (the victim is unknown to the violator); date/acquaintance rape (rape by one known socially); mate rape (forced sex by a spouse); and gang rape (sexual assault by two or more violators).[4] Tamar was ravaged by someone we can assume she trusted. Trust was breached, and she felt great shame. This was evident in how she reacted to Amnon's violation of her most precious possession. Let's continue with the story . . .

In 2 Samuel 13:18–20, how did Tamar react to her violation?

Scripture gives several indications of Tamar's humiliation and shame. She tore her robe which, as a virgin, was worn as a symbol of honor and purity. Dr. Sam Meier, expert in Hebrew and Semitic languages, tells us "that the destruction of one's own proper garment was an . . . intense drama portraying an invisible reality. One might describe the deliberate tearing of one's garment as a formal enactment of the rending of oneself. The sorrow that precipitated such a violent display was often of sufficient intensity to mark the end of one's former life and its continuation (if at all) only in a modified fashion . . . Life had been diminished even for those who continued to live: the rape of Tamar forever changed her life, a boundary which she marked by the tearing of her garment (2 Sam. 13:19)."[5]

Tamar also covered her head with ashes as well as with her hand, both signs of mourning and humiliation—*shame*.

By law, Amnon should have married Tamar in order to redeem her, but instead he rejected her completely; he utterly destroyed her. She lived *"desolate in her brother Absalom's house"* (v. 20). The Hebrew word for desolate, *shamem*, powerfully describes this "new" woman. It means "ruined, wasted . . . an extreme destruction that has lasting effects and causes all people to stand up and take notice of what has happened."[6]

And Amnon didn't care. Not only had he planned, deceived, seduced, and raped Tamar (which was also incest), but he also created an even greater sin by abdicating his moral responsibility to marry her and care for her for the rest of her life (Deuteronomy 22:28–29).

In 2 Samuel 13:21–22, we see that deception and distrust have a long shelf life. What are the reactions of Tamar's father and brother to Amnon?

Is it any wonder that David responded the way he did? He himself had violated Bathsheba. He acted on the counterfeit (lust), and it revisited his kingdom through his son. David's sin with Bathsheba was not lost on Amnon.

David's sin against Bathsheba and Amnon's sin against Tamar were egregious breeches of trust. Tamar had learned that she could not trust family. She could not trust her father. Not only had he led her as a lamb to the slaughter, even if unknowingly, but he failed as a father to defend her honor. She could not trust her brothers, one who had violated her, the other who seemed indifferent to her pain and disgrace although he plotted his revenge against Amnom and carried it out two years later. Even the servants abdicated their responsibilities to the king and his family by allowing Tamar alone with Amnon and presumably ignoring her protests and cries. As a result of the failure of everyone who should have protected her, Tamar faced the rest of her life as a desolate woman.

If you have been betrayed in a way similar to Tamar, did it shake your ability to trust? If so, who is difficult to trust now, and in what way?

Can you see how Amnon's act of deception poisoned every aspect of Tamar's future and everyone in it? If you were sexually violated, do you still embrace a mantle of shame? How has this affected your perspective on sex in general? If you are married, how has this affected your sexual relationship with your husband?

If we've been sexually violated, what comfort can we derive from Psalms 10:17–18 and 34:18?

> *"The Lord is near to the brokenhearted*
> *and saves the crushed in spirit."*
>
> Psalm 34:18 (ESV)

In her book, *Enhancing Your Marriage*, Judy Rossi writes:

> Although we can't change a painful past, it doesn't have to ruin or run our lives. Wrongs that we committed or that were committed against us were done in the

presence of Almighty God. In His divine sovereignty, He knew that we would face these painful experiences. He did not abandon us there; He was with us. And He grieves with us...Satan would have us believe that our past defines our present and shapes our future. In Jesus, however, it does neither. With the indwelling of His Spirit, everything we are and everything we can become is now found in Christ alone, regardless of our history.[7]

 IN HER SHOES

"There are times I am reminded of the event, and for many years I could not participate in conversations related to the topic of rape or sexual assault. But God has used these experiences to enable me to understand what others are experiencing. The love and prayers of friends and family speed the healing. The scars are still present, but instead of scabs ripped off when discussing this topic, I can feel the numbness of a scar and not relive the events."

If you have been sexually violated, how do you respond to the reality that God was with you? Has God been a part of your healing? If so, in what way? If not, where have you gone for healing?

Without Jesus, we can never wholly trust again. We close off our vulnerability, become hardened, brittle, even cynical. Distrust leads to desolation and isolation. The enemy's purposes have been accomplished through the counterfeit—separation from God, separation from others.

Here's a tough truth: Unless the violation is redeemed through Christ, the violator forgiven in Christ, and the mistrust yielded to God, fear, shame, doubt, and suspicion will have power over us, taint every relationship, and thwart the healing process.

CHOOSE H.E.A.L.I.N.G.

H-ope, not heartache: When we choose hope, we choose healing. If we choose heartache, we will remain entrenched in our pain. What assurance does Psalm 147:3 give us? What are the instructions in Hebrews 10:23 and why? Consider: What must you do to embrace hope?

E-ternal, not temporal (the big picture, the spiritual perspective): Read Romans 8:18–25. Our lives are subject to everything this fallen world has to offer. Nothing in this temporal life is guaranteed except our saving relationship with Jesus Christ. Consider: How can your experience be reshaped by this biblical perspective?

_____

_____

_____

_____

A-cceptance, not avoidance: We won't be able to accept what happened to us unless we believe that the Sovereign God had a divine purpose for our suffering. What happened to us was not good but evil. And God knew. Only God can redeem our past and our pain in a way that has meaning and can serve others. Read Luke 22:31–32. Consider: How can these verses shed light on what your future can look like, especially after this kind of suffering?

_____

_____

_____

_____

L-ight, not lies: Understand that you become the lies you believe. In the columns that follow, how does each truth (Light) address the lies (Darkness)?

Lies (Darkness)	Truth (Light)
This is too hard...I can't do this.	John 15:5
I am unacceptable, unclean.	Colossians 1:22
I can't get it together emotionally.	Philippians 4:4–8
I can't trust anyone.	Colossians 3:12–14

I can't trust God.	Jeremiah 17:5–8 and 29:11–13
If I let go of this anger, my violator will be let off the hook.	Psalm 37:1-8 and Romans 12:19
Fear will always be my companion.	Psalm 27:1-2; Proverbs 29:25; 2 Timothy 1:7

I-nsight, not ignorance: Read 1 Thessalonians 2:13. We shouldn't bury an experience that can benefit others who are or will be in the same place. Consider: How can God's truth help you deal with the issues surrounding your violation? How will you develop insight into your experience?

Choose to believe that God won't waste what you've experienced; He saved you for a reason. Discover it!

Get in and stay in God's Word. If you don't know where to begin, start with the Gospel of John. There you will learn of our Savior's power.

Seek godly biblical counsel to keep you moving forward.

Your issues may be layered. Resolve each issue as it surfaces.

N-ew life, not old: Faith through forgiveness brought us to new life in Christ. Exercising that faith to forgive our violator will *free us* to live our lives as Christ intended. (Did you do this in lesson 9?) To remain in the old life of bitter unforgiveness is its own bondage which thwarts God's transforming power. Therefore, we continually and with determined purpose let the Holy Spirit transform and free us little by little. "In order to get free, [we] must identify wholly with Christ and so be transformed. And this involves a conversion of the will . . . a persistent willingness to die to falsehood and embrace what is real and true."[8] Some of us will choose to live as perpetual victims rather than persevering victors. But God didn't save us to wallow in self-pity or to spend years licking our wounds. He has so much more in store for us when we choose forgiveness—when we choose *life*. Read 2 Corinthians 3:17-18 and 1 Corinthians 15:49. Consider: Have you forgiven your violator? If not, are you willing to forgive? Said another way, do you want to be freed from the burden of keeping your violator roped to your back? If so, please return to lesson 9 and walk through day 4. In your journal, replace the old thoughts with a truth from God as you choose forgiveness.

_____

_____

G-od, not circumstances: If we are more focused on the circumstance than we are on God, we have strayed from God. Choose to trust Him and let Him work out the healing that has already been done in you through Jesus Christ. Read Psalm 141:8 and 1 Peter 2:24–25. Consider: Where is your focus? If necessary, what must you do to recalibrate your focus?

_____

_____

_____

Some of us have already moved victoriously to new life through Jesus Christ. Others of us may have responded to violation by living a life of sexual sin; still others by shrinking from sexual freedom with our spouses. Whatever the response, we can choose to move from our past into God's present. He is willing and eager to let His life renew and flow through us so that in due time, our healing will be a healing balm in the lives of others.

> Prayer: I call upon You, LORD, since You are worthy to be praised, and I am saved from my enemies. The cords of death encompassed me, and the torrents of ungodliness terrified me. The cords of hell surrounded me; the snares of death confronted me. In my distress, I called on You and cried to You for help. You heard my voice out of Your temple, and my cry for help before You came into Your ears. Thank You, Lord, for Your divine rescue (from Psalm 18:3–6).

DAY 2

MY DARKNESS IS A CHOICE

 IN HER SHOES

"My husband and I were completely torn open. I would wake up in the middle of the night to my husband's sobs or find him in the shower with scalding hot water running over his neck in an attempt to feel something other than the emotional devastation he couldn't escape. Witnessing his pain made me finally realize what my choices had done, what my web of lies had created."

If you are struggling with sexual sin, when was the last time you entered into the presence of the Lord with free abandon? When was the last time that you felt whole? Recall the story of the prodigal son. It is as much about the search for wholeness as it is about his descent into darkness. And the story points to this conclusion: We were meant to dwell in our Father's house, in His abundance, in His loving embrace.

Let's return there for a minute. Can't you imagine the son's relief as he turned toward home? Behind him lay the waste and ruin of his foolish choices. The home he once considered his prison, the place that once felt oppressive, narrow, and limiting now represented everything that was good, abundant, and free, and he knew he desperately needed to get back there. With each step toward home, the shackles loosened. His step quickened until eventually he was abandoned to his father's welcoming arms. So relieved to be home. So totally, utterly relieved.[9]

Like the prodigal, we were born for better than the profane. We were designed to dwell in the light of God's love—fully, wholly, holy. And something deep within us knows this, longs for this, and cries out to return to His divine design. Ephesians 1:4 says that *"He chose us in Him before the foundation of the world, that we should be holy and blameless before Him."* There is peace in dwelling there. There is rest in finding our way back to Him.

As author John Eldredge puts it, there is "the utter relief of holiness."[10] When we understand the principles that break bondage, we find our relief—His name is Jesus.

Let's journey into our own prodigal hearts. The most pressing source of our sexual struggles and sufferings results from choices that create and foster areas of moral compromise and darkness. And Satan will always exploit those choices! For someone stuck in these depths, there is a way home. Moral darkness is "not simply the absence of light; it is the absence of God, who is light."[11] His grace will always meet us where our sin is deep. Only the Light of Life can make righteousness a habit, but we must choose to turn from darkness to light.

How would you answer this question: Are the things I'm suffering today the harvest of what I planted yesterday?

Are you tired of where you are? Read John 5:1–9. Why wasn't the man at the pool healed after thirty-eight years? How would you qualify his answer?

What question did Jesus ask the man who sought healing? What's critical about this question?

How would you respond if Jesus asked you the same question He asked the man who languished in his condition for so long (v. 6)?

You might answer with this question: *I don't know. What's it going to cost me?* Here's a bottom-line answer in the form of a question: What will it cost you if you won't give up the darkness? How does Matthew 5:29–30 answer this question?

_____

_____

_____

👣 IN HER SHOES

"I was unfaithful to my partners and husbands over a period of twenty years. I would be okay for a year or two, and then I would stray. This happened while I was married and also while I was single. I craved physical touch and somehow equated it to love. I was very confused. I wanted encouragement and positive words, and I felt sex met that need. But it didn't really."

YES, IT IS DARK IN THIS PLACE!

Is your life out of control? Are you living in a dark place? Are you tired of what your sin habit is doing to you and others? It takes courage to break the silence in our hearts and admit weakness—to resist denying, to reject rationalizing, or to refuse justifying any longer.

Do you want to be free from this bondage? If so, why? If not, why not?

_____

_____

_____

Perhaps we think we're "safe"—not convinced that our sin will find us out and take its toll. But it's already well known by the very One who is jealous for us and grieves over the competition for our affections.

Let's put Jesus' grief into personal perspective. In Luke 19:42, He wept over the people who had rejected Him, saying, *"If you had known in this day, even you, the things which make for peace! But now they have been hidden from your eyes."* Oswald Chambers has wonderful insight: "God's words here cut directly to the heart, with the tears of Jesus behind them. These words imply responsibility for our own faults. God holds us accountable for what we refuse to see or are unable to see because of our sin. And 'now they are hidden from your eyes' because you have never completely yielded your nature to Him"[12].

How do Isaiah 5:20 and 1 John 1:5–6 describe the behavior of a darkened, unyielding heart?

_____

_____

_____

The Bible is clear about our darkness in Matthew 6:22–24. What's the message?

_____

_____

_____

A darkened heart is an impoverished heart for which there is only one remedy. Read Psalms 70:5. According to this Scripture, what is the plea?

_____

_____

_____

Is there any darkness in your life that you know needs to be exposed to the Light, but you will not yield? God knows that you will never be whole if you are not holy, and you will never be holy if you continue to walk in darkness. If darkness is your choice, how is that playing out in your life?

_____

_____

_____

HELP! TURN ON THE LIGHT!

God is not in the darkness. From the beginning, He separated darkness from light with just a word. Separating darkness from light was also God's first work through Jesus Christ in the hearts of humanity. What does John 1:1–5 reveal about the light?

_____

_____

What does Jesus reveal about Himself in John 8:12? What choice does He give us?

_____

_____

Read Ephesians 5:8–15. Why do we need the light?

_____

_____

_____

If we recognize that we need God's help, the only relief is to turn our darkened hearts toward Him. When we do, He will withhold no good thing. Based on Matthew 5:3, how do we know?

_____

_____

_____

What do you think it means to be "poor in spirit?" Why do you think Jesus said they would be "blessed?" What good can come from being spiritually needy? How can this benefit one who is stuck in sexual sin?

Based on all the Scripture verses you have just read, how would exposing your darkness to the light benefit you personally?

DONE WITH THE DARKNESS

When we choose darkness, we choose idolatry. These idols turn our hearts from the Living God. According to Matthew 22:37–38, on whom should we focus our allegiance and entire devotion? How are we to do this?

What truths in 1 John 4:4 and Romans 6:14 empower us to choose the light?

 IN HER SHOES

"[After repeated infidelity and three divorces,] today I am married to a young Christian who is slowly developing a relationship with God and Jesus and leading our marriage. I have been faithful to him since we started dating. More importantly, my relationship with God has stayed the course. He has given me the vision of love I have so desired."

Entire devotion means a "deep, consistent love for God. This kind of complete surrender displays a singleness of heart toward God, leaving no room for rivals. If sin amounts to idolatry—idolatry of self or of others—then entire devotion is the cure."[13]

Our allegiance and devotion must change. To choose life is to choose the light and to be done with the darkness. Following Jesus is loving God. Let's think back to the Prodigal. He could not get home until he chose to turn from the life of darkness and return to the life his Father offered. The offer stands. Will you turn?

> Prayer: Lord, I choose the light. I choose life. I choose *You*. In the mighty name of Jesus, my Savior and Light, Amen.

DARKNESS EXPOSED (DON'T FOOL YOURSELF)

 IN HER SHOES

"I discovered that old habits die hard. Although I was now a Christian, I would frequently find my life back in the same rut that was carved into my life by years of pornography and abuse."

HOLY ILLUMINATED

Jesus will deliberately craft whatever circumstance is necessary to lovingly expose things we want to hide in the dark. When Jesus went to Galilee, He had to pass through Samaria. This was curious since the religious Jews avoided that route, even though it was shorter. They looked on the part-Jew part-Gentile inhabitants of Samaria with such disdain that they believed entering the town would defile them. Jesus disagreed. It was noon (the sixth hour) at Jacob's well, and there He met a Samaritan woman.

Read John 4:7–30. What transpired between Jesus and the woman at the well (vv. 7–9)?

Since women drew water in the cool of the day, morning and evening, it was odd that this woman came at noon when no others were around. It was also odd that Jesus' disciples happened not to be around, since they would likely have reminded Him of the cultural impropriety of engaging a Samaritan woman. But not just any Samaritan woman. She was an immoral woman whose shame isolated her from the others.

What was Jesus conveying to this woman in verses 10–15, and what do you make of her response?

Although the Samaritan woman didn't quite understand the spiritual significance of her "thirst," she did desire what Jesus offered—not to be thirsty again. Their conversation took a turn in John 4:16–26. What did Jesus reveal about her and about Himself?

We can only speculate why this woman had five husbands and was now living with a man outside of marriage. Perhaps she could neither satisfy or be satisfied by these relationships. Perhaps she thirsted for more, for better, hoping that the next one would treat her better, value her, meet her deepest longings. But Jesus knew, and undaunted by her sin, he ventured into her heart. With gentle compassion He revealed her thirst, and Himself as the Messiah, the Living Water that could quench her thirsty soul. And she received it.

Based on verses 27–30, how do we know that the Samaritan woman received Jesus' words for herself?

_____

_____

Has Jesus approached you as He did the Samaritan woman, telling you all the things that you have done? What inner thirst has He revealed that He wants to quench with only Himself?

_____

_____

_____

God is serious about sin in our lives. He loves us that much. His love won't cover over our hidden darkness; instead, His love reveals the darkness by exposing it to His light in whatever way He chooses for us —"holy illuminated." The fact that Jesus tenderly and without condemnation speaks conviction of sin into our souls indicates that He desires to do something about that sin. This is evidence that we are secure in Him, secure in His love. We can do nothing to make Him love us any more. We will do nothing to make Him love us any less.

 IN HER SHOES

"The scales had finally fallen from my eyes, and I could see the lies that I had believed that almost cost me everything—the lies from my childhood that had taught me that I was created for sex, to serve men, and to never say no; the lies that my thoughts would stay private and would never cause pain or heartache; and the lies that my feelings were the ultimate authority and determined God's perfect plan for my life. I desperately needed to be set free and healed by truth."

God promises freedom from our poor choices—freedom from our brokenness, our bondage, our guilt, our lies, our shame, our denials, our recrimination, our condemnation, our darkness. Once we admit the truth about ourselves (whole truth holy illuminated), and truly desire freedom from sin more than the sin itself (repentance), it is in God's divine plan to set us free (John 8:31–32, and 36; 1 John 1:9).

Take a good, prayerful look at yourself right now. God will help you. In order to keep the truth before you, a personal accounting is helpful. Let Psalm 139:23–24 guide your prayer as you answer the following questions in your journal:

What does God say about my sexual sin?

What drives me to my sin? What does my sin reveal about God's presence in my life?

What do I tell myself, others, and God about my sin and darkness? What lies am I living out in order to cover my sin?

What truths about my sin am I still denying, rationalizing, minimizing, and justifying?

What is my sexual sin costing me personally? Physically? Emotionally? Spiritually? Financially? Relationally? On the job? In the ministry? Other? What is my sin costing those I love—family members, friends, others?

List reasons why I should stop my sexual sin *now*:

What new truths have I discovered about my sin and Savior today?

THE ROAD HOME

It's important to remind yourself of God's freeing gift of salvation. He hasn't changed His purpose for you or His promise. Let His process continue to unfold in your life! Return to the personal accounting questions you just answered in your journal. As you ponder your answer, ask the Holy Spirit to lead you (Psalm 139:23-24).

Pray for Jesus' holy illumination in your life (Psalm 32:1–2).

Speak back to God whatever sin the Holy Spirit has "holy illuminated" to you (confession) (Psalm 32:5).

Openly express that you desire freedom from your sin more than the sin itself (repentance and return).

Receive God's forgiveness (Psalm 32:5).

Believe that you have been heard and met with open arms (reconciliation and restoration) (Psalm 32:6–7).

Ask for His help on this journey (accountability) (Psalm 32:7–8).

When you have done this, you are ready for the critical next thing.

WHOLLY ILLUMINATED—INTO THE LIGHT

If you choose to walk into the Light, God will move you to the next healing step: confessing your sins to a biblically grounded sister you trust. There is reason for this, and it's found in James 5:16. Why should you confess your sins to another? What quality should this person possess and why?

In no way do we minimize the potential difficulty of this task. However, once our sin is exposed, it breaks the power of secrecy. The light illuminates the darkness. Every time.

 IN HER SHOES

"God brought a beautiful, godly woman to walk alongside me, to mentor me. I shared my story of my abortion with her. She was safe and nonjudgmental. We met for many months, and she shared God's love and compassion with me through His Word, through prayer, and through friendship. She sharpened me and kept me on the straight and narrow path, always guiding me to the Savior."

What concerns you most about confessing to another? What do you think is the worst that can happen if you confess?

_____

_____

_____

Does your concern expose any new lies? Are you hopeful that you can be set free on your own terms? What are they? What does this reveal to you?

_____

_____

_____

Prayerfully consider the righteous women in your sphere of influence—women who will pray fervently for you. List their names in your journal. Does one stand out among the others? If so, circle her name.

The old adage holds here: To not decide is to decide. We must make fearless, brutally honest decisions about sin in our lives. We cannot move forward into healing if we are unwilling to be healed. If you have settled on your trustworthy friend, pray for God's timing. You will know when to move forward. And she'll be ready.

When you have done this, you are ready for the critical next thing.

> Prayer: Lord, I don't want to fool myself anymore. Thank You that Your Spirit will help to keep me accountable. Thank You for Your provision of a righteous friend with whom I can remain accountable. Above all, thank You for Jesus, my Living Water.

DAY 4

SEEN IN GOD'S LIGHT

SEEN IN NEW LIGHT

When we turn from our sin and return to God, He won't leave us where we are or where we've been, since *"He who began a good work in you will perfect it until the day of Christ Jesus"* (Philippians 1:6). The more we pursue Him, the more we resemble Him and become who we really are. This is a process.

Matthew 16:24–25 illuminates this process. Jesus gives three requirements for those would "come after" Him? What are they? What do you think each means? Why would we do this?

_____

_____

_____

We deny ourselves when we die to our self-will. We disown, renounce, surrender, hand over our lives and the right to our lives to Jesus Christ. We can only save our lives by *not* saving our lives. Anything short this is "self". Only when we deny self for His sake is the next thing possible: pick up our cross.

We pick up our cross when we embrace God's will, whatever the cost. We demonstrate that we are under Christ's rule when we willingly endure our sufferings or trials. Anything short of this is rebellion. Only when we pick up our cross for His sake is the next thing possible: to follow Jesus.

We follow Jesus when we actively cleave "to Him in believing trust and obedience...follow His leading and act according to His example."[14] We walk the road He's walked and faithfully follow His teaching. Anything short of this is following the enemy. Only when we follow Jesus for His sake is the next thing possible: change.

> "Then Jesus said to His disciples, 'If anyone wishes to come after
> Me, he must deny himself, and take up his cross and follow Me.
> For whoever wishes to save his life will lose it; but whoever loses his
> life for My sake will find it."
>
> Matthew 16:24–25 (NASB)

What does denying yourself look like in your sexual struggle? What are you willing to suffer (pick up your cross) for the sake of Christ? Are you willing to follow Christ? If not, what is keeping you from doing so?

_____

_____

_____

In Philippians 3:12–14, Paul declares that he's not yet perfect. He's "still involved in the struggles of life in a fallen world and hence he still sins."[15] This admission should be comforting to every Christian! But let's not get comfortable with it. What's his message?

_____

_____

_____

Paul was a grateful man, willing to leave all for Jesus. What has God called you to leave behind? What goal has He called you to strain toward for the upward call of Christ?

_____

_____

_____

Based on what you've just learned, turn to Romans 12:1–2. In verse 1, what does it mean to *"present your bodies as a living sacrifice"* (ESV)? What does it mean to you to be *"holy and acceptable"* to God? Why is this offering considered a way we worship God (*see* Romans 6:13 for more insights)? How does this apply to our sexual selves?

_____

_____

_____

According to verse 2, how do we remain holy and acceptable, especially as it relates to our sexual urges or passions?

_____

_____

By way of reminder, why are we to have transformed minds? What does that mean for us as it relates to our choices?

_____

_____

Because God spared us, we give *all* of ourselves back to Him as a living sacrifice in grateful response to His mercies. What would this worship look like in your life?

_____

_____

THE LIGHT AT THE ALTAR

Offering our bodies as living sacrifices is a daily form of worship. It is integral to the process of becoming more like Jesus. This is good news. However, sexual sin always impacts someone else's life. We must recognize and address the damage that we may have done.

 IN HER SHOES

"My husband and I continued marriage counseling, but I still couldn't tell him the whole truth. I was sure that if he knew what I really did he would take our kids and leave me with nothing. Every time I heard the doorbell or the phone ring, my heart would stop, terrified that the neighbor or his wife (who must have known by now) would come to tell my husband the truth. I became convinced that if my husband found out from anyone other than myself, our marriage would really be over. I finally told him the whole truth in the counselor's office. And by God's grace, my husband and everyone else that I had hurt forgave me. The complete truth allowed healing to begin."

Revisit Matthew 5:23–24 and 18:15. What do these passages address? Why do you think it is important to deal with unresolved offenses?

_____

_____

_____

Being at the altar is being in the presence of God. That's where the light is. That's where His Spirit reminds us that we have some amends to make and until we do so our worship is hindered. We can't remain at the altar and feign righteousness when we have treated someone unrighteously, whether by giving offense or by holding onto offenses. The altar is a critical place of transformation.

We're talking about honesty and integrity in our hearts before God. If we resist being honest about people we've offended, then we're re-inviting denial into our lives and relationships. What does Romans 12:18 say is our responsibility?

_____

_____

_____

We're called by God to reconcile offenses regardless of who committed them. However, "Paul recognizes it is not always possible to be at peace with everyone, even when one makes the effort."[16] But an effort must be made, with one exception: "We make direct amends to people we've harmed whenever possible, except when to do so would injure them or others."[17] For example, making direct amends would probably include family members and loved ones, but would probably not include former sex partners from "way back" who now have families of their own. Talk over making amends with your trusted friend. Ultimately, it's a matter of prayer and Holy Spirit guidance.

> "We don't get to go to the altar and feign righteousness when we have treated someone unrighteously, whether by giving offense or by holding onto offense. The altar is a critical place of transformation."

Let's go to the altar. As the Spirit leads, list the following in your journal: the names of those you offended, how you offended them, and the impact you think your offense had on them.

With whom are you prompted to reconcile your offense? Circle them.

Now ask this question as it relates to each person circled: _Would my effort to make direct amends to this person do more damage than good to him/her or others?_ Write your answer beside each name. If the answer is yes, leave it be, and make your amends with the Lord only over this person. If the answer is no, continue with the following:

Pray that God would provide 1) the opportunity to make amends, 2) His timing, 3) the preparation of the heart of the one offended, 4) the preparation of your heart, and 5) the words you speak.

As God leads you to each person, be sure and come back to your journal, and note the date and the outcome.

Not everyone will receive you or your attempt to make amends. But you will have done the right thing. Even if you have not made peace with that person, you will be at peace with God.

> Prayer: Now may the God of peace equip you with all you need for doing His will. May He produce in you, through the power of Jesus Christ, every good thing that is pleasing to Him. All glory to Him forever and ever! Amen (from Hebrews 13:20–21 NTL).

DAY 5

REMAINING IN THE LIGHT

 IN HER SHOES

"For several months following the confession of my affair, I felt like a big red 'A' was painted on my chest. Over time, God again set me free by His truth. He called me by name, and when I turned to Him, I did not find shame or condemnation but His loving arms open wide. I fell into His arms, and He reminded me that my sin was not my identity. God's truth is this: Jesus came as the Redeemer for people just like me; people who have been stained and broken by [sin and bondage], either their own or others.' I am a work in progress, not perfect but forgiven, with a broken heart that has been bound up, released from the darkness of sin and abuse, and wearing a crown of beauty not ashes (Isaiah 61:1–3). What an amazing God!"

STANDING IN THE LIGHT

You're on a newly illuminated glide path. Do you perceive it? Perhaps up until now, Jesus has only been your Savior. Now He is your Lord. This lesson will help you to stand firm on this path.

In your journal do the following and keep notes. (Solicit the help of a biblically grounded sister, if necessary):

Daily acknowledge that you need God to help you choose His divine design for your sex life whether married or single. Read Matthew 6:33. Ask God to give you a Scripture to help you choose purity when otherwise tempted. If you're married, decide to be sexually committed to your husband in your heart, in your mind, with your body. Only this will fill the hole in your soul. Lust will never care for you the way God cares for you. Pornography will never provide for you the way God provides for you. An adulterer will never love you the way God loves you. Premarital sex will never fulfill you the way God fulfills you. Alternate lifestyles will never satisfy you the way God satisfies you.

Daily keep short accounts with God. Read 1 John 2:1. You are saved and free, but you may still stumble. If you stumble, repent and return. God will eagerly forgive and move you forward. Always forward!

Remember to examine your thoughts. They'll keep your temptations in check. Revisit 2 Corinthians 10:5 and Philippians 4:8. Are you telling yourself the truth about you, about your circumstance, about your temptations, about _____ (fill in the blank)? What must you guard your mind against?

Remember to examine your emotions and bring them in line with truth: *"Lord, You know. How would You have me respond?"* How do Psalm 139:1-12, 23-24 and Proverbs 24:10 help temper those temptations that give you the most trouble? Why should God's perfect knowledge of your circumstance strengthen you to stay the course?

Cultivate healthy friends and activities. Practice new, healthy, active habits every day, such as a daily devotional time, Bible study, physical activity, craft activity—especially with a fellowship of sisters. Read 1 Corinthians 9:24-27 and 1 Thessalonians 5:11. What new thing(s) will you add? What friends do you consider healthy?

Daily examine your "house": Read Luke 11:24–26. Cleanse your home, workplace, automobile, computers, iPod, iPhone, and television of all pornographic materials, phone numbers, e-mail correspondence and addresses, social networks, chat rooms, Web sites—anything that throws temptation in your face. These are not harmless! (Note: Visit www.covenanteyes.com. This organization provides software that will monitor Internet usage and send weekly reports to an accountability partner [necessary] and to a spouse [highly recommended]. The program can be downloaded onto every tool that gets Internet access.) Instead, *fill* every space with godly friends, godly materials, music, media, talk, laughter. What house cleaning must you do immediately?

Daily examine the boundaries you should set and then set them: Read Psalm 1:1–3 and 2 Timothy 2:22. Who or what tempts you toward sexual sin? Who tempts you with his or her presence? Where are you when your temptations begin, strengthen, or are strongest? When are you tempted most? What state of mind leads you toward temptation? In each case, determine beforehand what your boundaries are and how you will adhere to them. Have an alarm go off in your head (the Holy Spirit!) when you perceive that a boundary is being breached. Have a plan when that alarm goes off. Call your mentor or sister in Christ. Engage in a diverting activity. What's your plan?

_____

_____

_____

> *"Now flee from youthful lusts and pursue righteousness, faith, love*
> *and peace, with those who call on the Lord from a pure heart."*
>
> 2 Timothy 2:22 (NASB)

Daily examine your accountability before the Holy Spirit as well as before your mentor, other biblically grounded sister(s), or an accountability group. Read Deuteronomy 6:12–14. At the end of the day, what is the Holy Spirit prompting you to tell your mentor or accountability group?

_____

_____

_____

Memorize and recite specific Bible verses or passages that lift you up. Read Psalm 56:10-13 and John 14:26. The Holy Spirit will bring just the right ones to your remembrance when you perceive a weakness or temptation. Examples of verses to memorize: John 5:4, 15; 1 Corinthians 10:12–13; Philippians 1:6; 4:4–8, 13; 2 Peter 1:3. There are so many more. As you continue reading the Word daily, God will bring a verse that comes alive in your heart. That's the one you should memorize. Write them all in your journal, and visit them regularly.

Daily express to God your gratitude for this new glide path. Read Matthew 5:14–16. In due time, He will free you to share your story with specific others who are where you have been—for their good and for His glory. Are you grateful?

_____

_____

_____

_____

Prayer: Lord, You are my Master, and I thank You for loving me enough to set me free from a life of darkness. I need You to speak truth into my deceptions, peace into my emotions, purity into my activities, and courage into my temptations. Give me the discipline to purge my house and fill it with what is profitable, the strength to stay Your course, the diligence to maintain my boundaries, and the humility to seek accountability. Lord, I need You.

LESSON 12

NAKED AND UNASHAMED

In the last eleven lessons, we've built a foundation that will help us stand firmly for God's divine design for sex. In these last five days we'll address how to choose God's battle plan against the enemy who wants to derail our resolve, face lingering trust issues with God and/or with others; tap the joy of choosing satisfaction in God, and harness the value of choosing purity so that we can truly live naked and unashamed.

DAY 1

CHOOSING GOD'S BATTLE PLAN

Someone once said, "Safety is not found in the absence of danger but in the presence of God." But just as we must not forget the power of our Savior, we must not forget the ploys of our enemy. Edith Schaeffer wrote, "The only way in which Satan can persecute or afflict God is through attacking the people of God." [1] So we need to be ready. If we're going to do battle, we must have the heart of God (Ephesians 5:1), the mind of Christ (1 Corinthians 2:16), and the power of the Holy Spirit (Acts 1:8), who is equipping us with all three.

Let's understand Satan's schemes as they relate to our personal circumstances. According to 2 Corinthians 11:3, 14 and 1 Peter 5:8, what tactics does Satan use?

Even the apostle Paul raised concerns that our choices may cooperate more with the enemy than with God. Whatever choices are before us, we're to follow Christ's example *"so that no advantage would be taken of us by Satan, for we are not ignorant of his schemes"* (2 Corinthians 2:11). Or are we? Understand this: "The devil can traffic in any area of darkness, even the darkness that still exists in a Christian's heart." [2] We get to choose who wins this battle.

Christians may underestimate the power and wiles of Satan. Christ didn't, and if He considered Satan a formidable foe, then so should we. Just so there's no misunderstanding, Satan is no match for Jesus Christ! Jesus gave His life to undo Satan's damage, and this same life is now in us. We can face this foe with courage and do battle alongside God because *"he who is in you is greater than he who is in the world"* (1 John 4:4 ESV).

Military members train daily for battle against our country's flesh-and-blood enemies. We, too, must train daily, because the enemy of our souls is not going to let up until the Lover of our souls returns. The battle not only includes our trials, our tests, our hardships, our heartaches, but also our daily face-off with *"the lust of the flesh and the lust of the eyes and the boastful pride of life"* (1 John 2:16). Succumbing to these or to sexual temptations can break fellowship with the One who loves us and the ones we love.

Scripture is very clear about how we are to ready ourselves for battle. According to Ephesians 6:10–12, where does our power come from for our battle (v. 10)?

Why will we need battle gear (v. 11)?

Who is not our enemy (v. 12)? What do you think this means? Describe our enemy (v. 12). What do you think this means?

What protects us, and why are we commanded to put it on (v. 13)?

Remember that neither our loved ones nor we are the enemy. The enemy (Satan) is the enemy, and he will use us like pawns in a chess game in order to derail our relationship with God and with each other. Temptations will harass us every day. It's a reality of life, but we don't have to fall victim to the tempter's schemes. In this next exercise: How can each piece of armor (Column 1) help you in your sin struggle or with your reaction to sin against you or a loved one (Column 2)?

Armor of God	Protection Against Sin
Belt of truth: committing to truthfulness and personal integrity so that your walk will match your talk	
Breastplate of Righteousness: doing what is right so that your heart is protected	
Feet Shod with Gospel of Peace: knowing that Christ joins you in battle so that you proceed with peace and stability	
Shield of Faith: trusting God resolutely so that the enemy's accusations and temptations will be thwarted in your mind	
Helmet of Salvation: protecting your mind with the truth of Whose you are so that Satan can't shake the assurance of your salvation	
Sword of the Spirit: using God's Word consistently (offensively and defensively!) so that you can counter the enemy's lies, deceptions, and schemes (his battle plan!)	

According to Ephesians 6:18, what part does prayer play in our battle?

_____

_____

_____

We handle all things with prayer, at all times, in the Spirit who will align us with God's will and with all perseverance. We don't give up, give over, or give in to the enemy.

 IN HER SHOES

"Adoration, Scripture, and praise music were a part of my weekly routine in just trying to make it through. Tears once again fill my eyes this time in gratitude for how far the love and provision of Christ had brought me. He is faithful no matter what circumstance I find myself in. He comes alongside me and gives me the strength I need to go through whatever is going on in my life. I must choose to trust in His love and goodness, even when all evidence points the other way. Time after time He shows up and carries me through. His love holds me up and comforts me if I will just let it."

Read Romans 8:31–39. What is your encouragement in battle? How is your victory described?

_____

_____

_____

If God brought us to this battle, then we're either all in or we're not in at all. He is _for_ us, and has equipped us with the finest battle gear in all eternity. We are not only "striving towards victory but fighting from the position of victory." [3] He has shown us that we can endure anything if we depend on Him for everything. Conquerors—just like Jesus!

> Prayer: God, I acknowledge You as Lord. Thank You that You love me, that You promise to protect and rescue me. Thank You that You answer me when I call and are with me in my trouble. You are my Deliverer and I rest in Your shadow. (From "The Soldier's Psalm"—Psalm 91.)

Day 2

Choosing Trust in God

 IN HER SHOES

"The enemy of our souls tried to get me to agree with him that I was a failure as a mother, and I felt very inadequate as a Christian parent."

Throughout this study we have referred to the deadly nature of sexual sin. In a world where we have access to every human drama known at the push of a button, to say sex apart from God's divine design is deadly may sound like mere hyperbole. It is not. It ravages the very foundation of "naked and unashamed"—_trust_. And while all relationships can suffer the effects of breached trust, in no other relationship does the dagger go more deeply than in marriage. When trust is ravaged, the condition under which a married couple is able to be sexually and emotionally vulnerable and give themselves with abandon is destroyed.

However the pain of sexual sin is experienced, we often react by closing ourselves off to any future risk of damage by developing a brittle mantle of anger, fear, rejection, and isolation. If that happens, mistrust can systematically shut down our relationships one by one, beginning with our relationship with God. Should this occur, there are far reaching outcomes.

Consider the following scriptures from the perspective of these far reaching outcomes. How do they affirm why we should trust God (especially when trusting a loved one is challenging or even unfeasible)?

Psalm 9:9–10

Psalm 37:3–6

Psalm 56:10–11

Psalm 73:24–26

Proverbs 3:5–6

John 14:1 (to believe means to trust in, rely upon, cling to, depend upon)

When we're in relational crises, we may perceive that trusting another (or others) is risky, perhaps even dangerous—a perception that we can also readily transfer to God. However, when applied to relational crises, these scriptures assure us that *not* trusting God is both risky and dangerous.

When we pull away from the very One who desires to guide us through life, the long-term damaging effects of mistrust impact every aspect of our being and relationships.

Our open communion with God is hindered and our ability to trust others is undermined.

When trust is breached by someone we love, particularly a spouse, we have a choice: We can "collapse in bitterness, isolation, and the most destructive self-reliance of all: never wanting anything from anyone again. Or we can choose to believe that all relational pain is a means to convert us to a radical reliance on God . . . "[4] According to Proverbs 18:1, what results from an isolationist response to betrayal? What can this mean when it comes to rebuilding trust? What can reliance on God mean when it comes to rebuilding trust?

Identify a specific relationship where trust was breached. Did it shake your trust in God? If so, how? What was the outcome of that relational crisis? What did you do with your anger, fear, anxieties, sorrow, bitterness? How were they resolved? What fruit did they bear in your life? In that relationship?

How might radical reliance on God have influenced your response and the outcome of this relational crisis?

When it comes to trusting God to help you rebuild a relationship (perhaps the one identified), where are you on a scale of 1 to 10 (1 being *I'm not there at all*; 10 being *I'm radically relying on Him*)? How could radical reliance on God free you from being bound to mistrust? How can radical reliance on God teach you the appropriate ways to rebuild trust and with whom?

When we choose to radically rely on God, we have both the freedom and the foundation on which to do the work of rebuilding trust in our broken relationships with others *as God leads*.

> Prayer: Lord, I choose to trust You—radically rely on You—in every-thing.

CHOOSING TO BUILD TRUST

Nothing rocks our world like sexual betrayal. Our reactions are quick and visceral. We often experience fight-or-flight—the first sign that we are threatened to our very core. And we defend against future attacks by closing ourselves off, leaving no vulnerabilities exposed. Relationally, we cease to trust. In the case of betrayal, this is wise until trustworthiness is proven. (Note: When it's *dangerous* to trust someone, safety must be secured before trust can be rebuilt. Professional help is essential to this end.)

In marriage, betrayal shatters everything that binds us to our mates. When this happens, the last place we want to go is to a vulnerable physical, emotional, or sexual place of oneness. "Naked and unashamed" seems unattainable, perhaps not even desirable.

When we live in constant mistrust with a repentant mate or others with whom we're close, we choose the worst kind of loneliness. Walled-off isolation precludes our ability to rebuild damaged relationships that could otherwise be healed and ultimately thrive. So the first step to rebuilding damaged relationships is to *choose* to—to be willing to step out based on our radical reliance on God.

 IN HER SHOES

"The temptation not to trust my husband is strong. He knows this is a normal consequence of his actions. We were broken and dying as a couple, and God in His infinite mercy and grace redeemed our marriage by redeeming us. Our marriage is stronger now than ever before. We fight longer and harder against things that threaten it. We make daily choices to protect our marriage. We celebrate it. We know that God can redeem anything."

Trust is developed over time as the relational parties experience trustworthiness in each other. It must be earned, nurtured, and purposefully built between two people. Constant reassurance is essential. And although one person can reach out to another, without reciprocal trust the openness needed to build mutual trust shuts down.

Choosing to build trust must be based on our understanding of what God commands regarding our hearts. Read Proverbs 4:23, 28:13–14 and Psalm 51:6. How does the condition of our hearts equip and prepare us for the hard work of relationship building? What needs to be the focus of this hard work?

In Colossians 3:12–17, summarize God's direction for building relationships. Practically speaking, what does this look like in relationship-building? How does it apply to *your* broken relationship?

_____

_____

_____

When we choose to trust God in our broken relationships, particularly in a broken marriage, we have hope that love can rebuild the perfect bond of unity.

 IN HER SHOES

"After several weeks, I felt the Holy Spirit prompting me. He asked me difficult questions like, 'Do you believe that the best way to help your [repentant] husband stay spiritually and physically faithful to you is to deny him access to you?' I fought against it for a while, but I soon began to see my husband through God's eyes, and I knew that I needed to take the first step toward reconciliation. It was absolutely an act of sacrifice. There was no joy in that sexual encounter for me. I'm not sure there was joy for my husband, either. We both cried all the way through it. We knew that those moments were the holiest sexual encounter we would ever experience. It got easier after the first time. Several months later, I realized after an evening together that the thoughts of other women had not entered my mind at all. What a joyful moment that was!"

That said, let us be clear: Trusting another is not the same as loving (*agape*) another. Nor is it the same as forgiving another. God requires both from us no matter what the circumstance (Matthew 5:43–48); however, trust must be earned in the rebuilding process. And if we have betrayed others, we must earn their trust one building block at a time.

Let's look at some basic trust-building tools:

Agape Love: Repairing relationships requires *agape*, since it's the only love that acts as a bulwark in the face of betrayal. God's love in and through us cannot be destroyed, since it's not dependent on another's trustworthiness. Therefore, God's *agape* will not fail us or others. Read John 13:34–35 and 15:10–17. What kind of love is Jesus talking about? How is it manifest in our relationship with others? How can *agape* rebuild trust?

_____

_____

_____

If trust has been broken with another, how will *agape* help you rebuild that trust? If trust has been broken with your spouse, how will *agape* help you rebuild the "naked and unashamed" (spiritual, physical/sexual, emotional, relational) quality of relationship between you and your husband, whether you are the betrayed or the betrayer?

_____

_____

_____

Amazing Grace: Imbedded in *agape* is grace. Someone wisely said that when we gratefully acknowledge the grace we've received, we freely give it to those in need. Just as God's grace frees us from guilt, extending grace to another frees them (and us) to participate in the trust-building process. Consider 2 Corinthians 9:8 and 12:9. Who is the recipient of God's grace? For what purposes? Why is extending grace so important in rebuilding trust? How can grace rebuild trust?

If trust has been broken with another, how will grace help you rebuild trust? If trust has been broken with your spouse, how will grace help you rebuild the "naked and unashamed" quality of relationship between you and your husband, whether you are the betrayed or the betrayer?

Resolute Commitment: Committing to do God's work in all things includes the hard work of restoring relationships. It only takes one willing and determined heart to initiate the rebuilding process. As the Lord's servants, how do 2 Corinthians 5:16–20, Philippians 2:12–16, and 2 Timothy 2:24–26 counsel and encourage us in this process, whether we are the betrayer or betrayed? How can resolute commitment help to rebuild trust?

If trust has been broken with another, how will resolute commitment help you rebuild that trust? If trust has been broken with your spouse, how will resolute commitment help you rebuild the "naked and unashamed" quality of relationship between you and your husband, whether you are the betrayed or the betrayer?

Honest Communication: Honest and open communication (truth) can lead to genuine understanding. Truth is the cornerstone for trust leading to restored relationships. What wise guidance does Ephesians 4:29 offer for positive results? How can the following help to rebuild trust?

Be approachable, receptive, a safe place with and for another:

_____

_____

Say what we mean, and mean what we say:

_____

_____

Say it with kindness (the tougher the message, the gentler the delivery):

_____

_____

Listen with your ears as well as with your heart:

_____

_____

Seek to understand rather than to be understood:

_____

_____

If trust has been broken with another, how will your candid and honest expression of your thoughts and feelings (truth) help you rebuild that trust? If trust has been broken with your spouse, how will your candid and honest expression of your thoughts and feelings help you rebuild the "naked and unashamed" quality of relationship between you and your husband, whether you are the betrayed or the betrayer? How can receiving candid and honest expression of your husband's thoughts and feelings help rebuild the "naked and unashamed" quality of your relationship?

_____

_____

_____

_____

Proven Repentance: God has given us "proof" of the trustworthiness of His love through the life and death of Christ. So, too, earthly relationships need proof of trustworthiness. Trust is not built on words. Trust is built on what we do that demonstrates our trustworthiness. Based on 2 Corinthians 7:9–10, what is required of us or a loved one before we can prove repentance? What is God's role in our or another's efforts to prove repentance? How can proven repentance help to rebuild trust?

_____

_____

_____

_____

If trust has been broken with another other than your spouse, how will proven repentance help you rebuild that trust?

_____

_____

_____

In cases of marital betrayal, in order for healing to take place and trust to be rebuilt, there needs to be a clear change of behavior that can be seen and assessed. This is the outward action of the inward change of a heart (repentance). Consider the following trust-builders. They are reasonable, realistic, attainable, and tangible actions that are required when sexual sin has broken trust:

- Allowing the time it will take to rebuild trust
- Agreeing to individual as well as couple Christian counseling
- Being real—open and honest—and communicating accordingly
- Gradually and intentionally rebuilding connection and becoming more a part of each other's lives and activities (the dating/courting process)
- Keeping nothing secret (bank accounts, post-office boxes, credit cards, bills)
- Cancelling whatever remains tethered to the betrayal
- Where applicable, temporarily ceasing sexual intimacy until God frees you both to open the door again
- Where applicable, eliminating the fear of an STD by being willing to be tested
- Limiting computer activity when together or apart
- Securing the computer with filters and accountability sites
- Cancelling overnight trips for a time
- Eliminating patterns, activities, and places that have led to temptation
- Changing jobs, even cities, if necessary
- Confessing/repenting of future failures and asking forgiveness
- Other? _____

If trust has been broken with your spouse, how will proven repentance help you rebuild the "naked and unashamed" quality of relationship between you and your husband, whether you are the betrayed or the betrayer?

_____

_____

_____

If you have betrayed a loved one, write a list of reasonable, realistic, attainable, tangible requirements that you should offer to the one you betrayed.

_____

Caution: Trust requires proof, and that's fair. It also requires consistency. Whichever side of betrayal you're on, rebuilding will take time, effort, patience, and solid, unwavering dependence on the Holy Spirit. He will reveal motives that want to remain hidden, emotions that need to be expressed or dealt with before God alone. Work with Him so that God can bring about His best in your efforts.

Genuine Forgiveness: When one is willing to prove his or her repentance, the other is called by God to forgive from the heart (recall Lesson 9). Read Psalm 103:10–13 and Hebrews 8:12. Just as God does with our repentance, we demonstrate true forgiveness by not using the offense against the one who hurt us. How can genuine forgiveness help to rebuild trust?

_____

_____

_____

_____

If trust has been broken with another, how will genuine forgiveness help you rebuild that trust? If trust has been broken with your spouse, how will genuine forgiveness help you rebuild the "naked and unashamed" quality of relationship between you and your husband, whether you are the betrayed or the betrayer?

_____

_____

_____

 IN HER SHOES

"After having lived my whole life with secrets, I needed to learn how to be an open book so my husband could start to trust me again."

Tender Humility: When we consistently humble ourselves before God, we are reminded of Who's in charge and to Whom we are ultimately accountable in our relationships. But humility doesn't come naturally or easily, which is why God commands it. Read Philippians 2:3. When we choose humility, the Holy Spirit will develop in us what we need to take baby steps toward another's heart. In marriage, taking baby steps is critical toward rebuilding sexual intimacy. This process requires tender humility as a couple depends on Holy-Spirit patience, peace, prompting, and timing. How can tender humility help to rebuild and reinforce trust?

_____

_____

_____

If trust has been broken with another, how will tender humility help you rebuild and reinforce that trust? If trust has been broken with your spouse, how will tender humility help you rebuild and reinforce the "naked and unashamed" quality of relationship between you and your husband, whether you are the betrayed or the betrayer?

Will you *choose* to rebuild trust?

> Prayer: Lord, I trust You to direct my path in every aspect of this trust-building process—moment by moment.

DAY 4

CHOOSING SATISFACTION

Married or single, God's divine design is first that we would experience the beauty of "naked and unashamed" intimacy *with Him* so that in marriage, His divine design for sexual intimacy would reflect that same beauty, depth, sacredness, safety, and therefore, satisfaction—"naked and unashamed".

In John 4, when Jesus revealed Himself to the Samaritan woman as living water, He knew her deep spiritual need and its link to her poor sexual choices. He proclaimed that her deeper need could only be met in Him. In John 6, Jesus further revealed Himself as the Bread of Life. But this seemed to be a particularly difficult teaching, and many followers chose to withdraw from Him. What did Jesus ask when He turned to His Twelve in John 6:66–67? How did Peter respond in verses 68–69 and why?

The disciples chose belief and had "come to know" this Holy One of God. It was as if they were saying, *Lord, we have learned to have faith in, trust in, rely on, and cleave to You. Now we have come to know You intimately.* How satisfied they must have been in Him! Why would they go anywhere else?

Choosing satisfaction in Jesus Christ means *learning* to be satisfied with and by Him, satisfied with His provision, satisfied with and in His presence. This satisfaction deepens our intimacy with Him and makes everything different in life. In the same way, *learning* to be satisfied with and by our spouse, satisfied with his provision, satisfied with and in his presence—deepens our intimacy with him. It makes everything different in marriage.

Have you heard the echo, *You do not want to go away also, do you?* If your answer is, *Lord, to whom shall I go? You have…* how would you complete this sentence? He has what?

_____

_____

Our lives—to include our sex lives—can glorify God. Renowned author and pastor John Piper claims, "God is most glorified in us when we are most satisfied in Him." [5] Does something interfere with your satisfaction in God? What does this reveal about your belief in Him? How is that interference reflected in your sexual choices?

_____

_____

How can we reach that place of satisfaction in God, where belief in and intimacy with Him consistently meet each other until they are inseparable? The verses that follow—when consistently practiced—unfold a powerful pathway toward satisfaction in God. Note that the simple instructions in these verses are commands rather than suggestions.

IN HER SHOES

"If it weren't for my relationship with Jesus Christ, I would still be in the throes of sexual sin or under the weight of its guilt."

REJOICE!

Read 1 Thessalonians 5:16–18, then write 1 Thessalonians 5:16 here:

_____

_____

Why do you think we're commanded to *"rejoice always"*?

_____

_____

To rejoice means to practice joy. It's curious that in this verse there is no object of our rejoicing. Typically, we experience joy over someone or something that satisfies. But this rejoicing has a bit of a different focus, especially as it relates to how or why we can be satisfied in God.

Read Romans 12:12. In what are we to rejoice?

_____

_____

_____

Hope! Unlike any other beings, Christians, above all, have the capacity to hope! How is this possible? Read Romans 15:13.

According to Habakkuk 3:17–18, under what circumstances can we express our hope with rejoicing?

_____

_____

_____

We can rejoice because we have a firm hope. What do the following scriptures say about hope? Romans 8:24, Colossians 1:27, Hebrews 11:1, and 1 Peter 1:20–21.

_____

_____

_____

_____

How does rejoicing in hope build intimacy with God? How does rejoicing in hope influence your satisfaction with God? Your satisfaction with where He has you in life?

_____

_____

_____

When we choose to rejoice always because of our hope in God, we proclaim total dependence on Him during overwhelming odds or weaknesses. We are saying, _You are enough. I choose to be satisfied._

PRAY!

Write 1 Thessalonians 5:17 here:

_____

_____

Why do you think we're commanded to "pray without ceasing"?

_____

_____

_____

What do you think it means to pray "without ceasing"?

_____

_____

_____

Because prayer is the deepest place of intimacy with God, we must keep it fresh and ongoing. This doesn't mean that we're supposed to be on our knees in a prayer closet 24/7. It does mean that we seek to remain in an attitude of prayer where we are always open to His approach and confident that we can approach Him at any time with whatever is on our hearts (just read David's psalms). Prayer becomes an attitude of the heart.

The Holy Spirit makes it possible to always be open to fellowship with God. According to Romans 8:26–27, what part does the Holy Spirit play in our prayers? Does this give you comfort? Why or why not?

Consider the Holy Spirit's role in our prayer life: Why should prayer be important in a believer's sex life? Regardless of her marital status, how should a believer pray in relation to her sex life?

Imagine that, at our request, the Holy Spirit intercedes in our lives for our good and God's great glory! Why would we not pray! Isn't it comforting to know that when we can't express our deepest pain or longings to God, the Holy Spirit will do it for us? Isn't it satisfying to know that God will hear and work through our prayers in accordance with His will?

Do our prayers respond to God's holiness, reflecting our reverence for Who He is? How do our prayer lives reflect/address/tackle our sexual selves—our sexual longings, our sexual frustrations and disappointments, our sexual sins and setbacks? God calls us to be fully expressive, fully honest, fully abandoned—"naked and unashamed" before Him.

How does your prayer life build intimacy with God? What will you do to strengthen that intimacy? How does your prayer life influence your satisfaction with God? How can your prayer life with God influence your sexual satisfaction with your spouse?

BE THANKFUL!

Write 1 Thessalonians 5:18 here:

What does it mean to you to give thanks? What do you think "everything" means?

Psalm 145 is a beautiful benediction of praise to God for His goodness. This psalmist truly knew God intimately. And the psalmist's satisfaction and joy in that intimacy was almost beyond his capacity to express. Read this psalm carefully. Why was this psalmist so grateful?

_____

_____

David wrote Psalm 145. The same David whose spouse despised him, whose father-in-law betrayed him, who lost a lifelong friend who was closer than a brother, who lost several of his children, and who knew the shame and sorrow of his own depraved choices, and yet he praised God with abandon. Perhaps it was because of all of David's sufferings and failings that he understood God's great grace, mercy, and goodness.

We can be thankful because God is good. Most of us define _good_ in the earthly, fleshly sense, but God's goodness is seen in light of the bigger picture—in light of eternity. Even when life disappoints, we can still be thankful, because God is still good, and His eternal plan for us will not disappoint.

In light of your circumstances, how would you answer the question, "Is God still good?" How can being thankful build intimacy with and satisfaction in God? How can being thankful bring you peace with where you are or need to be in God's divine design for sex?

_____

_____

But be thankful in _everything_? Why? Because _"this is God's will for you in Christ Jesus"_ (5:18). "This"—referring to all three commands—is God's will for us all the time and in every circumstance. You may ask yourself, _Rejoice, pray, give thanks before things get better? Those don't seem like natural responses when life hurts._ We're not talking about natural responses. We're talking about spiritual responses. Rejoicing, praying, and giving thanks satisfy us _in_ our circumstances. This satisfaction comes not from the external, but from the eternal.

These three verses are neither platitudes nor pointless pabulum. God commands them because He knows they work! When we choose to _"rejoice always"_, He satisfies us with hope. When we choose to _"pray without ceasing"_, He satisfies our need for intimacy with Himself. When we choose to _"in everything give thanks"_, we acknowledge God's great goodness in our lives and in our circumstances. All three are the response of our hearts to the heart of God—naked and unashamed.

> Prayer: Lord, remind me to rejoice always, to remain in an attitude of prayer so I can hear Your voice, to give thanks in all circumstances. You are enough and I choose to be satisfied.

CHOOSING PURITY

When we think of the word *purity*, virginity often comes to mind. But just what is purity? Simply stated, it's a state of cleanness, blamelessness or innocence,[6] which for the believer begins with the cleansing blood of Jesus Christ. In a larger sense, purity addresses the whole person of the heart. It is a walk and a work, a place and a perspective. It is not just a destination, but a direction (1 John 3:3).

THE IMPORTANCE OF A PURE HEART

According to Titus 1:15-16, how are the pure and impure described?

_____

_____

_____

Consider this: A pure heart desires to be pure about *all* things. A pure heart will not lead someone to impure activities. Conversely, someone who is engaged in impure activities does so out of an impure heart. And a genuinely pure heart will not offend God in her response to another's sin.

Let's revisit 1 John 2:15–17 and recall the three sources that feed into impurity. What do Psalm 51:10 and 2 Timothy 2:20–22 tell us to do and why?

_____

_____

_____

Unrecognized impurities in your heart will eventually be borne out in your choices. Do you recognize any area of impurity in your heart? What will you do to "clean house"? According to 2 Corinthians 11:3 and 1 John 3:1–3, how will we develop a pure heart?

_____

_____

_____

_____

Jesus set the stage for the profound value of a pure heart. Read Matthew 5:8. What is it?

_____

_____

_____

Blessed! The pure in heart will be fully satisfied regardless of circumstances because of the indwelling of Jesus Christ. Seeing God is the believer's ultimate satisfaction! And as His, He'll continue to purify our hearts by cleaning the smudges, dirt, and darkness left in its nooks and crannies. It's a process of His loving, faithful cleansing every time we confess sin to Him (1 John 1:9). This is a glorious hope since His cleansing can make each moment and each day new.

Purity enables us to be naked and unashamed before God, vulnerable and totally abandoned to Him without blushing (1 John 4:16-19). This makes the battle to be pure-hearted the most important battle in God's divine design.

THE PROOF OF A PURE HEART

Read Psalm 24:3–5 and Proverbs 4:23–27. What is the evidence of a pure heart? What is the blessing?

_____

_____

_____

Purity will be reflected in a believer's *faith*. In what ways is this implied in 1 John 5:4–5? How will our faith influence our sexual choices? How will our faith influence our response to another's choices?

_____

_____

_____

Purity will be reflected in a believer's *wisdom*. Read James 3:13–18. Why is it important that our wisdom is first pure? How will *"wisdom from above"* (pure wisdom) influence our sexual choices? How will our wisdom influence our response to another's choices?

_____

_____

_____

Purity will be reflected in a believer's *motives*. Read Psalm 15:1–2 and 51:6. Where are our motives hidden? What will keep our motives pure? How will pure motives influence our sexual choices? How will pure motives influence our response to another's choices?

_____

_____

_____

Only God's Truth will unearth hidden motives, and only His Truth will purify them.

Purity will be reflected in a believer's *thoughts and attitudes*. Based on Philippians 2:4–5, how will a pure heart be reflected in our thoughts and attitudes? How will pure thoughts and attitudes influence our sexual choices? How will pure thoughts and attitudes influence our response to another's choices?

_____

_____

Purity will be reflected in a believer's *words*. According to Luke 6:45 how does the heart influence our words? How will pure words influence our sexual choices? How will pure words influence our response to another's choices?

Purity will be reflected in a believer's *desires*. Read Exodus 20:14 and 17 and Psalm 37:4. How will pure desires influence our sexual choices? How will pure desires influence our response to another's choices?

Purity will be reflected in a beliver's *conduct*. Read Proverbs 21:8 and Luke 6:46-49. What is the connection between our conduct and how we listen to God? What is the outcome when we listen? What is the outcome when we don't? How will pure conduct influence our sexual choices? How will pure conduct influence our response to another's choices?

Purity will be reflected in a believer's *love (agape)*. Read 1 John 5:1-3. Love for Whom? What does this love look like? How will this love influence our sexual choices? How will this love influence our response to another's choices?

Author Chris Tiegreen encourages us, "God knows the frailities of our character. The human heart is a fickle thing; it caves in to the voices of this world and the compulsions of our flesh. But it is redeemable, utterly redeemable...Have we forgotten the call of the Holy God? He understands our imperfections, but He calls us above them. The pure in heart—the steadfast, passionate, faithful lovers of the Savior—are a work in progress. But it is a relentless work. Our direction never changes. God will always show more of Himself to those blessed enough to crave purity." [7]

That's good news! Who could want more than the supreme satisfaction of being in the presence of our Bridegroom—"naked and unashamed"!

> Prayer: As you close out this study, *"May the God of peace Himself sanctify you through and through—that is, separate you from profane things, make you pure and wholly consecrated to God—and may your spirit and soul and body be preserved sound and complete [and found] blameless at the coming of our Lord Jesus Christ, the Messiah. Faithful is He Who is calling you [to Himself] and utterly trustworthy, and He will also do it [that is, fulfill His call by hallowing and keeping you]"* (1Thessalonians 5:23–24 AMP). Amen.

ABOUT THE AUTHORS

JUDY ROSSI has been a Bible study teacher, workshop leader, and international conference and retreat speaker since 1986, addressing women in the areas of marriage, parenting, and other women's issues. She has a degree in Speech Pathology and Audiology. Married for forty years to John, a retired Army officer, they have two married daughters and six grandchildren.

SANDY TROUTMAN has practiced in family counseling, drug and alcohol rehabilitation, and medical social work, and has worked as an educator on issues of abuse, addiction, anger management, and drug and alcohol related issues. She has a B.S. in Social Work and Psychology and an M.S. in Social Work. She and her husband Mark, a retired Army officer, have been married for twenty-eight years. They have two children, Anna and Nathan.

ENDNOTES

Lesson 1

1. Spiros Zodhiates and Warren Baker, Hebrew-Greek Key Word Study Bible (Chatanooga: AMG, 2008), #7225, 2020.

2. Walter C. Kaiser Jr., Peter H. Davids, F. F. Bruce, Manfred T. Brauch, *Hard Sayings of the Bible* (Downers Grove: InterVarsity Press, 1996), 808.

3. Zodhiates, Hebrew-Greek Key Word, 1.

4. R. C. Sproul, *Essential Truths of the Christian Faith* (Carol Stream: Tyndale, 1992), 37.

5. Sproul, *Essential Truths*, 59.

6. Zodhiates, Hebrew-Greek Key Word, #2896, 2892.

7. Ibid., #3615, 1902.

8. Jerry Bridges, *The Pursuit of Holiness* (Colorado Springs: NavPress, 1990), 26–27.

9. Spiros Zodhiates and Warren Baker, eds., *The Complete Word Study Dictionary, Old Testament* (Chattanooga: AMG, 1994), #6754, 2358.

10. Kaiser, et al, *Hard Sayings*, 808.

11. John and Stasi Eldredge, *Captivating: A Guided Journal, Unveiling the Mystery of a Woman's Soul* (Nashville: Thomas Nelson, 2005), 31.

12. Ibid.

13. Ray C. Stedman, *Adventuring Through 1 Timothy, 2 Timothy, and Titus* (Grand Rapids: Discovery House, 1997), 20.

14. John MacArthur, *The MacArthur Study Bible* (Nashville: Word, 1997), 21.

15. Glenn Kreider, Transcript from "Soteriology: Sin and Hope" (Dallas: Dallas Theological Seminary, Spring 2014).

Lesson 2

1. R. C. Sproul, "Beware of Idolatry," (Sanford, FL: Ligonier Ministries, the Teaching Fellowship of R. C. Sproul), http//www.ligonier.org/learn/devotionals/beware-idolatry.

2. *English Standard Version Study Bible* (Wheaton: Crossway, 2008), 2159.

3. Ibid., 2158–2159.

4. Oswald Chambers, ed. James Reimann, *My Utmost for His Highest: The Golden Book of Oswald Chambers* (Grand Rapids: Discovery House, 1992), July 21.

5. Spiros Zodhiates and Warren Baker, eds., *The Complete Word Study Dictionary, New Testament* (Chattanooga: AMG, 1992), #4100, 1162.

6. Ibid., #3340, 969.

7. John Eldredge, *The Utter Relief of Holiness: How God's Goodness Frees Us from Everything That Plagues Us* (Nashville: FaithWords, 2013), 106.

8. Ibid., 107.

9. Billy Graham, *Unto the Hills: A Daily Devotional* (Nashville: Thomas Nelson, 2010), July 21.

10. Chambers, ed. Reimann, *My Utmost*, July 1.

11. Graham, *Unto the Hills*, August 1.

Lesson 3

1. J. D. Watson, *A Word for the Day: Key Words from the New Testament* (Chattanooga: AMG, 2006), 20.

2. Ed Wheat, *Love Life for Every Married Couple: How to Fall in Love, Stay in Love, Rekindle Your Love* (Grand Rapids: Zondervan, 1980), 61–75.

3. Rory C. Reid and Dan Gray, *Confronting Your Spouse's Pornography Problem* (Chicago: Silverleaf Press, 2006), 74.

4. D. Guthrie and J. A. Motyer, *The New Bible Commentary,* Revised (Grand Rapids: Eerdmans, 1970), 519.

5. Ibid., 870.

6. *English Standard Version Study Bible* (Wheaton: Crossway, 2008), 1644.

7. Joe Stowell, *Our Daily Bread* (Grand Rapids: Radio Bible Class, April 11, 2013).

8. Charles F. Pfeiffer and Everett F. Harrison, eds., *The Wycliffe Bible Commentary* (Chicago: Moody Press, 1962), 1264.

9. Ibid., 1280.

10. James MacDonald, *When Life Is Hard* (Chicago: Moody Press, 2009), 136.

11. Spiros Zodhiates and Warren Baker, *The Complete Word Study Dictionary, New Testament* (Chattanooga: AMG, 1992), #2744, 854.

12. Ibid.

13. Spiros Zodhiates and Warren Baker, *Hebrew-Greek Key Word Study Bible* (Chattanooga: AMG, 2008), 1545.

14. John Piper, *A Godward Life, Book Two* (Sisters, Ore.: Multnomah Books, 1999), 290.

15. Julie Ackerman Link, *Our Daily Bread* (Grand Rapids: Radio Bible Class, April 18, 2013).

16. Oswald Chambers, ed. James Reimann, *My Utmost for His Highest: The Golden Book of Oswald Chambers* (Grand Rapids: Discovery House, 1992), October 31.

17. Ibid., May 8.

Lesson 4

1. J. D. Watson, *A Word for the Day: Key Words from the New Testament* (Chattanooga: AMG, 2006), 32.

2. John MacArthur, *The Truth War: Fighting for Certainty in the Age of Deception* (Nashville: Thomas Nelson, 2007), xv.

3. Spiros Zodhiates and Warren Baker, *Hebrew-Greek Key Word Study Bible* (Chattanooga: AMG, 2008), 327.

4. Billy Graham, *Unto the Hills: A Daily Devotional* (Nashville: Thomas Nelson, 2010), July 3.

5. Rick Renner, *Sparkling Gems from the Greek: 365 Greek Word Studies for Every Day of the Year to Sharpen Your Understanding of God's Word* (Tulsa: Teach All Nations, 2003), 493.

6. Ibid.

7. Ibid., 493–494.

8. Watson, *A Word for the Day,* 71.

9. Jonathan Leeman, *Reverberation: How God's Word Brings Light, Freedom, and Action to His People* (Chicago: Moody Press, 2011), 48.

10. English Standard Version Study Bible (Wheaton: Crossway, 2008), 961.

11. Chambers, ed. Reimann, *My Utmost,* June 24.

1. Marva J. Dawn, *Sexual Character: Beyond Technique to Intimacy* (Grand Rapids: Eerdmans, 1993), 39–40.

2. Tim Alan Gardner, *Sacred Sex: A Spiritual Celebration of Oneness in Marriage* (Colorado Springs: WaterBrook, 2002), 4.

3. Ibid., 13, 16.

4. Ibid., 59.

5. William M. Struthers, *Wired for Intimacy: How Pornography Hijacks the Male Brain* (Downers Grove: InterVarsity, 2009), 136.

6. Harry Schaumburg, *Undefiled: Redemption from Sexual Sin, Restoration for Broken Relationships* (Chicago: Moody Press, 2009), 14.

7. Douglas E. Rosenau, *A Celebration of Sex: A Guide to Enjoying God's Gift of Sexual Intimacy* (Nashville: Thomas Nelson, 2002), 164.

8. Tim and Beverly LaHaye, *The Act of Marriage: The Beauty of Sexual Love* (Grand Rapids: Zondervan, 1998), 35.

9. Louann Brizendine, *The Female Brain* (New York: Three Rivers, 2006), 40–41, 70–71.

10. Joe S. McIlhaney Jr. and Freda McKissic Bush, *Hooked: New Science on How Casual Sex Is Affecting Our Children* (Chicago: Northfield, 2008), 56.

11. Sean McDowell, "Why Modern Evolutionary Theory Is Wrong about Sex": HYPERLINK, http://www.seanmcdowell.org/index.php/science/why-modern-evolutionary-theory-is-wrong-about-sex/

12. Gardner, *Sacred Sex*, 55.

13. Joe S. McIlhaney Jr. and Freda M. Bush, *Girls Uncovered: New Research on What America's Casual Culture Does to Young Women* (Chicago: Northfield, 2011), 61.

14. *English Standard Version Study Bible* (Wheaton: Crossway, 2008), 1218.

15. Spiros Zodhiates, Warren Baker, eds., *The Complete Word Study Dictionary, New Testament* (Chattanooga, AMG, 1992), #2133, 680.

16. Robert Lewis and William Hendricks, *Rocking the Roles: Building a Win-Win Marriage* (Colorado Springs: NavPress, 1991), 82.

17. Ibid., 128.

18. Ibid., 129.

19. Tim Challies, *Sexual Detox: A Guide for Guys Who Are Sick of Porn* (Adelphi, MD: Cruciform Press, 2010), 39–40.

20. John Piper and Wayne Grudem, eds., *Recovering Biblical Manhood and Womanhood: A Response to Evangelical Feminism* (Wheaton: Crossway, 1991), 49.

21. Juli Slattery and Dannah Gresh, *Pulling Back the Shades: Erotica, Intimacy, and the Longings of a Woman's Heart* (Chicago: Moody Press, 2014), 21.

22. Zodhiates, *Word Study Dictionary*, #2776, 860.

23. Stu Weber, Tender Warrior: *Every Man's Purpose, Every Woman's Dream, Every Child's Hope* (Sisters, OR: Multnomah Press, 1999), 87.

24. English Standard Version, 2206.

25. Adapted from Rev. Michael Easley's sermon (Alexandria, VA: Immanuel Bible Church, Spring 2002).

26. Piper and Grudem, *Recovering Biblical Manhood*, 47.

Lesson 6

1. Spiros Zodhiates and Warren Baker, *The Complete Word Study Dictionary, New Testament* (Chattanooga: AMG, 1992), #5401, 1450.

2. Spiros Zodhiates and Warren Baker, *The Complete Word Study Dictionary, Old Testament* (Chattanooga: AMG, 1994) #2490, 2316.

3. *English Standard Version Study Bible* (Wheaton: Crossway, 2008), 2298.

4. Ibid., 2199.

5. Rory C. Reid and Dan Gray, *Confronting Your Spouse's Pornography Problem* (Chicago: Silverleaf Press, 2006), 74.

6. Compilation derived from Patrick Carnes, *Don't Call It Love: Recovery from Sexual Addiction* (New York: Bantam, 1991), 11–12 and Mark R. Laaser, *Healing the Wounds of Sexual Addiction* (Grand Rapids: Zondervan, 2004), 63–69.

7. Charles M. Sell, *Achieving the Impossible: Intimate Marriage* (Portland, OR: Multnomah Press, 1982), 81.

8. Ed Vitagliano, "Bonded in the Brain: New Science Confirms Biblical View of Sex," *AFA Journal* (October 2010): 15.

9. John Piper and Wayne Grudem, eds. *Recovering Biblical Manhood and Womanhood: A Response to Evangelical Feminism* (Wheaton: Crossway, 1991), 47.

10. John Blake, "Why Young Christians Aren't Waiting Anymore," CNN, September 27, 2011, 08:39 a.m. ET, http//religion.blogs. cnn.com/2011/09/27/why-young-christians-arent-waiting-anymore/

11. Janice Shaw Crouse, "The Myths and Reality of Living Together Without Marriage," 2007, http://www.crosswalk.com/family/marriage/the-myths-and-reality-of-living-together-without-marriage-11531429.html.

12. Willard Harley, "Living Together Before Marriage," Letter 2, *Marriage Builders*, http://www.marriagebuilders.com/mb.cfm/4/31/240.

13. Nicholas Sparks, *The Wedding* (New York: Warner, 2005), 29–30.

14. Sam Margulies, "Virtual Infidelity," *Psychology Today*, March 30, 2008, http://www.psychologytoday.com.

15. Douglas E. Rosenau, *A Celebration of Sex* (Nashville: Thomas Nelson, 2002), 344.

16. Wesley Hill, *Washed and Waiting: Reflections on Christian Faithfulness and Homosexuality* (Grand Rapids: Zondervan, 2010), 19.

17. Andrew Comiskey, *Strength in Weakness: Healing Sexual and Relational Brokenness* (Downers Grove: InterVarsity Books, 2003), 192.

18. Piper and Grudem, eds., *Recovering Biblical Manhood*, 47.

19. Harry W. Shaumburg, False Intimacy: *Understanding the Struggle of Sexual Addiction* (Colorado Springs: NavPress, 1997), 38.

20. Tim Challies, Sexual Detox: *A Guide for Guys Who Are Sick of Porn* (Adelphi, MD: Cruciform Press, 2010), 38–39.

21. Tim and Beverly LaHaye, *The Act of Marriage After 40* (Grand Rapids, MI: Zondervan Publishing House, 2000), 189.

22. Dannah Gresh and Juli Slattery, *Pulling Back the Shades: Erotica, Intimacy, and the Longings of a Woman's Heart* (Chicago: Moody Press, 2014), 9, 134.

23. Ibid., 24.

24. Holly Finn, "Online Pornography's Effects and a New Way to Fight Them," *The Wall Street Journal*, May 3, 2013, http://online.wsj.com/article/SB10001424127887323628004578456710204395042.html.

25. Joshua Harris, *Sex Is Not the Problem (Lust Is): Sexual Purity in a Lust-Saturated World* (Colorado Springs: Multnomah Books, 2003), 105–106.

26. Vitagliano, "Bonded in the Brain," 15.

27. Josh McDowell as spoken to John Stonestreet, "Beyonce and the Super Bowl Guinea Pig Kids," *Break Point*, February 7, 2013, http://www.breakpoint.org/bpcommentaries/entry/13/21434.

28. Crystal Renaud, *Dirty Girls Come Clean* (Chicago: Moody Press, 2011), 23.

29. Ibid., 26.

30. Challies, *Sexual Detox*, 17.

31. Holly Finn, "Online Pornography's Effects."

32. Thomas E. Schmidt, *Straight and Narrow? Compassion and Clarity in the Homosexuality Debate* (Downers Grove: InterVarsity Academic, 1995), 11.

Lesson 7

1. Charles F. Pfeiffer and Everett Harrison, eds., *The Wycliffe Bible Commentary* (Chicago: Moody Press, 1962), 981.

2. Ibid.

3. Andrew Comiskey, *Strength in Weakness: Healing Sexual and Relational Brokenness* (Downers Grove: InterVarsity Press, 2003), 69.

4. Gary Foster, "For the Record: The Foster Report," *Christian Counseling Connection*, vol. 18, issue 4, 15.

5. Brooke Westphal, "How Many Americans Are Affected by Depression?" eHow Health, http://www.chow.com/about_5649169_many-americans-affected-depression_html.

6. Sharon A. Hersch, *Begin Again, Believe Again: Embracing the Courage to Love with Abandon* (Grand Rapids: Zondervan, 2010), 167.

7. Sarah Young, *Jesus Calling* (Nashville: Thomas Nelson, 2004), 210.

8. Robert Farrar Capon, *Daily Christian Quote*, http://dailychristianquote.com/dcqgrief.html.

9. J. W. Gray, "Ethics and Rationalization," May 24, 2011, http://ethicalrealism.wordpress.com/2011/05/24/ethics-and-rationalization/

10. John MacArthur, *The MacArthur Study Bible* (Dallas: Word, 1997), 42.

11. J. D. Watson, *A Hebrew Word for the Day* (Chattanooga: AMG, 2010), 333.

12. John Eldredge, *The Utter Relief of Holiness* (New York: FaithWords, 2013), 17.

13. Spiros Zodhiates and Warren Baker, *The Complete Word Study Dictionary, New Testament* (Chattanooga: AMG, 1992), #3811, 1088.

14. Ibid., 948.

15. Oswald Chambers, ed. James Reimann, *My Utmost for His Highest: The Golden Book of Oswald Chambers* (Grand Rapids: Discovery House, 1992), August 10.

16. Kevin Goodrich, "Preaching Change in a Pill-Popping Culture: Toward a Stronger Gospel Message," *Christian Counseling Connection*, vol. 18, issue 4, 14.

17. Beth Moore, *Jesus, the One and Only* (Nashville: LifeWay, 2000), 53.

18. Sharon A. Hersh, *Begin Again, Believe Again: Embracing the Courage to Love with Abandon* (Grand Rapids: Zondervan, 2010), 161–162.

Lesson 8

1. *English Standard Version Study Bible* (Wheaton: Crossway, 2008), 621.

2. John MacArthur, *The MacArthur Study Bible* (Nashville: Word, 1997), 494.

3. *New American Standard Bible* (Grand Rapids: Zondervan, 1995), 472.

4. Chris Tiegreen, *At His Feet* (Carol Stream: Tyndale, 2003), 176.

5. Spiros Zodhiates and Warren Baker, *The Complete Word Study Dictionary, New Testament* (Chattanooga: AMG, 1992), #498, 195.

6. Ibid., 888.

7. W. E. Vine, Merrill F. Unger, and William White, eds., *An Expository Dictionary of Biblical Words* (Nashville: Thomas Nelson, 1985), 336.

8. Beth Moore, *Jesus, the One and Only* (Nashville: LifeWay, 2000), 76.

9. (No info. on this)

10. John F. Walvoord and Roy B. Zuck, *The Bible Knowledge Commentary: New Testament* (Colorado Springs: David C. Cook, 1983). 650.

11. J. D. Watson, *A Word for the Day: Key Words from the New Testament* (Chattanooga: AMG, 2006), 286.

12. Charles F. Pfeiffer and Everett F. Harrison, *The Wycliffe Bible Commentary* (Chicago: Moody Press, 1962), 1054.

13. Oswald Chambers, ed. James Reimann, *My Utmost for His Highest: The Golden Book of Oswald Chambers* (Grand Rapids: Discovery House, 1992), December 7.

14. Rick Renner, *Sparkling Gems from the Greek* (Tulsa: Teach All Nations, 2003), 864–865.

15. Walvoord and Zuck, *Bible Knowledge*, 487.

16. Ibid., 655.

17. Mark Buchanan, *Your God Is Too Safe: Rediscovering the Wonder of a God You Can't Control* (Belmont, Mich.: Multnomah Books, 2001), 204.

Lesson 9

1. Spiros Zodhiates and Warren Baker, *The Complete Word Study Dictionary, New Testament* (Chattanooga: AMG, 1992), #863, 299.

2. Judy Rossi, *Enhancing Your Marriage: A Women's Bible Study* (Chattanooga: AMG, 2004), 129–132.

3. Andrew Comiskey, *Strength in Weakness: Healing Sexual and Relational Brokenness* (Downers Grove: InterVarsity, 2003), 136.

4. June Hunt, *Counseling Through Your Bible Handbook: Providing Biblical Hope and Practical Help for 50 Everyday Problems* (Eugene, OR: Harvest House, 2008), 186.

5. Rory C. Reid and Dan Gray, *Confronting Your Spouse's Pornography Problem* (Sandy, UT: Silverleaf Press, 2006), 147.

6. Meg Wilson, *Hope after Betrayal: Healing When Sexual Addiction Invades Your Marriage* (Grand Rapids: Kregel, 2007), 114.

7. Hunt, *Counseling*, 187.

8. Wilson, *Hope after Betrayal*, 115.

9. Tim Alan Gardner, *Sacred Sex: A Spiritual Celebration of Oneness in Marriage* (Colorado Springs: WaterBrook, 2002), 214.

10. Oswald Chambers, ed. James Reimann, *My Utmost for His Highest: The Golden Book of Oswald Chambers* (Grand Rapids: Discovery House, 1992), February 3.

1. Harry W. Schaumberg, *False Intimacy: Understanding the Struggle of Sexual Addiction* (Colorado Springs: NavPress, 1997), 103.

2. Rory C. Reid and Dan Gray, *Confronting Your Spouse's Pornography Problem* (Sandy, UT: Silverleaf Press, 2006), 14.

3. Frank York and Jan LaRue, *Protecting Your Child in an X-Rated World* (Wheaton: Tyndale, 2002), 218.

4. Ibid., 220–221.

5. June Hunt, *Counseling Through Your Bible Handbook: Providing Biblical Hope and Practical Help for 50 Everyday Problems* (Eugene, OR: Harvest House, 2008), 34–35.

6. Tim Clinton and Ron Hawkins, *The Quick Reference Guide to Biblical Counseling* (Grand Rapids: Baker Books, 2009), 131.

7. Shaumburg, *False Intimacy*, 123.

8. Web site Resources: www.hopeafterbetrayal.com; www.settingcaptivesfree.com; www.freedomeveryday.org; www.faithfulandtrueministries.com; wwwhopequestgroup.org; www.purelifeministries.org; www.harvestusa.org; www.bebroken.org; www.freedombeginshere.org. Counseling Resources: Contact www.Newlife.com or 1-800-newlife. Contact American Association of Christian Counselors at www.aacc.net or Ecounseling at www.counseling.com. These organizations provide Christian counselors nationwide.

9. Shaumburg, *False Intimacy*, 53.

10. Ibid., 104–105.

11. Reid and Gray, *Confronting*, 38.

12. Henry Cloud and John Townsend, *Boundaries: When to Say Yes, How to Say No to Take Control of Your Life* (Grand Rapids: Zondervan, 1992), 29–30.

13. There is an exception. Refer to 1 Timothy 3 where overseers and deacons are required to manage their children and keep them under positive control.

14. Mark Laaser, *Healing the Wounds of Sexual Addiction* (Grand Rapids: Zondervan, 2004), 141–142.

15. Shaumburg, *False Intimacy*, 53.

16. *English Standard Version Study Bible* (Wheaton: Crossway, 2008), 948.

17. Steve Gallagher, *At the Altar of Sexual Idolatry* (Dry Ridge, KY: Pure Life Ministries, 2007), 117–118.

18. Oswald Chambers, ed. James Reimann, *My Utmost for His Highest: The Golden Book of Oswald Chambers* (Grand Rapids: Discovery House, 1992), August 10.

19. Hunt, *Counseling*, 72.

20. Ibid., 69.

21. Clinton and Hawkins, *Biblical Counseling*, 225.

22. Ibid., 223.

23. Hunt, *Counseling*, 70.

24. Ibid., 70–71.

25. Tim Clinton, "Does Jesus Have Boundaries?" *Christian Counseling Connection*, vol. 19, issue 1, 2.

26. Hunt, *Counseling*, 74.

27. York and LaRue, *Protecting Your Child*, 131.

28. Resources on sex education for children: Stan and Brenna Jones, *How and When to Tell Your Kids about Sex* (parents' guide). The Jones have a four-part age-oriented series on teaching your kids about sex: *Book 1: The Story of Me* (ages 3–5); *Book 2: Before I Was Born* (ages 5–8); *Book 3: What's the Big Deal? Why God Cares about Sex* (ages 8–11); *Book 4: Facing the Facts: The Truth about Sex and You* (ages 12–14); *A Chicken's Guide to Talking Turkey with Your Kids about Sex* by Kevin Leman and Kathy Flores Bell; *Talking to Your Kids about Sex* by Mark Laaser. For Teens: *The Dirt on Sex* by Justin Lookadoo; *Technical Virgin* by Hayley DiMarco; all Hayley DiMarco books such as *How Far Is Too Far?* All Michael DiMarco books such as *Almost Sex: 9 Signs You're about to Go Too Far (or Already Have)*; a helpful and informative pamphlet: *Why Wait? 24 Reasons to Wait Until Marriage to Have Sex* (pamphlet, Rose Publishers, set of 10.)

29. York and LaRue, *Protecting Your Child*, 131.

30. Clinton and Hawkins, *Biblical Counseling*, 221.

31. For more on raising children to become responsive to Jesus Christ, see Judy Rossi's *Raising Responsive Children: A Bible Study for Moms* at any Christian bookstore or online bookseller.

Lesson 11

1. Diane Langberg, "The Modern Day Assault on Women: Rape, Abuse, and Trafficking," *Christian Counseling Today*, vol. 20, no. 1, 27.

2. Spiros Zodhiates and Warren Baker, *The Complete Word Study Dictionary, Old Testament* (Chattanooga: AMG, 1994), #157, 2298.

3. Charles F. Pfeiffer and Everett F. Harrison, eds., *The Wycliffe Bible Commentary* (Chicago: Moody Press, 1962), 297.

4. June Hunt, *Counseling Through Your Bible Handbook* (Eugene, OR: Harvest House, 2008), 326.

5. Sam Meier, "Let Your Garments Always Be White." http://www.xenos.org/ministries/crossroads/onlinejournal/issue5/garments.htm), 2000.

6. Spiros Zodhiates and Warren Baker, Hebrew-Greek Key Word Study Bible (Chattanooga: AMG, 2008), #8076, 2052.

7. Judy Rossi, *Enhancing Your Marriage: A Women's Bible Study* (Chattanooga: AMG, 2004), 70.

8. Andrew Comiskey, *Strength in Weakness: Healing Sexual and Relational Brokenness* (Downers Grove: InterVarsity Books, 2003), 188.

9. John Eldredge, *The Utter Relief of Holiness: How God's Goodness Frees Us from Everything That Plagues Us* (Nashville: FaithWords, 2013), 17–19.

10. Ibid., 17.

11. Francis Frangipane, *The Three Battlegrounds* (Cedar Rapids, IA: Arrow, 1989), 12.

12. Oswald Chambers, ed. James Reimann, *My Utmost for His Highest: The Golden Book of Oswald Chambers* (Grand Rapids: Discovery House, 1992), April 3.

13. Diane Leclere, "The Broken, Messy—and Holy—Church," *Christianity Today*, April 2014, 53.

14. Zodhiates, *Word Study Dictionary*, #190, 112.

15. *English Standard Version Study Bible* (Wheaton: Crossway, 2008), 2286.

16. Ibid., 2179.

17. Ben Colter and Paul Hardy, *Stop the Madness: Findi*

18. *ng Freedom from Addictions* (Nashville: Serendipity House, 2006), 7.

Lesson 12

1. Schaeffer, Edith. *Take My Heart, Oh God: Riches from the Greatest Christian Writers of all Time* (Grand Rapids, MI: Worthy Media, Inc., 2010), January 12.

2. Francis Frangipane, *The Three Battlegrounds* (Cedar Rapids, IA: Arrow, 1989), 12.

3. ten Boom, Corrie. *Take My Heart, Oh God: Riches from the Greatest Christian Writers of all Time* (Grand Rapids, MI: Worthy Media, Inc., 2010), March 13.

4. Sharon A. Hersh, *Begin Again, Believe Again: Embracing the Courage to Love with Abandon* (Grand Rapids: Zondervan, 2012), 166.

5. John Piper, *Desiring God* (Sisters, OR: Multnomah Books, 1986), 50.

6. Spiros Zodhiates and Warren Baker, *The Complete Word Study Dictionary, New Testament* (Chattanooga: AMG, 1992), #47, 72.

7. Chris Tiegreen, *Walk with God* (Carol Stream, Illinois: Tyndale House Publishers, Inc., 2004), 230.

When you buy a book from **AMG Publishers**, **Living Ink Books**, or **God and Country Press**, you are helping to make disciples of Jesus Christ around the world.

How? AMG Publishers and its imprints are ministries of **AMG** (*Advancing the Ministries of the Gospel*) **International**, a non-denominational evangelical Christian mission organization ministering in over 30 countries around the world. Profits from the sale of AMG Publishers books are poured into the outreaches of AMG International.

AMG International Mission Statement

AMG exists to advance with compassion the command of Christ to evangelize and make disciples around the world through national workers and in partnership with like-minded Christians.

AMG International Vision Statement

We envision a day when everyone on earth will have at least one opportunity to hear and respond to a clear presentation of the Gospel of Jesus Christ and have the opportunity to grow as a disciple of Christ.

To learn more about AMG International and how you can pray for or financially support this ministry, please visit

www.amgmissions.org